A RIVER IN TIME

The Yadkin-Pee Dee
River System

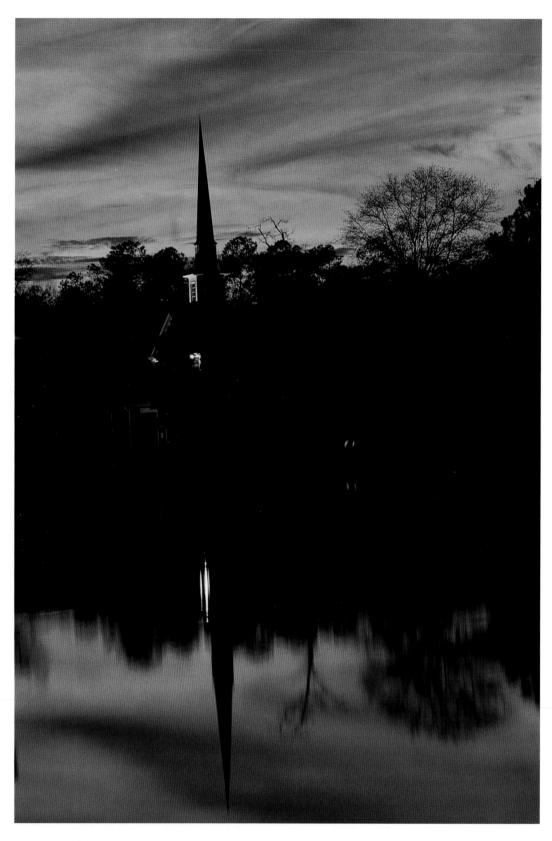

The waters of the river, like its history, reflect both nature and civilization. Here a tributary of the Pee Dee captures the reflection of Reedy Creek Baptist Church in Marion County. *Charles McRae.*

A RIVER IN TIME

The Yadkin-Pee Dee
River System

Suzanne Cameron Linder

with

Emily Linder Johnson

Palmetto Conservation Foundation

© 2000 Palmetto Conservation Foundation
Palmetto Conservation Foundation
PO Box 1984
Spartanburg, SC 29304

1 0 9 8 7 6 5 4 3 2 1

Printed in Hong Kong on recycled paper by
C & C Offset Printing Company, Ltd.

LIBRARY OF CONGRESS CARD NUMBER: 00-105613

ISBN 0-9679016-3-4

Book design and layout by the
South Carolina Department of Archives and History

Contents

Acknowledgements

This study originated as a Ph.D. dissertation at the University of South Carolina. I am indebted to Dr. Walter Edgar for directing my research and sharing his vast knowledge of regional history. Other members of the dissertation committee, Dr. John Winberry, Dr. John G. Sproat, and Dr. Lacy Ford also offered constructive criticism and valuable advice. I appreciate the appointment as research fellow in the Institute for Southern Studies, which makes available its scholarly associations and programs and the resources of the outstanding university libraries. I am especially grateful to Director Allen Stokes, Robin Copp, Beth Bilderback and the other capable staff of the South Caroliniana Library and Director Bruce Rippeteau, Chester DePratter, and Stanley South of the Institute for Archaeology and Anthropology.

A dissertation is by necessity a scholarly exercise in which readability is not the primary objective. I am indebted to my daughter, Emily Linder Johnson, for judiciously editing it to turn it into a form designed for the popular audience. Together, we added the last two chapters to bring the narrative up to date.

Several friends have adopted local history as an avocation. They have provided information not available from any other source. The late Dana Crosland of Bennettsville made a life-long study of the Pee Dee and kindly shared his knowledge. Dr. Ernest Helms provided information, encouragement, and found the unusual picture of the fisheries. Peggy and Bill Kinney of Bennettsville offered their comprehensive collection of local history material and copies of historical articles that have appeared in the *Marlboro Herald-Advocate,* which Bill publishes. Sarah Spruill of Cheraw, Horace Rudisill of Darlington, and Ned Sloan made available their wonderful collections as well as their valuable insights.

Emily Garner researched illustrations and secured copyrights, shot original photos, and worked in the darkroom as needed. Her skill and artistic eye contributed greatly. I appreciate the help of my research associate, Marta Thacker, and thank Dr. Miles Richards for contributing the piece on Stephen Foster.

We were extremely fortunate to have Dr. Charles McRae of Marion, a prize-winning nature photographer, contribute his work. Thanks also to John Davis of South Carolina Wildlife magazine, Anne Schneider of the State Library, Virginia Skinner of Georgetown, Glen Simmons of the Winston-Salem City and County Planning Board, Jeff Michael of The Land Trust for Central North Carolina, Steve Spratt and Michele Ackerman of Yadkin/Pee Dee Lakes Project, Erin Allen of Stanly County Public Library, Frank Deal of Thyatira Church, Gene Ellis of Yadkin, Inc., Diane Kuchen of North Carolina Department of Natural Resources, Jamie and Marcia Constance, Judge Peter Hairston, Chalmers Hammet of Williamsburg Historical Society, Lon and Donna Outen, and many members of Historic Ricefields Association.

Richard Watkins kindly shared his lifetime interest in environmental concerns and contributed immeasurably to chapter ten. He also accompanied me on various explorations of the river and took some of the photographs in the book. I am grateful to him for his support throughout and for bringing my work to the attention of PCF.

Thanks to Dr. Rodger Stroup of the South Carolina Department of Archives and History for his interest and guidance and to all of the staff at the Archives who make it such a pleasant place to work. Special thanks to Judith Andrews for editing and book design and Tim Belshaw for maps. Finally, I am most grateful to Roche Carolina and the Palmetto Conservation Foundation for making the publication of this book possible.

Suzanne Linder

Foreword

Dear Reader,

Roche Carolina is proud to sponsor *A River in Time.*

The Pee Dee is our home. It's where we work, where we live and where we are raising our children. Roche as a corporation is dedicated to improving the quality of life around the world.

We are delighted to be able to help in local efforts to secure the quality of life we enjoy today and for future generations.

Sincerely,

Don Herriott
President and General Manager
Roche Carolina Inc.

The Roche Group is one of the world's leading research-based healthcare groups active in the discovery, development and manufacture of pharmaceuticals and diagnostic systems. With locations all over the world, Roche is active in the areas of pharmaceuticals, diagnostics, monitoring and treatment of diseases and on the promotion of general well-being.

Roche Carolina is located in Florence, South Carolina.

Sunrise over Leggett's Mill Pond near Centenary, South Carolina. *Charles McRae.*

PREFACE

How does one capture the essence of a river? In many ways the river is a process, a cycle, ever changing yet ever the same. Drops of water collect in the mountains to form a tiny stream. An irresistible force propels each drop toward the sea. Streams tumble over mountain rocks and join to form great rivers that slow down, like a person nearing life's end, and meander to the sea. Then warm sun draws the drops of water into the atmosphere forming clouds that blow back to the mountains. Rain falls on steep slopes, and the cycle begins again. Leonardo da Vinci saw rivers as the veins of the planet, nourishing the earth and its creatures.[1] Rivers also carry a rhythm, like the heartbeat of the universe. Water is the life-blood of all existence and the vehicle for the beginning of all living creatures.

The Yadkin-Pee Dee River System covers over 18,000 square miles in the Carolinas and a small part of Virginia. It is the second largest river system in drainage area on the Atlantic coast, emptying into the Atlantic Ocean at Winyah Bay, near Georgetown, South Carolina. Small streams come together near Blowing Rock, North Carolina, to form the Yadkin, which comprises about half the length of the river system. Many people do not realize that the Yadkin and the Pee Dee are actually one great river. One purpose of this

Elk Creek, a picturesque tributary of the Yadkin River in Wilkes County, North Carolina. *Suzanne Linder.*

study is to point out that this is indeed true, and for this reason it is often useful to refer to the Yadkin-Pee Dee River. A study of settlement patterns will show that some people came up the Pee Dee through Winyah Bay to populate the South Carolina portion of the river. Other settlers came down the great wagon road through the Shenandoah Valley of Virginia to develop the Yadkin Valley. Yet the names Yadkin and Pee Dee came from earlier tenants of the land. The Native Americans who moved up and down the river with the seasons or built elaborate towns along its banks provided the two names for the two very different sections of the same river system.

Long before human beings arrived, somewhere in the mists of time more than thirty million years ago, the river began its journey. As people moved into the region, they gravitated to its banks, and it formed an integral part of their existence. Through the centuries uses of the river have changed, yet its importance has remained. Native Americans and early settlers found it a source for water and food as well as a transportation route. Rice planters near the coast harnessed the tidal flow for irrigation and motive power while settlers in the piedmont and mountains built sawmills and gristmills. Canoes and rafts gave way to teamboats and steamboats. Then railroads and highways eclipsed the river as a means of transportation. In the twentieth century the river remains important in the production of electric power and as a source of water for industry and human consumption. It is a primary resource for recreational pursuits like fishing, boating, or simply enjoying nature. With the advent of modern industry and the growth of population, people began to realize the need to protect the river from pollution.

Barry Beasley, manager of the Land and Water Stewardship Program in the South Carolina Department of Natural Resources, recently said that there are four components in effective river conservation: sound ecological science, aesthetics and established cultural connections, an understanding of the place of humans in nature, and an "ecological conscience."[2] We hope that this book, by providing an overview of the history of the region, will contribute to an understanding of cultural connections and a greater appreciation of the river and its role throughout time.

Critics will undoubtedly say this topic is much too broad and there is no way one book could adequately cover the subject. They would be right. The authors have felt overwhelmed with the immensity of the project. We are acutely aware of the limitations of time and space. Yet we believe there is a need for a survey, an overview of the entire Yadkin-Pee Dee River system. We do not claim that this study is comprehensive, only that it is a beginning.

We lived in Bennettsville, South Carolina, on Lake Paul Wallace, part of the Pee Dee watershed, for about twenty years. We watched the sun rise over the lake and light the pond lilies and wild wisteria. The wood duck nested in our yard; wild geese paid an annual visit; huge flocks of migrating yellow evening grosbeaks visited our bird feeder. Orchard orioles hung graceful swinging nests in the elm just outside an upstairs window where we could see the yellow-green female and the orange and black male feed their hungry babies. Gray foxes and raccoons came to steal a bite of dog food from our yard. A beaver kindly removed a tree that was blocking our view. We developed an appreciation for the water and the wild things it attracted, and we felt a part of the whole. Drinking water for the community came from the Crooked Creek, a Pee Dee tributary, and treated wastewater funneled back. Since our bodies are about seventy percent water, we were actually a part of the river, and the river was a part of us.

In the Yadkin portion of the river as well as in the Pee Dee, families have lived in the same communities for many generations. An appreciation for history and a sense of continuity are pervasive. We hope this study will reinforce this appreciation, preserve the story for future generations, and encourage people to protect and preserve this great natural resource.

A red maple tree signals the coming of winter in a Marion County swamp.
Charles McRae.

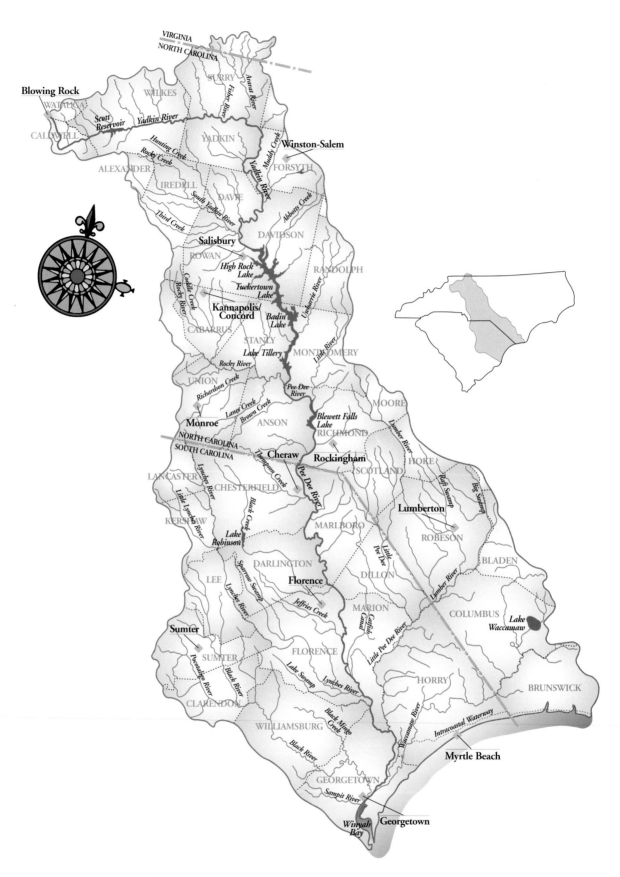

The Yadkin-Pee Dee river system in North and South Carolina. *Tim Belshaw.*

CHAPTER 1

The Source

*"The earth is the Lord's, and
the fulness thereof,
the world and those who dwell
therein;
for he has founded it upon the
seas,
and established it upon the rivers."*
Psalm 24

The river has stories to tell. Some it holds deep within its dark waters and some it shares as history plays out upon its banks. We know stories of Indian princesses, of brave explorers, of teamboats and steamboats and plantations where life on the river was both graceful and hard.

We have learned of nomadic hunter-gatherers, of conquistadors and chieftains, and of indigo vats and rice fields echoing with the sound of laboring slaves. We are only recent tenants on an ancient soil creating our own stories as we respond to the music of the river—the unheard harmony of water, earth and sky that sings of the very beginning of life itself. From the headwaters of the Yadkin tumbling and skipping over mountain rocks to the gentle meanders of the Great Pee Dee in the coastal plain, the river draws its inhabitants into their own distinctive "life on the river."

History reveals stories of diverse people, from the first explorers to modern outdoorsmen, who have sought and shared the secrets of the river. A young man of German origin, John Lederer, provided one of the first written records of the Yadkin/Pee Dee basin as it existed before European colonization. A resident of Hamburg, Lederer was about twenty-six years old in 1670 when he explored the backcountry of Virginia and the Carolinas on behalf of Governor William Berkeley of Virginia. To travel into unknown territory and to face wild beasts or Native Americans who were possibly hostile required great courage. Yet the young German described his adventures in matter-of-fact terms. Writing in Latin, he produced a detailed record of his journey, including descriptions of the people he met, the wild animals he encountered, and the land he saw. His background as a scholar and physician enabled him to make pertinent comments on a wide variety of subjects.[1]

Although Lederer was interested in trade with Native Americans as well as the country's natural resources, his primary purpose was to find a way through the Appalachian Mountains and to discover what lay beyond. Because the geography of America was still vague in the seventeenth century, many theorists at that time hoped to locate an inland passage to the Far East.[2]

The young German adventurer made three journeys of exploration. With three Indian companions, he traveled to the vicinity of present-day Charlottesville, Virginia. Using customary understatement, he said that on his first night in the forest he encountered "nothing remarkable" except a rattlesnake at least two and a half yards long and as big around as a man's arm. Having killed and dissected the rattler, he found a whole squirrel inside. The Indians told him that rattlers could mesmerize squirrels by staring at them and thus cause them to fall from the trees to be devoured. Lederer said he doubted that story and thought snakes could climb trees and surprise squirrels in the nest.

The next day Lederer recounted "a Doe seized by a wild Cat crossed our way; the miserable creature being even spent and breathless with the burden and cruelty of her rider, left not sucking out her bloud until she sunk under him. . . . " He described the wildcat as slightly bigger than the English fox, "fierce, ravenous and cunning." He deduced that the wildcat would watch from the branch of a tree and jump down onto the back of a deer to kill it.[3]

Nearing the mountains, Lederer found "Isinglas" [mica] about four inches square, a "transparent stone like Crystal that cut glass" [quartz], and "Marchasite" [crystallized iron pyrite]. When he first saw the Appalachians he could hardly tell if they were mountains or clouds until his Indian guides prostrated themselves in adoration and "howled out after a barbarous manner, 'Okeepoeze,' i.e. 'God is nigh.'"[4]

Lederer's adventures continued when he barely avoided death in quicksand while crossing a river. At every river he observed beaver and otter, and the woods were full of grey foxes. He reported great herds of red and fallow deer, old world varieties that he probably confused with the white-tailed deer native to Carolina. He also saw bears "crashing Mast like swine," and small leopards, which were likely wildcats or small panthers since leopards are not native to the region. "The wolves in these parts are so ravenous," he said, "that I often in the night feared my horse would be devoured by them." Although his horse was tethered to the same tree under which he and the Indians slept, he was still apprehensive and hoped the fire would keep the wolves at bay.[5]

Lederer's second journey began in May of 1670 at the falls of the James River in Virginia where he was accompanied by Major William Harris, a militia officer, twenty colonists on horseback, and five Indians. They traveled almost due west for about two weeks, after which Major Harris and the colonists decided that the glories of discovery did not equal the comforts of home, and they decided to return. Lederer turned southward toward the Carolinas and continued on with one Susquehanna Indian guide, Jackzetavon.[6]

Following a well-worn Indian trail, Lederer crossed the Yadkin at the Trading Ford about six miles northeast of present day Salisbury, North Carolina. He found the Sara Indians at this location.[7] The Sara colored their faces with cinnabar, which Lederer correctly identified as "Quicksilver" or mercury. Lederer also commented on cakes of salt he observed in the Sara village. He noted, ". . . many other rich Commodities and Minerals there are undoubtedly in these parts, which if possessed by an ingenious and industrious people, would be improved to vast advantages by Trade."[8]

The young German adventurer found that the Sara were so fond of their children that they would not reprimand them for mischief. By avoiding arrows aimed at his person and his horse, Lederer "caused such a meeting amongst the Youth of the Town, that the Seniors taking my horse and self into protection, had much ado (and that by intreaties [sic] and prayers, not commands) to appease them. . . . "[9]

After leaving the Sara, Lederer traveled south to Wisacky [Waxhaw] and visited the Catawbas near present-day Rock Hill, South Carolina. He then headed east and north, crossing the Pee Dee and the coastal plain of North Carolina to get back to Virginia. The difference between Lederer's conception of the terrain based on contemporary maps he studied and the topography of the region derived

The Yadkin River at the Trading Ford visited by John Lederer has remained a major crossing to the present day. (Highways 29, 70, 52 and I-85.) *Suzanne Linder.*

from modern, accurate maps has created some disagreement about the exact location of Lederer's route. He reported a large savanna, a lake, and a barren desert that seem contradictory to modern geography. It is important to note, however, that Lederer's native language was German, that he wrote in Latin, and that he probably communicated with his Indian guides through English, a second language for all. Sometimes he based his observations on information derived from sign language with the Indians.[10] Even so, his report was valuable as one step in the process of exploration. His descriptions of life among the Native Americans and of natural phenomena give a rare glimpse of the unspoiled wilderness.

Translated from Latin and published in England in 1672, Lederer's work was available for use by later explorers and traders. Although he did not find the pathway he sought, Lederer helped to open the way for trade with the Native Americans in the Piedmont region. He received little credit for his endeavors, but he might have said as he did when he commented on another situation, "I have lost nothing by it, but what I never studied to gain which is popular applause."[11]

Once called a "sad start for a proud river," the Yadkin-Pee Dee River today begins as a small spring beneath the parking lot at Green Park Inn in Blowing Rock, North Carolina. *Suzanne Linder.*

THE BIRTH OF A PROUD RIVER

The Great Pee Dee as we know it today is not only a river but a region and, perhaps to some, a way of life. Although there is an old tale that early settlers found the letters "P.D." carved in the bark of a tree and thus named the river, other theories are more believable. The name possibly derives from one of two Catawba Indian words: *piri*, meaning "something good," or *pihere*, meaning "smart, expert, or capable."[12] Pedee, Peedee, and Pedea were other early spellings. It is possible that settlers who recalled one of the Dee rivers in the British Isles corrupted the original Indian name.[13] The most likely explanation seems to be that the river takes its name from the Pedee Indians who lived along its banks.

North Carolinians call the upper part of the river the Yadkin from an Indian word first recorded by Virginia trader Abraham Wood in 1674. Wood told of the journey of James Needham, a gentleman of some prominence in Virginia, to "Yattken Town at Yattken River." The exact meaning of the word from the Sioux language is unknown, but Indian scholar Douglas Rights said that it possibly meant "big tree" or "place of big trees."[14]

Once called "a sad start for a proud river,"[15] the source of the Yadkin/Pee Dee River is a small spring just below the eastern continental divide near Blowing Rock, North Carolina. A likely watering spot for bear, deer, and Native Americans, the spring was later marked by a fancy little springhouse, which enabled guests of the nearby Green Park Inn to imbibe in style. Before the development of vitamins, this mineral spring was a great asset for a resort. In modern times, however, the need for a parking lot eclipsed the value of mineral water, and owners of the hotel paved over the spring. Today runoff from the parking lot flows with spring water into a culvert that carries it to the edge of the hillside.

Despite its humble beginning the river has exerted a powerful influence on the history of the region and the inhabitants of the area. It has offered life-sustaining water and food for man and beast, fertile flood plains for growing crops, and an artery of transportation to and from the sea. Be it the earliest humans huddled around a small stone hearth on a bluff, fur traders in periaugers searching for deerskins, Welsh farmers, lumber rafters, steamboat captains, or twentieth-century sportsmen in motorized water-craft, all have gravitated to the river and its tributaries. In modern times, the river has provided hydroelec-tric power and the tremendous amounts of water necessary for paper mills and textile factories.

CHARACTERISTICS OF THE YADKIN-PEE DEE: FORMATION, DRAINAGE, AND TRIBUTARIES

Second only to the Susquehanna River Basin in drainage area on the Atlantic coast, the Yadkin-Pee Dee Basin covers over 18,000 square miles in the Carolinas and a small portion of Virginia. The basin includes all land whose waters drain into Winyah Bay at Georgetown, South Carolina, with the exception

The Yadkin River from Ferguson Bridge. *Suzanne Linder.*

The Pee Dee River enters the Atlantic Ocean through Winyah Bay at Georgetown, South Carolina.
Phillip Jones. Courtesy South Carolina Department of Natural Resources.

of the Sampit watershed. Thirty North Carolina counties and fourteen South Carolina counties are entirely or partially included in the area. Fifty-nine percent or 10,600 square miles is in North Carolina and forty percent or 7,300 square miles is in South Carolina. Only one percent, or about 180 square miles, lies in southwestern Virginia.[16]

The Yadkin and the Pee Dee have different names because different groups explored the upper and lower portions of the river at different times, and it was not immediately apparent that they were the same river.[17] The Yadkin flows northeast from its source for about one hundred miles. Its headwaters form a trellis-like arrangement that is typical of mountain rivers.[18] Some geologists believe the Yadkin was once part of a huge prehistoric river that flowed in a northeasterly direction and emptied into the Atlantic about where the Potomac does now. About 30 million years ago, there was a land shift known as the last rise of the Blue Ridge Scarp. The shifting tectonic plates of the earth's crust tipped the North Carolina piedmont toward the southeast, and the river followed a new southerly course toward the Atlantic. The turn known as Big Bend near the present town of East Bend in Yadkin County, North Carolina, marks this shift.[19]

From its sources near Blowing Rock, North Carolina, to the end of Scott Reservoir near Wilkesboro, the Yadkin falls about 3,000 feet. From there, the river drops another 965 feet to sea level.

The river continues to meander from the fall line for about two hundred miles through bottom-land and swamps overlooked by occasional bluffs before it enters the Atlantic through Winyah Bay at Georgetown. Shifting tides flood and drain the marsh systems adjacent to the bay. In the estuary, the river's fresh water mixes with the ocean's salt water. The river's discharge is nearly 15,000 cubic feet per second, exceeded in South Carolina only by the Santee with 20,000.[20]

The many tributaries of the Yadkin-Pee Dee contribute to this large volume of discharge. The major tributaries of the Yadkin are the South Yadkin, which joins the main channel just north of High Rock Lake, and the Uwharrie, which winds through a range of ancient mountains of the same name and meets the Yadkin at Lake Tillery to form the Pee Dee. Tributaries of the Pee Dee include the Rocky River, the Lynches River, the Lumber River, the Little Pee Dee, the Black River, and the Waccamaw.

The Rocky River rises in Iredell County, North Carolina, at an elevation of about 800 feet above mean sea level. For about twenty-four miles, the average fall is 11.1 feet per mile. It continues easterly through a deep narrow valley over many rapids and then flows through a wider alluvial valley to its confluence with the Pee Dee north of Wadesboro, North Carolina. The valley of the Rocky River contains springs the Indians called "the place of healing waters." In the antebellum period, planters from the coastal plain visited Rocky River Springs resort to escape the greater incidence of malaria at lower elevations and also to partake of the mineral waters. In an 1825 advertisement in a Cheraw newspaper, the proprietor, C. C. Coppedge, declared, "The efficacy of the water of these Springs in eradicating bilious or debilitated complaints has long been established." Modern analysis shows that the waters contain iron, sulphur, mild arsenic, and magnesia.[21]

The Lynches River originates in the piedmont region of North Carolina in Union County. For the greater part of its length it winds through a swamp choked with debris. It flows southeasterly for about 120 miles to its junction with the Pee Dee near Johnsonville, South Carolina. To the north of the Great Pee Dee, the Lumber River rises in Moore County, North Carolina. Its swift current and sparkling black water produce cool temperatures even in summer. Rotting vegetation in the swamps produces tannic acid, which stains the water the color of weak coffee. Riverton, near Wagram, North Carolina, is well known for its broad and deep "swimming hole." In the days before air conditioning, it provided a place to cool overheated bodies. A refreshing swim in the strong current could set teeth chattering and lower the body temperature enough to remain cool for hours afterward.[22]

The Lumber River flows past Riverton, southeast between Scotland and Hoke counties, and into Robeson County, where local people sometimes call it the Lumbee. Below Lumberton, the river turns sharply southwest to meet the Little Pee Dee just beyond Nichols, South Carolina. This confluence forms the largest tributary of the Great Pee Dee, draining about 3,110 square miles with a discharge of 3,186 cubic feet per second. Many elevated sand ridges, swales, creeks, and relict oxbow lakes interrupt the smooth flow of the Little Pee Dee as it curves across a broad floodplain.

The second largest tributary to the Great Pee Dee is the Black River. Many small creeks near Bishopville, South Carolina, join to form the Black River, which drains 2,030 square miles and joins the Pee Dee four miles north of Winyah Bay. Its path is entirely within the coastal plain, and it is a lowcountry river overhung by giant cypresses and prolific Spanish moss.[23]

Tree branches lean out over the river, and many a fisherman has been unpleasantly surprised when a snake dropped from a limb into his boat. One shocked angler immediately pulled his gun, shot the snake, then recoiled in dismay as the water swiftly bubbled up through the hole in the bottom

Possibly a half million "Carolina Bays" appear in the Coastal Plain from Maryland to Florida. They occur frequently in the Pee Dee Basin. *Ted Borg. Courtesy South Carolina Department of Natural Resources.*

of his boat. Perhaps getting wet was preferable to a moccasin's bite. More experienced boatmen say the snake generally wants to get out more than he wants to bite, and a little help with a paddle can gently nudge him over the side.[24]

Another lowcountry river, the Waccamaw, joins the Pee Dee at Winyah Bay. Its headwaters come from the drainage of a large swamp and from waters that flow from Lake Waccamaw in Columbus County, North Carolina. Fed by springs, the lake has a bottom and shore of white sand. Swimmers can see the lake bottom through perhaps twenty feet of clear water.

Lake Waccamaw is a natural lake located in a depression known as a Carolina bay. Possibly a half million of these peculiar landforms appear in the coastal plain from Maryland to Florida, and they occur frequently in the Pee Dee Basin. The name may derive from bay trees that often grow around the edges of the oval or elliptical depressions.

The origin of the landforms known as Carolina bays remains a mystery. One theory holds that the depressions are scars left by a huge meteor that broke into pieces that dug depressions into the earth's surface. A second theory holds that the peculiar shape of the bays results from prevailing winds that cause basins to form ovals whose axes are perpendicular to the wind direction.[25] Another possible explanation is that marine currents and eddies of former seas under prevailing winds produced the strangely similar landforms.[26] Although a definitive explanation of the Carolina bays remains elusive, they are an important feature of the Pee Dee Basin landscape.

EARLY MAN AND THE RIVER

The origin of man in the region also remains mysterious. Scholars believe that humans lived in what are now the Carolinas as early as 13,000 to 11,000 B.C., but there is little evidence to identify their way of life. One reason for the lack of evidence of early man may be that sites of occupation were located in part of the coastal plain now covered by water. The continental shelf was habitable during parts of the Pleistocene epoch when sea level declined and exposed the continental shelf up to fifty miles off shore. Another reason may be that the area lacks the caves that would have attracted early man and preserved his remains.[27]

It is probable that at some time before 10,000 B.C., nomadic hunters and gatherers lived in what now are the Carolinas. Some scholars believe they hunted now extinct megafauna like mammoth, mastodon, or great bison. Other scholars say definitive evidence of this is unavailable. There is evidence, however, that megafauna lived in the area. Archaeologist James Michie reported the remains of a juvenile mastodon near Myrtle Beach, South Carolina. Michie argued that the dispersal of early tool types suggests that during the same period people were living along major river valleys and large creeks, especially within the valley of the Great Pee Dee.[28]

During the Paleo-Indian period from 10,000 B.C. to about 8,500 B.C., temperatures warmed, and the forest composition gradually changed from spruce and jack-pine to northern hardwoods like birch, hemlock, beech, and elm, with later additions of oak, hickory, and sweet gum. With forest changes, the Indians developed a new way of life that led to the Archaic Horizon about 8,000 B.C. The Archaic way of life included evidence of fishhooks and use of a mortar for grinding, and the diet

An artist's reconstruction of Indians at Sara's Ridge, one of many important pre-historic sites from the Archaic period. Many similar sites were excavated along the Yadkin-Pee Dee.
Artist's reconstruction by Martin Pate. Courtesy Southeast Archaeological Center, National Park Service.

consisted of fish, shellfish, deer, raccoon, turkey, opossum, squirrel, waterfowl, and turtle, along with acorns, hickory nuts, walnuts, roots, and seeds.[29]

Archaeologists have excavated a number of Archaic sites along the Yadkin-Pee Dee River.[30] Joffre Lanning Coe, formerly director of the Research Laboratories of Anthropology at the University of North Carolina, reported two sites at either end of the Narrows of the Yadkin that contributed extensive information beginning with the transition from the Paleo-Indian to the Early Archaic period and continuing to about 1700 A.D. Coe's work was especially important because he found sites that had been successively occupied for thousands of years and yielded stratified deposits that made it possible to differentiate artifacts of various ages and cultures.[31]

Certain geographic features at the Yadkin Narrows attracted inhabitants. According to Coe, the Yadkin is "ultimately drained through a gorge at the Narrows like sand in an hourglass." When primitive people moved up and down the river, they inevitably passed in the vicinity of the Narrows. The shallow water surrounding the falls and rapids assured an opportunity to catch fish and mollusks. The most important factor in the location of camps was the constricted valley and barriers to shore traffic. Travelers encountered a slim neck that limited the space available for camps along the river. The

While living along the Yadkin-Pee Dee, the Mississippians built large villages surrounded by stockades of pine poles such as this reconstruction at Town Creek near the Little River. *Suzanne Linder.*

Doerschuk Site, excavated by Coe, was the last bit of level ground suitable for camping on the east side of the river below the Narrows.[32]

Other evidence suggests many sites of occupation along the Yadkin and Pee Dee with the most notable being people of the Mississippian cultural tradition around 1300. The Mississipian culture took shape along the middle Mississippi River between 700 A.D. and 900 A.D. The building of flat-topped, pyramidal earthen mounds that served as the foundations for temples or other important buildings characterized this culture. The Mississippians built large villages surrounded by stockades of pine poles set close together with one or more watchtowers to afford protection. Inhabitants built houses by setting a framework of poles in the ground in a circle and tying the tops together with rope made of hemp.

The Mississippian subsistence base focused on agriculture, especially corn, squash, beans, and tobacco. This economy increased the land's carrying capacity, and population therefore increased. Although Mississippian people hunted many small animals, the most important object of the hunt was the deer. A skillful hunter could disguise himself in a deerskin and stealthily slip into a group of feeding deer to shoot his arrow at close range. Women mixed the venison with beans, corn, and nuts

THE EARLIEST GUIDEBOOK FOR
RIVER TRAVEL

The work of German explorer John Lederer might be viewed as one of the first travel handbooks to the Yadkin-Pee Dee River. Lederer shared his own observations as well as what he had learned from the Indian guides to make it easier for those who would follow. Through his writings, Lederer made recommendations to future explorers. He noted that moss usually grew on the north side of trees and that this was helpful if a compass was not available. He also suggested making notches on trees with a small hatchet to mark one's trail. His experience showed that parched maize was better food for the pack than the biscuit Englishmen usually carried because the maize did not mold. For trading goods he advised coarse cloth, axes, hoes, and any edged tools. For Indian nations in more remote areas, he suggested trading trinkets and beads. He noted that guns, powder, and shot were in great demand but forbidden for trade by the English government.[1]

In dealing with the Native Americans, he advised traders to be firm in price and never compromise. He suggested being wary of ambushes in late evening and at dawn. Traders should never enter a home until invited and then must seem unafraid when led pinioned like a prisoner. That, Lederer said, was a ceremony used for both friends and enemies.[2]

in large clay pots to make stew. Early European visitors reported that this succotash was a delicious dish. The hide of the deer was useful for bedding or clothing. In addition to leather clothing, the Mississippians had cloth woven from plant fibers, opossum hair, or fine feathers.[33]

In the Little River near the Town Creek village, stones that formed a fish weir or trap are still visible. Indians piled rocks to form a v-shaped dam across the river, with the v pointing downstream. Fish swam into conical traps at the apex of the v, and the current prevented them from swimming back out.[34]

Religion was an integral part of daily life for the Mississippian people. Beginning with a ritual bath in the river each morning, religious observations included prayer offered before planting seeds or killing deer and elaborate ceremonies held in the temple at night. The ceremonial center was a special place where chiefs and leading warriors from each town could get together to discuss important matters. Archaeologists have excavated and restored such a center at Town Creek located in Montgomery County, North Carolina, on the Little River, a tributary of the Great Pee Dee.

A raised pyramid built of dirt carried in baskets on the backs of people from many towns and crowned by a temple or chieftain's dwelling dominated the palisaded enclosure. Inside the temple, priests kept a perpetual fire with four logs facing the cardinal points. Ceremonies inside the temple consisted of pipe smoking, feasting, drinking, singing, and sometimes entertainment by groups of dancing girls, who danced for several hours at a time.

By day, warriors from different towns played ball games around the large ball post topped by a bear skull and scalps located in the open area at the base of the temple mound. Two teams would hit a ball made of deerskin stuffed with hair. Their rackets were similar to lacrosse sticks, and the game was violent. Next to warfare, ball games gave a warrior an opportunity to distinguish himself and gain honors.[35]

In addition to more sophisticated ceremonial and social traditions, Mississippian people developed large political units called chiefdoms. Nevertheless, their occupation of the Pee Dee Basin lasted only two or three centuries. It is possible they moved south and west to become the forebears of the Creek Indians, but local tribes may have absorbed some.[36] After the Mississippian culture declined, there is evidence that Indians of Siouan stock occupied the Pee Dee region in the sixteenth century. Their way of life, however, was already threatened by the presence of Europeans.

After the coming of the first Europeans, the world of the Indian, which had changed little in thousands of years, would face a harsh and rapid transformation, but the geographical factors that gave the river its powerful influence would remain to provide elements of cultural continuity to future inhabitants.

Hernando de Soto. *Courtesy South Carolina Department of Archives and History.*

CHAPTER 2

Conquistadores and Chieftains

". . . brown of skin, well-formed and proportioned . . . [and]
more civilized than any people seen in all the territories of Florida."
The "Gentleman of Elvas" describing Native Americans in the
Carolinas while traveling with Hernando De Soto.

The stories of Spaniards in the Carolinas are tales of intrigue, adventure, and discovery. Sadly, however, they are also tales of historic depopulation, military conquest, and slavery. Spanish explorers originally came to the Carolinas in search of precious metals, a land route to Mexico, and a suitable place for settlement close to the sea route from the West Indies to Spain. The Spanish visits are significant because reports of chroniclers give eyewitness accounts of the Native American civilization in the sixteenth century.

Geographical factors brought the first Europeans to the mouth of the Pee Dee River. Winyah Bay, a wide estuary where the Pee Dee, the Black, the Waccamaw, and the Sampit rivers enter the Atlantic, provided a sheltered harbor for Spanish caravels, the sailing vessels used in the fifteenth and sixteenth centuries. Although the Spaniards visited the interior only briefly, their incursions had a significant impact on the society of Native Americans, which rested on a somewhat fragile balance of human and environmental factors.

THE FIRST SPANIARDS ARRIVE

One of the first Spaniards to show interest in the land to the north of Florida was Lucas Vazquez de Ayllon. Ayllon, a wealthy and educated nobleman, sent out ships at his own expense to explore large portions of the Atlantic coast.

In 1520, Ayllon sponsored a ship under Francisco Gordillo. It was to explore northward from the Spanish capital at Hispaniola—today's Dominican Republic. Gordillo possibly traveled as far as present-day New York. On his return voyage he encountered another Spanish ship in search of natives to be sold as slaves. Its captain, Pedro de Quexos, persuaded Gordillo to accompany him on a slave-hunting expedition. Although this mission was against Ayllon's orders, Gordillo agreed. The two ships sailed together for some days, after which "they were driven by a sudden tempest which lasted two days, to within sight of a lofty promontory . . . "[1]

The natives first flocked to the beach to see the ships, then fled when the Spanish launched a landing party. The mariners, however, were able to capture a man and a woman whom they took on board and showered with presents before letting them return to their people. These natives were later identified with the Shakori Tribe, recorded by the Spaniards as Chicora.[2]

Having convinced the natives they meant no harm, the captains sought a suitable place to anchor their ships. On St. John the Baptist's Day, June 24, 1521, they sailed into a great river, which they named San Juan Bautista. Quexos recorded the latitude as 33.5 degrees, which corresponds closely to that of Pawley's Island, South Carolina.[3]

The native chief who called his land Chicora sent fifty men to the ships with presents of food. He also provided guides to lead the Spanish in an exploration of the bay and countryside. The Spaniards repaid the hospitality with cruelty. After luring 140 Indians on board ship under pretext of entertainment, they set sail for Hispaniola. When one ship sank on the way, the survivors crowded onto the second ship. Cramped conditions and unfamiliarity with Spanish food, however, made them sick and starved by the time they reached Hispaniola.

Although slaves were much in demand for work in agriculture and in mines, this particular capture was unauthorized. The local Spanish council of government, presided over by Diego Columbus, son of Chistopher, judged the Indians free and issued an order for their return to their native land. The order was never enforced.[4]

NATIVE AMERICAN FRANCISCO CHICORA ENTHRALLS THE SPANISH COURT

Ayllon hastened to Spain to secure his discoveries and to seek a commission from Spanish ruler Charles V to explore and settle the new land. He took along one of the captive Indians, whom he called Francisco Chicora. This able Native American adopted the Christian religion and soon learned to converse in Spanish. He enthralled the Spanish court with fantastic tales of his homeland. Chicora's stories provide valuable insight into the myths and legends as well as the realities of Native American culture in the Pee Dee region.

Historian Peter Martyr explained that since the natives had no written language, Indian traditions and folk tales were handed down from father to son. Chicora recounted the tale of Datha, a king of gigantic size, and of his wife, who was also large. There were two explanations for their unusual stature. One theory held that while they were infants, their bones were softened with an ointment of strange herbs to make them pliant. After their limbs were stretched, the infants were wrapped in warm covers and revived with milk from a nurse who had eaten special food. Having received this treatment many times, the royal children grew to great size.

Martyr questioned this story and found more believable an explanation given to a priest by other captives. The priest reported that a diet of crushed herbs was given at puberty to stimulate growth. Although Martyr was not fully convinced, he advised the Spaniards to investigate the matter quickly, lest some enemy uncover the secret first.[5]

Martyr questioned another account. "In place of horses," he related "the king is carried on the shoulders of strong young men, who run with him to the different places he wishes to visit." Martyr's

The colony of San Miguel de Gualdape may have been located near the mouth of the Waccamaw River, across Winyah Bay from present Georgetown. *Suzanne Linder.*

priestly informant had never heard of this, but Francisco Chicora—supported by Ayllon—insisted it was true. Later European visitors would find that it was customary for native chiefs to ride on litters carried on the backs of warriors. It is possible that when Chicora spoke, something was lost in translation.[6]

Chicora also told the story of men with alligator-like tails a meter long and as thick as a man's arm. To sit, they had to accommodate their tails by finding a seat with an open bottom or digging a hole of over a cubit. Martyr declared, "Such is the story told to me, and I repeat it for what it is worth. Your Excellency may believe it or not."[7] This tall tale was as fantastic as reports that surfaced in modern times of a "Lizard Man" along the Lynches River.

SAN MIGUEL DE GUALDAPE: THE FIRST COLONY

Chicora's master, Ayllon, obtained a patent to return to the new land as governor and establish a colony. An eminent jurist and a knight of the Order of Santiago, Ayllon was not a professional soldier. Unlike the numerous Spanish conquistadors who sought wealth and power through war, Ayllon was a man of peace. He tried to settle disputes by arbitration and accepted a patent from Spanish monarch Charles V specifying that Indians were not to be made slaves unless captured in war. Another provision, possibly recommended by Ayllon, required truthful and fair dealings with the Indians. Although his subordinates were sometimes cruel and treacherous, there is no record that shows Ayllon himself failed to live up to the ideals of his patent.[8]

After several delays, Ayllon set sail from Hispaniola in July 1526 with a fleet of six ships carrying five hundred men with additional women and slaves destined for the land of Chicora. After a mistaken landfall to the north, the Spaniards made their way again to the river they had named San Juan Bautista. Here they established a colony and called it San Miguel de Gualdape.

There is controversy over where San Miguel was located. Paul Hoffman, an authority on Spanish settlement, has placed the colony on Sapelo Sound about halfway between present-day Savannah and Brunswick, Georgia. The exact site will remain inconclusive until further archaeological evidence is found.[9]

Although Spanish mariners of the period were fairly accurate in determining latitude, they could not judge longitude. South Carolina historian Paul Quattlebaum did much research comparing the Spanish archival materials with the geographical features of the coastline. He placed San Miguel near the mouth of the Waccamaw River on lower Waccamaw Neck, across Winyah Bay from today's Georgetown. Archaeologists have excavated in the area but have found no evidence of a Spanish settlement. If this location is correct, Winyah Bay at the mouth of the Pee Dee River has the distinction of being the site of the first Spanish settlement on the American continent north of Mexico.[10]

The approximately six hundred settlers arrived at San Miguel sometime in August 1526. Ayllon appointed a mayor or chief magistrate to direct the affairs of the town. The King's patent instructed Ayllon to include a surgeon, a physician, an apothecary, as well as monks and priests. They built houses and a ship or barge that either oars or sails could propel. Although the craft was open, the crew could cover the hold to protect supplies from the weather. The barge could travel up river where the water was too shallow for the caravels. With the exception of Indian dugouts, this was the first recorded instance of shipbuilding on the Pee Dee River as well as on the Atlantic coast.[11]

Francisco Chicora and other Indians who had been trained as interpreters escaped from the Spanish at the first landfall. An accomplished storyteller, Chicora must have fascinated his people with tales of his incredible journey.[12]

Even without interpreters, the Spanish had contact with the Native Americans, and their accounts provide some of the first information available about the people of the Pee Dee area. The colonists recorded that as many as two hundred natives lived in one large communal house constructed of two rows of tall pines between fifteen and thirty feet apart—apparently still standing in the ground. Their top branches were intertwined to form a roof and the whole structure was covered with matting woven between the trunks and branches. The houses were three hundred or more feet long and, although numerous, were some distance apart. The Spanish also took note of "mosques" or temples made of stone with oyster shell mortar on islands that also served as burial grounds where the principal people were buried in temples by themselves.[13]

The settlers at San Miguel had a difficult time. Many died of an illness that one Spanish historian recorded as malaria. Ayllon himself became ill. After having received the sacraments, repented of his sins, and sorrowed for the plans of his fleet, he died on St. Luke's Day, October 18, 1526.[14]

Following the death of their leader, the settlers' difficulties increased. In mid-winter, they decided to abandon the colony and return to Hispaniola. The weather was so cold that seven men froze

THE MELUNGEONS

Since the mid-1600s, a group of people of unknown origin called Melungeons have lived in the southern Appalachians. Although there are several theories as to the origin of these dark-skinned people, one of the most probable explanations has an interesting South Carolina connection.

The Melungeons maintain their unique identity today and recent DNA evidence does not contradict their claim to be descendants of Spanish and Portuguese explorers. From the South Carolina viewpoint, one of the explorers linked to the Melungeons is Juan Pardo. More specifically, descendants of soldiers stationed at Juan Pardo's outposts near the Yadkin River, joined by refugees from Santa Elena and possibly others, may have survived in the area and intermarried with Carolina and Virginia Native Americans to eventually become the Melungeons.

A comparison of Santa Elena surnames with best-known Melungeon surnames shows an amazing similarity.[1]

to death on board the ship, *Santa Cathalina*. Of the original settlers who set out with such high hopes, only 150 sick and despondent Spaniards reached home early in 1527. The ill-fated colony had lasted less than six months. The town of San Miguel de Gualdape disappeared and has not been found to this day.[15]

Tales of the giants and "alligator men" of Chicora and reports of the good harbor and fertile land of the River of St. John the Baptist would fascinate explorers and historians for centuries to come. In a world of conquest, deception, and frantic search for easy wealth, Lucas Vazquez de Ayllon envisioned the peaceful settlement of a fair and fertile land. The history of the region might have been different had he lived.

HERNANDO DE SOTO FINDS COFITACHEQUI

The next Spaniard to approach the vicinity of the Pee Dee was Hernando de Soto, a veteran of the conquest of Peru. He landed at Tampa Bay in 1539 with an army of six hundred men with horses, a herd of pigs, and war dogs outfitted with spiked collars. For the next four years De Soto explored what is now the southeastern United States looking for precious metals and ruthlessly exterminating those who stood in his way.[16]

The accounts of the De Soto chroniclers provide the first eyewitness descriptions of the Native Americans of the inland Carolinas. One of the most prosperous chiefdoms the Spaniards visited was Cofitachequi. Earlier scholars located the kingdom at Silver Bluff on the Savannah River, but historians Charles Hudson, Marvin T. Smith, and Chester B. DePratter place it east of the Wateree River and just south of present-day Camden, South Carolina.[17]

De Soto had been seeking Cofitachequi ever since he began his journey at Apalachee, near present-day Tallahassee, Florida. On April 30, 1540, he encamped near a large river and sent a small party ahead to Cofitachequi to arrange for interpreters and canoes for crossing the river. On May 1, De Soto arrived at the crossing that lay opposite the town.[18] Four canoes approached. In one of them was a young kinswoman of the chieftain. She greeted De Soto and said:

> My sister sends me to salute you, and to say, that the reason why she has not come
> in person is, that she has thought to serve you better by remaining to give orders on
> the other shore; and that, in a short time, her canoes will all be here, in readiness to
> conduct you thither, where you may take your repose and be obeyed.[19]

Soon the cassica, or chieftain, arrived on a litter covered with a delicate white material. She was a young girl of fine bearing, and Indians of rank bore her litter on their shoulders with much respect. She sat on cushions under an awning in the canoe that took her across the river. Speaking to De Soto quite gracefully and at ease, she took a string of pearls from her neck and put it on De Soto to show her good will.[20]

She invited him to her town and provided abundant hospitality. The "Gentleman of Elvas" who accompanied De Soto related, "The country was delightful and fertile, having good internal lands upon the streams; the forest was open, with abundance of walnut and mulberry trees." He found the people to be "brown of skin, well formed and proportioned . . . [and] more civilized than any people

An engraving by Theodore de Bry based on a drawing by Jacques le Moyne de Morgues (1588) illustrates how the French explorers saw an Indian princess. *Courtesy South Caroliniana Library.*

seen in all the territories of Florida." They wore shawls of thread made from the bark of trees or feathers—white, gray, vermillion, and yellow, rich and proper for winter. They also made shoes, stockings and hose of well-dressed deerskins with designs drawn in colors. Rodrigo Ranjel, De Soto's private secretary, found the people "very clean and polite and naturally well conditioned."[21]

Elvas noted large vacant towns grown up in grass. The Indians explained that many had died of "a pest in the land" two years before and the others had moved away to avoid a similar fate. Ranjel recorded that in Talimeco, one of the deserted towns, the house of worship was on a high mound. The caney, or house of the chief, was large, high, and broad. The mats the former inhabitants had decorated it with were so skillfully done they seemed to be one. There were many cabis, fine fields, and a pretty stream. Walnuts, oak trees, pines, live oaks, cedars, and groves of liquid amber—sweet gum—grew nearby. At Cofitachequi, De Soto's men had found glass beads, rosaries, crosses, and Biscayan axes made of iron they supposed must have come from Ayllon's colony nearly fifteen years earlier.[22] The epidemic that decimated the towns might have been caused by the transmission of European diseases.[23]

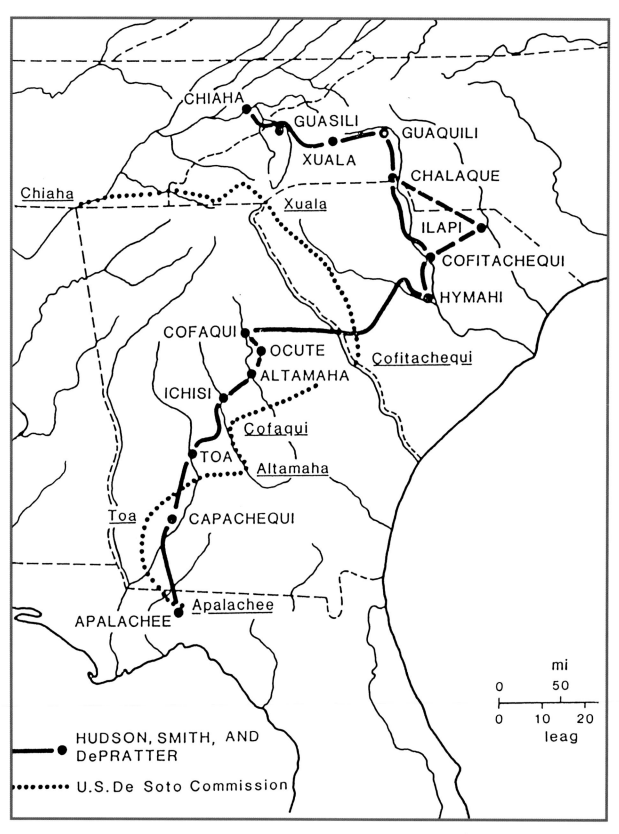

De Soto's route through what is now the Southeastern United States. *Courtesy South Carolina Institute of Archaeology and Anthropology/University of South Carolina.*

When De Soto departed, he forced the Lady of Cofitachequi—the chieftain or possibly her niece—to accompany him so that when he encountered her people along his march, carriers would be readily available. He forced her to march on foot among her slaves. After passing Xuala, however, she managed to escape. She joined a slave who had escaped from Spanish nobleman Andre de Vasconcelos and, as Elvas said, ". . . it was very sure they lived together as man and wife, and were to go together to Cutifachiqui [sic]."[24]

De Soto's visit was brief, but the accounts of the expedition's chroniclers provide valuable insights into the Native American culture of the period. Cofitachequi was a powerful chiefdom with influence possibly extending from the Atlantic coast to the Appalachians and northward to Town Creek on the Little River, a tributary of the Pee Dee. Cofitachequi was a part of the Mississippian tradition. At the apex of its development this tradition represented the highest cultural achievement in the Southeast and probably in North America.[25]

SANTA ELENA: A BASE FOR LAUNCHING EXPEDITIONS INTO THE INTERIOR

The chiefdom[26] was still powerful more than twenty-five years later when Spaniards again visited the area. In the interim, the French had established Charlesfort, a short-lived outpost on present-day Paris Island, South Carolina, and a larger fort near what is now Jacksonville, Florida. In response to the French incursions, Pedro Menendez de Aviles, a Spanish nobleman, with support from King Philip II of Spain, arrived in Florida in 1566. He routed the French and built a fort at St. Augustine. Menendez then founded the town and fort at Santa Elena on Parris Island at the site of the abandoned Charlesfort.[27]

Juan Pardo made two expeditions from Santa Elena into the interior between 1566 and 1568, traversing the length of what is now South Carolina into western North Carolina and eastern Tennessee. Because the Spaniards were dependent on trade with the Indians for their food supply, Pardo arrived with items like chisels, wedges, hatchets, knives, necklaces, mirrors, and cloth. Pardo's mission was to pacify with goodwill, not to conquer by force, to attract the natives to the service of God and His Majesty, and to take possession of the land in the name of the Spanish king.[28]

Pardo took his evangelical mission seriously and had powers of persuasion. He said, "I spoke to them about God and His Majesty, as it [was] commanded to me, and they answered that they were ready to obey His Holiness and His Majesty . . . ."[29] The local chiefs asked Pardo to leave Christians behind to teach the people on at least three occasions—twice at Guatari, a location Pardo called "one of the good lands of the world."[30] Pardo complied.

DePratter, Hudson, and Smith have located Guatari on the Yadkin River near Salisbury, North Carolina. This location would correspond to what was later called the "Trading Ford" of the Yadkin.[31] At Guatari Juan Pardo once found "more than thirty chiefs and a great number of Indians," and spent "about fifteen or sixteen days" before leaving his chaplain, Sebastian Montero, and four soldiers as teachers. Later, Pardo spent seventeen or eighteen days there, built Fort Santiago, and left seventeen soldiers with a squad leader.[32]

Juan de la Vandera, the expedition's scribe, recorded that at Guatari were two female chiefs "who are ladies, and no less, in comparison with other chiefs, for in their retinue they are served by pages and ladies." Vandera said it was a rich land with villages of good houses and earthen huts, "round and very large and very good." He called it "a land of mountains and good arable land" near "a very great river which empties at Saupa [Sampit?] and Usi, where it becomes salty, near the sea, sixty leagues from Santa Elena."[33]

The Pardo expedition also visited another site on the same "great river." This was Ylasi, the site the DeSoto chroniclers called Ilapi, located on the Pee Dee near Cheraw, South Carolina. For both De Soto and Pardo, Ylasi proved to be a good place to find food. On his final return to the coast, Pardo stopped there for corn.[34]

When Pardo returned to Santa Elena on March 2, 1568, he induced the Indians to build a string of buildings to house corn and other stores for the Spanish to use. His soldiers built small forts at six sites, including Guatari and Cofitachequi, and small detachments stayed to man these forts. Pardo, hoping to win friends for Spain and guarantee food supplies, distributed trade goods to the Native Americans.[35] He also introduced the use of metal implements to some Indians who had known only stone tools. The more positive contributions of the Spanish to local culture, however, were counteracted by the fact that the Spaniards unintentionally introduced European diseases as well.[36]

EUROPEAN CONTACT HAS DEVASTATING RESULTS

In the period following Spanish exploration, cultural and population collapse was rapid, probably occurring in less than sixty years. Although the period of Spanish exploration was of limited duration, indirect European influence persisted for more than a century, primarily through the spread of disease. Epidemics can be documented by multiple burials that were numerous between 1540 and 1565 and again between 1600 and 1630.

Native American civilization in the Southeast reached the zenith of its cultural development in the Mississippian tradition in the early sixteenth century. The Spanish conquistadors may have contributed to this development in some small ways, but the fragile balance of human and environmental factors that supported these early civilizations could not withstand the ravages of disease that followed contact with Europeans. The Indian population of 15,000 in 1600 had declined dramatically by 1715.[37]

Perhaps the Spanish explorers would not have been able to settle in the area of the Yadkin-Pee Dee without the aid of the Native Americans. Because of the generous gifts of food to early settlers and Spanish armies, however, and because of the the Native Americans who served as guides for expeditions of exploration, the Spanish were possibly responsible for settlements at Winyah Bay and at the Trading Ford of the Yadkin. Whether or not San Miguel de Gualdape was located at the mouth of the Pee Dee, the Spanish definitely had a settlement at Santa Elena—Parris Island, South Carolina—from 1566 to 1587.[38] It is highly likely that expeditions from Santa Elena reached the Yadkin-Pee Dee basin.

Native American civilization in the Southeast reached the zenith of its cultural development in the Mississippian tradition in the early sixteenth century. When the first permanent European settlers came to the Pee Dee region in the early 1700s, they found a land still wild after these early attempts at settlement, and a native population weakened both culturally and militarily by disease.

Spanish explorers found a delightful and fertile country graced by wildflowers and insects such as this pickerelweed and yellow butterfly. *Charles McRae.*

Sunset from Morrow Mountain near the site where the Yadkin and Uwharrie join to form the Pee Dee. *Richard Watkins.*

CHAPTER 3

Voices in the Wilderness

*"Nor could all Europe afford a pleasanter Stream, were it
inhabited by Christians, and cultivated by ingenious Hands."*
Explorer John Lawson describing the Yadkin.

Before Europeans settled the Carolinas, a vast wilderness stretched from coastal beaches westward into the Appalachian Range. Exactly what this wilderness was really like is a question that has intrigued conservationists, sportsmen, and all those who love nature. The desire for profit from trade with Native Americans or from exploitable natural resources motivated early explorers who were willing to risk the unknown in search of fortune. The Yadkin-Pee Dee River was a principal avenue of trade and settlement, and glimpses of this unspoiled area are available through written records of a few courageous visitors.

JOHN LAWSON'S RECIPE OF THE "DELICIOUS COUNTRY" WHETS APPETITE FOR TRADE

Trade with the Indians of the interior was flourishing by 1700 when the Lords Proprietors of Carolina appointed John Lawson, a recent immigrant from England, to make a reconnaissance of the interior. At that time there were still no adequate maps of the region. Lawson's journey took him from Charleston up the coast to the Santee River. He followed the river northwest to the Waxhaw settlement, then east to the confluence of the Rocky River and the Yadkin.[1]

On the trip from Waxhaw, Lawson noted that his spaniel did not find one partridge. He described killing several ducks of a strange kind, however, "having a red Circle about their Eyes, like some Pigeons that I have seen, a Top-knot reaching from the Crown of their Heads, almost to the middle of their Backs, and abundance of Feathers of pretty Shades and Colours. They prov'd excellent Meat."[2] These ducks may have been wood ducks, year-round residents of the Carolinas, whose excellent flavor came from a diet of vegetation instead of fish.

Lawson said the pigeons were so numerous that one might see millions in a flock. They sometimes split off the limbs of stout trees upon which they roosted at night. The Indians killed large numbers with long poles with which they hit the pigeons at roost. They used the pigeon fat like butter. The flocks were so large they almost obstructed the light of day as they passed over.[3]

John Lawson crossed the Uhwarrie River and remarked that he was impressed with the quality of stones available. Photo in the Uwharrie National Forest. *Suzanne Linder.*

Upon reaching the Yadkin River region, Lawson called it a "delicious country" exceeded by none he had ever seen. He observed grass six feet high along the banks of pleasant rivulets. "Nor could all *Europe* afford a pleasanter Stream, were it inhabited by *Christians*, and cultivated by ingenious Hands."[4] The Indians lived in a cleared field of about a square mile near the river. Lawson saw numerous swans and other waterfowl as well as songbirds. He said that "the forward Spring welcom'd us with her innumerable Train of small Choristers, which inhabit those fair Banks; the Hills redoubling, and adding Sweetness to their melodious Tunes by their shrill Echoes."[5]

Lawson knew the Yadkin as the Sapona River. The Indian king of Sapona Town and his wife entertained Lawson and his party with great respect. They served swan, geese, and venison. The Indian doctor showed Lawson quantities of medicinal drugs and explained what great maladies he had healed through their use. For pains in the joints, the Indians had several *Bagnios* or sweating houses made of stone in the shape of large ovens.[6]

After leaving Sapona Town, Lawson and his party traveled through some rich valleys. About eight miles from Sapona, they reached the "Heighwaree" [Uwharrie] River. Lawson was especially impressed with the quality of stones. He said the area "affords as good blue Stone for Mill-Stones, as that from Cologn [*sic*], good Rags, some Hones, and large Pebbles, in great abundance, besides Free-Stone of several Sorts, all very useful." One of the hones "prov'd rather better than any from *Old Spain*, or elsewhere."[7]

The description of the Yadkin River region was but a small part of John Lawson's book, first published in London in 1709. It contained a journal of his travels and also detailed descriptions of land, vegetation, animals, insects, birds, and fish. He included extensive information about the Native Americans, possibilities for trade, and opportunities for settlement.[8]

INDIAN TRADE FLOURISHES ALONG THE PEE DEE

Although traders frequented the valleys of the Yadkin and its tributaries, they did not settle permanently there in the early years of the eighteenth century. Indian trade, however, was a principal motivation for settling the lower part of the river in the area of Winyah Bay.[9]

Trade with the Indians, especially in deerskins and Indian slaves, had become important to the settlement at Charleston, which had been established in 1670. The Yemassee War of 1715 caused Indian trade to the south of Charleston to diminish considerably. The General Assembly dealt with the problem by passing an act on June 30, 1716, which attempted to restore the Indian trade by establishing a public monopoly controlled by commissioners. Regulations at first limited trade to three sites: Savano Town—near present-day Augusta, Georgia; the Congarees—near present-day Columbia; and Winyah Bay, the mouth of the Yadkin-Pee Dee.[10]

In an effort to establish Indian trade to the north, the commissioners of Indian trade on July 10, 1716, appointed William Waties Sr. as factor—a merchant who secured products and arranged to transport them to market. Waties was to establish a trading post or "factory" at "the old Casekey's House on Black River [a tributary of the Pee Dee] at Wineau." The commissioners also authorized the purchase of a cargo of Indian trading goods to the value of two hundred pounds for the Wineau Factory.[11]

Waties's instructions authorized him to proceed to various branches of Wineau [Winyah] Bay at his discretion to trade for skins, furs, slaves, or other vendible commodities. He was not to buy knowingly any free Indian for a slave, however, or to make a slave of any Indian who belonged to a tribe that was friendly with the government. He was forbidden to sell arms or ammunition to hostile Indians. And he was to see that all skins, furs, and slaves were branded with the mark C over W. Another white man, John Vourmerl'n—who was probably an indentured servant—was to accompany Waties along with several Indian slaves. Later Meredith Hughes replaced Vourmerl'n. The Board instructed Waties to "go on board the Periago, and proceed with the Goods now laden in her, for the Wackamaws &c., according to his Instructions."[12]

In September 1716 Waties established a trading post at "Uauenee," or the Great Bluff, a place that would be convenient for the Pee Dee Indians, who were friendly with the settlers. With the help of a carpenter from Charleston, Waties built a twelve by ten-foot log house. Transportation to and from Uauenee on the Pee Dee River was by periauger.[13] Throughout the years, the spelling of Uauenee changed to Yourenee, Euhaney, Yauhaney, and finally Yauhannah. Although positive proof is not available, it seems likely that the bluff at present-day Yauhannah was the site of the early trading post.

THE PERIAUGER NAVIGATES THE PEE DEE

The "Periago" or periauger was a cypress dugout canoe that builders had enlarged by splitting it down the middle and installing boards for added width. Various models included a rudder, oars, sails, a tarpaulin, or even an awning to shade passengers. A large periauger could carry as much as one hundred barrels of pitch or tar and transport horses, cattle, and goods from one plantation to another. It was useful both for its speed and for its carrying capacity. It also provided comfort for passengers if equipped for that purpose.[1]

Although there was no set number, the standard crew was usually four to six oarsmen and the factor. The commissioners evidently preferred Indian over Negro slaves, but in emergencies they used British sailors. Indian slaves were available at three pounds per month. The charge for Negro slaves must have been higher because the commissioners refused Bartholomew Gallard's [Gaillard] offer for the use of his Negro slaves saying: ". . . we expected you would send some Wineau Indians instead of them, for the Periago goes up Pedea River and it would be very inconvenient to you and chargeable to us, to keep your Negroes for so long a Voyage. . . ."[2]

A VERSATILE VESSEL FOR RIVER TRANSPORTATION

The periauger, a dugout canoe, was a versatile and functional vessel for river transportation. The factor loaded it with trade goods such as cloth, blankets, tools, salt, gunpowder, guns, and rum (mixed with one third water) and sent it up the river. The distance by water from Winyah Bay to Charleston was about a hundred miles. The inland route, suitable for canoes or periaugers, could follow creeks that connected Winyah Bay with the Santee River and the Santee to Sewee Bay. The passage continued through Awendaw Creek to the Wando River, and finally to Charleston. Another route entered the Atlantic Ocean from Winyah Bay, passed the mouth of the Santee and entered Sewee Bay, then followed Awendaw Creek and the Wando to Charleston.[14]

Native Americans welcomed European textiles, and white settlers found deerskins useful for clothing, thus insuring an active exchange. The government monopoly over the Indian trade enabled the commissioners to fix prices and thereby try to ensure fair dealings with the Native Americans. The commissioners set a schedule listing the value of each item in deerskins. For instance, fifty bullets were worth one deerskin, while a "Duffield Blanket" was worth fourteen skins. A yard of "Strouds" sold for seven skins.[15] Mary Robinson, a seamstress in Charlestown, advertised ready-made buck and doeskin breeches, "either natural or black, purple, and cloth colours . . . She also dresses Deer Skins . . . dyes, washes, and mends buck-skin Breeches."[16]

Because the periauger available to navigate the Pee Dee in 1717 had no cabin, the skins were vulnerable to rain and rough seas. To make wet skins useful, they had to be "dressed" or tanned a second time. On June 18, 1717, the commissioners complained to Meredith Hughes, then factor at Wineau:

> We have yours of the 3rd Instant by the Bearer, with the Skins, but a great many
> of them are very much damaged and some quite spoiled and good for Nothing; and
> all (as we apprehend) for Want of being better placed in the Periaugoe which ought
> to be done highest in the Middle, arch-wise, that so the Rain and Water might run
> off, and not soak in, as it did in these, which please to mind for the future.[17]

Keeping the skins dry in an open boat in rough water was only one of the many problems encountered by the factor. The Pee Dee outpost was uncomfortable and vulnerable to dangers from potentially hostile Indians. The Cheraws were not friendly with the government, while the settlers complained that the Waccamaws stole their cattle. Waties resigned as factor in February 1717, leaving his post to his assistant, Meredith Hughes.

HOSTILITIES HALT TRADE

During the Yemassee War, Indians killed about four hundred colonists, about six percent of the white population, including numerous Indian traders. Only with help from other colonies and finally the Cherokee Indians were the Carolinians able to defend Charleston.[18] The Indian factors had reason to feel apprehensive. In the summer of 1717, Hughes moved from the Pee Dee back to Black River

Indians supplied deerskins, the principal export of South Carolina in the early-colonial period. *Engraving by Theodore de Bry based on a drawing by Jacques le Moyne de Morgues, 1588. Courtesy South Caroliniana Library.*

because he thought the post at Uauenee was too dangerous. On August 10, 1717, the commissioners wrote to Hughes, "We have considered the Subject of your several Letters, and find the Dread you have of the Charraws hath occasioned your Removal from our Trading House at YourEnee, and interrupted the Commerce you had with the Indians there." They instructed Hughes to come to Charleston to confer with them.[19]

Hughes appeared before the board on September 7 and indicated that he had brought with him such effects of the trading post as he could and housed the rest at the home of Andrew Collins, an inhabitant of Black River. On September 11 Hughes again appeared and asked the opinion of the board concerning a present of thirty deerskins that he received from the Cheraw Indians in recompense for one of the Cheraws trying to shoot him. The Board decided that the skins were "hereby adjudged to be the Publick's Due, and disposed of for the Good of the Trade."[20]

Even though Hughes had moved the trading post closer to the settlements at Black River, he continued to fear the Cheraws. In January 1718 he warned of possible trouble. The commissioners notified the governor but advised Hughes to take a firm stand. They said, "We would have you take no notice to the Indians of your Resentment of their Behaviour, but shew them you expect they should reform and submit."[21]

By May of 1718 the trade had diminished to the extent that Hughes decided to move back to Uauenee. The commissioners said they approved of Hughes' returning to Uauenee "which in all Likelyhood will revive the Trade now under management which hath declined so much of late." They also authorized Hughes to secure a constable to prosecute anyone who was trading with the Indians illegally. They were concerned not only that government profits would be eroded but also that illegal traders might cheat the Indians and thus promote warfare.[22]

Eventually hostilities became open. Although the tribe was already weakened by disease, a hundred Waccamaw warriors fought against the settlers in 1720. Of these, sixty were killed or captured and sent to the West Indies as slaves. This encounter marked the virtual end of the tribe as well as the end of the profitable Indian trade in the vicinity.[23] In the 1720s, the marketing of naval stores replaced the Indian trade as the principal means of livelihood for the settlers in the Pee Dee area.[24]

NATIVE AMERICAN CULTURES YIELD TO THE PRESSURE OF SETTLEMENT

Nothing could ever replace the Native American cultures that were gradually being destroyed by the pressure of settlement. The meetings of the Indian commissioners provided ample evidence of brutality and theft by traders, the abuse of rum to facilitate cheating such as the use of illegal weights and measures, enslavement of free Indians, and various other abuses.[25] The Native Americans were justifiably outraged, but they lacked the political organization needed to unify against the settlers.

Potential profits from trade with Native Americans had motivated exploration of the Yadkin/Pee Dee basin but ironically had led to destruction of Indian society. Familiarity with the Indian path to the Trading Fords of the Yadkin as well as knowledge of the fertile land that awaited served as a stimulus to settlement of the northern river basin and pushed the Indians even farther west. The profitable deerskin trade promoted settlement around Winyah Bay and demonstrated the usefulness of the periauger in transporting goods. Native Americans acted as guides and expert boatmen. In the 1720s, the periauger was to prove functional in transporting naval stores and enabling settlers to utilize the river to send cash products to market. The river served as a focal point for both trade and settlement in the early eighteenth century.

Numerous swamps in the Pee Dee Basin provided potential rice fields. *Phillip Jones. Courtesy South Carolina Department of Natural Resources.*

CHAPTER 4

Pine Trees, Rice, and Rivers

". . . we have the best conveniency in the
province for trade, a Fresh water River no
Worms and also the conveniency of vessels . . ."
From a Petition to the Assembly from the citizens of Santee and Winyah.

In the early eighteenth century, the Pee Dee was ripe for settlement and called out to those who could envision gold from pine trees and rich rice lands. The tidal swampland of the Pee Dee provided ideal fields for the cultivation of rice, while vast tracts of virgin pine furnished raw materials for the production of naval stores such as tar, pitch, and turpentine. The British needed vast amounts of tar and pitch made from pine resin for caulking the hulls of ships. Tall pine trees also provided excellent masts.

The production of naval stores and the development of rice culture motivated adventurous settlers to claim land along the rivers of the Pee Dee system in the coastal region. Access to a river was a necessity both for transporting the extremely heavy barrels of tar, pitch, and turpentine as well as for planting rice. To provide labor, South Carolinians imported such large numbers of slaves that the slave population soon outnumbered the free, and the province instituted the township system to entice white settlers to immigrate.

PERMANENT SETTLEMENTS BEGIN AROUND WINYAH BAY

Some of the first permanent settlers in the Winyah Bay area at the mouth of the Pee Dee were not on the bay itself, but on Black River. In early records, Wenea, Weenee, Wineau, Winyaw, and Winyah all refer to Black River or to settlements thereon.[1] Dugal McKeithen and John Nesmith each held tracts of 500 acres on Black River in 1698, and Francis Avant received 350 acres on the north side of the river in 1709.[2] Peter, son of John and Sarah Lane, was born at Black River on November 4, 1713.[3]

Despite evidence of a few settlers, a surveyor familiar with the area said in 1712 there were no more than five families north of the Santee River.[4] Possibly there were more than this because in 1714 the legislature authorized the appointment of an inspector or packer of commodities for the Winyah region. The packer's job was to certify that the product was of good quality and of standard weight or measure.[5] By 1716, Captain Robert Screven and Samuel Miller served as tax inquirers, indicating a sizeable population.[6]

Prince George Winyah Parish Church, Georgetown, South Carolina. *Suzanne Linder.*

The establishment of churches was further indication of permanent settlement. In March 1722 the legislature passed an act to establish the parish of Prince George with former Indian trader Meredith Hughes, John Lane, and John Hayes designated as commissioners to supervise building a church.[7] By 1723 there were evidently two communities, one on Black River and one on Winyah Bay. A petition, which was granted, requested that the church be built on Black River because more people lived in that community. Ten years later, the majority had shifted to Georgetown, and the Black River settlement became a part of Prince Frederick's Parish in 1734. The community was located near the intersection of Black Mingo Creek and Black River.[8]

Dissenters had established a meeting house on Black Mingo by 1726. The building was probably shared by Baptist followers of William Screven and his son, Elisha Screven, and Presbyterians.[9] William Screven, founder of the Baptist denomination in South Carolina, died at Winyah in 1713, but his son Elisha was also a Baptist minister.[10] Presbyterian records note the baptism of George and Helen Nelson's son "Mathew" in 1729.[11] By 1734, Black Mingo Church was definitely Presbyterian. The minister, Samuel Hunter, "a worthy and judicious minister of Christ," served the church about twenty years until his death in 1754.[12]

SETTLERS SEND GOODS TO CHARLESTON

After the Indian trade died out in the Winyah area, white settlers used the old Indian trade routes through the maze of waterways to paddle their canoes or periaugers loaded with barrels of rice, tar, beef, or pork to Winyah Bay. There they transferred the goods to larger vessels, usually sloops or schooners, for transportation to Charleston. In many cases, if a ship could cross the sandbar at the entrance to Georgetown Harbor, it could navigate some distance up the Pee Dee, Black, or Waccamaw.[13]

Passage was not always easy, for under the influence of tides and currents, shifting sands formed bars where heavily laden watercraft could easily go aground. In passing an act in 1738 to impose penalties for the obstruction of waterways, the legislature said it was "of great inconveniency and public detriment, that boats or pettyaugers of too great draught of water should be suffered to enter into the several creeks, cut-offs or water-passages . . . ." The act also addressed the problem of passage to and from Winyah, which was impeded by sand filling an area called the Breach, by directing commissioners to see that boats drawing up to four feet of water could be accommodated. [14]

Local craftsmen developed a type of vessel that was suitable for carrying heavy loads in shallow water. There was a flourishing shipbuilding industry in the Georgetown vicinity. The South Carolina Ship Register lists at least thirty-three vessels built in and around Georgetown before the Revolution.[15] It is likely that shipwrights built the ocean-going vessels, while plantation carpenters built smaller watercraft.

The fact that small ocean-going vessels, sometimes called coasters, could navigate directly to the plantations along the rivers made it difficult to collect customs duties.[16] The British Empire had strict navigation laws, and it was necessary for exports to pass through an official port with a customs inspector. This meant that to carry on legal trade, early settlers in the Pee Dee basin had to ship their goods through Charleston. Georgetown would not become a legal port of entry until 1732 when the population growth demanded it.[17]

In the early eighteenth century, the twin opportunities presented by rice and naval stores as marketable commodities stimulated settlers to seek suitable lands and to buy slaves to provide labor. When it became possible to generate wealth from tilling the soil rather than from the Indian trade, individuals who could be characterized as large planters began to emerge, and small farmers made their way into the back country.[18]

CAROLINA FORESTS ARE SOURCE OF FIRST LEADING EXPORT

In the Winyah Bay area, naval stores preceded rice as the leading export.[19] In an effort to encourage the production of naval stores, the British government offered a subsidy for their production. This bounty on naval stores made their manufacture profitable in Carolina.

Some British manufacturers complained that Carolina tar was too "hot," meaning that when it was applied to a rope as a preservative, the tar tended to scorch and thus weaken the rope. They attributed the problem to the fact that Carolinians made tar from dead wood, whereas, Swedes used recently cut trees to produce "green" tar.[20]

In Carolina forests there was much dead wood that could be gathered without harming growing trees. In addition, seasoned heart pine becomes highly flammable and is sometimes called "lightwood" or "lighter wood." According to Francis Yonge, South Carolina's representative to the Board of Trade in London, lightwood could produce three times as much tar as green wood. Yonge pointed out that if South Carolinians had to use the Swedish method, it would not be profitable to engage in the process. Yet, after September 29, 1724, Americans were required to use the Swedish method in order to claim the bounty.[21] The products of the naval stores industry were heavy and difficult to transport. Since there were very few roads, access to water transportation was almost a necessity. Some lands that were of limited worth for growing crops became valuable because stands of pine trees grew there. Harvesting tar required less capital than establishing a rice plantation; thus, the naval stores industry made considerable impact on the province's growth and on the dispersal of the population, especially along the rivers.[22]

By the 1720s, enough settlers had moved into the lower Pee Dee basin (which included the Black and Waccamaw rivers) to produce sufficient goods for export. In 1723, with the hope of reducing freight charges, the people of Winyah petitioned to become a port of entry so that local produce could be shipped directly to a foreign destination without going through Charleston.[23]

When the British removed the bounty on naval stores in the mid-1720s, the freight charges to Charleston became even more burdensome. The citizens of Santee and Winyah petitioned the assembly:

> tho we have paid so many taxes yet none of it is applied to our services in order to make a port. Tho'
> we have the best conveniency in the province for trade, a Fresh water River no Worms and also the
> conveniency for vessels which damages us for want thereof Ten Thousand pounds a year by carrying
> our produce to Town all which makes it the harder for us to pay Tax.[24]

Led by Landgrave Thomas Smith, George Pawley, and William Waties, a group of large landowners marched into Charleston and threatened the Council. Arthur Middleton, acting governor, arrested Landgrave Thomas Smith on charges of treason. When the legislature convened, riotous persons from the outlying parishes prevented the Assembly from passing a new tax act until their grievances were satisfied.[25]

HARVESTING TAR, PITCH, AND TURPENTINE

Workers put "V" shaped notches in trees to draw resin for turpentine production. *Suzanne Linder.*

To produce turpentine, workers gathered the resin or sap of the longleaf pine from live trees. Near the base of the tree, workers cut a pocket to catch the resin. Then they removed bark above the pocket and cut channels in a "V" shape to direct the resin to the pocket at the base of the tree. When the resin was distilled, the products were spirits of turpentine and the residue, rosin. In the colonial period, people also called raw resin "turpentine."[1]

To produce tar, the workers built a kiln by digging a hole in clay soil or lining sandy soil with clay. A trench from the center of the hole slanted downward and led to a lower level where dippers could collect the tar. When the excavation was complete, workers split about twelve to fifteen cords of dead pine into rails and arranged row upon row of rails pointing to the center. In the center, they put twisted knots, stumps, and gnarled bits of root. The kiln was sometimes seven feet high at the outer rim, topped with a roof of split rails.

The next step was to "flag the kiln" by placing a covering of pine boughs over the top and in the crevices of the sides. To "bank the kiln," men covered the boughs with green logs and then placed sod in the cracks, and the kiln was ready to burn. As the boughs smouldered, tar began to ooze out of the trench. To obtain pitch, the manufacturer distilled the tar by boiling it in a caldron or simply burning it in a round hole dug in the ground.[2]

GEORGETOWN BECOMES A PORT AND ENCOURAGES TOWNSHIP GROWTH

The new royal governor, Robert Johnson, recognized the need for a port at Winyah and began negotiations toward that end in 1730 before he left London. Likewise in 1730, George Hunter, later surveyor-general of the province, visited Winyah Bay and wrote on his map:

> At Wineaw Bar I sounded the Channel and at Low Water neap Tides found 10 foot water. At High Water Spring Tides there rise 16 ½ feet. And the same water, has at Georges Town on Sampit Creek 4 fathom. Georges Town was laid out in Lots & sold last year [1729] to people who are obliged to build a House in 15 Months. They expect there a port of Entry to ease them of the freight to Charles Town. They have one foot less water or thereabouts than Charles Town.[26]

By 1732 Georgetown had become an official port, with a collector of customs and a deputy to the naval officer stationed in Charleston. The naval lists are a tribute to the meticulous record keeping of the British Empire. In artistic script the naval officer recorded the date of entry, the vessel's name and home port, the master's name, type of ship, number of tons, guns, and men; when and where the ship was built and registered, and the owner's name. Further records showed what the ship carried, its destination, and date of departure.

Sloops, snows, brigantines and schooners with names like *Amelia* of Providence, *Dolphin* of New London, or *Success* of Bermuda brought manufactured goods from Europe, fruit and rum from the West Indies, and bricks and earthenware from New England. Categories of exports included rice, pitch, tar, turpentine, logwood—used to make dye—skins, sassafras, pork, corn, and peas.[27]

The establishment of a port at Georgetown was a decided advantage to prospective settlers of the Pee Dee Basin. It coincided with a plan for settling the middle region of South Carolina proposed by Governor Robert Johnson to the Board of Trade in London in March 1730. Johnson recommended that the crown grant ten townships of twenty thousand acres each on the frontier. The Board directed Johnson to lay out eleven townships on the banks of rivers about sixty miles from Charleston, two each on the Altamaha, Savannah, and Santee, and one each on the Pon Pon (Edisto), Wateree, Black, Pee Dee, and Waccamaw. The Altamaha became part of Georgia, so eventually only nine townships were surveyed.[28]

The plan had three purposes. The first was to encourage white Protestants to settle on the frontier to provide a buffer between the coastal region and the various dangers from Indians, French, and Spanish. The second purpose was to increase the ratio of whites to African Americans in the population. Because slaves outnumbered whites about two to one in South Carolina by 1730, additional white immigrants could help lessen the perceived danger of slave insurrection. Third, more settlers would increase the economic productivity of the colony.[29]

The township plan provided that each settler would receive a town lot and fifty acres of land for each head in the household, including slaves, but no grant could have a river front of more than one-fourth its depth. In addition a quantity of land not exceeding three hundred acres contiguous to the town would constitute a commons area. As further encouragement settlers could receive tools and provisions and a ten-year exemption from quit rents.[30]

BROWN'S FERRY VESSEL RAISED FROM
THE BLACK RIVER

In 1976, divers raised the remains of a small merchant vessel from the Black River.

Artifacts such as a pewter shoe buckle, a small white egg cup, and ceramic pipes dated the boat to about 1740, making it the oldest preserved vessel in America.[3] Known as the Brown's Ferry Vessel, the craft was flat-bottomed and keelless, apparently for the purpose of reducing draft. It was not a ferry boat but was so named because it sank at the location called "Brown's Ferry" carrying twenty-five tons of bricks. The boat had a complex framing plan, employing softly rounded hull sections amidships, compound shapes in the quarters, and a pointed bow and stern. The hull was shallow enough to operate in shoal waters but full enough in the hold to accommodate a thirty-ton burden. It was fifty feet, five inches long and fourteen feet wide.[4]

Although the vessel was found approximately twenty miles up river from Georgetown,[5] the damage on the hull from teredo, or shipworm,[6] showed it must have ventured beyond the confines of Black River into salt water. She was a practical working boat. She could run her flat bottom on a bank to load where there were no docks, and she could hoist sails to travel in the ocean along the coast. Poles and oars provided propulsion when wind was impractical.[7]

The vessel is now located in the Rice Museum in Georgetown. It is important as an example of the sturdy and practical boats that used the Pee Dee and its tributaries for river commerce in the early 1700s. (See page 46.)

KINGSTON: THE FIRST TOWNSHIP IN THE PEE DEE BASIN

Three of the proposed townships were in the Pee Dee Basin: Williamsburg on the Black River, Queensboro on the Pee Dee, and Kingston on the Waccamaw. Kingston was located with the northeast line close to and paralleling the North Carolina boundary. The township had three sides of a square, with the Waccamaw River forming the irregular side nearest the Atlantic Coast. The south side ran just below the Little Pee Dee River.[31]

Official surveyors laid out the town of Kingston on a bluff near the center of the township where a large creek or "lake" flowed into the Waccamaw. This community later became the town of Conway. When first surveyed, Kingston was a wilderness. A young gentleman from England visited the area early in 1734 and published an anonymous account of his travels. His narrative gives a graphic picture of the wildness of the region and the courage and fortitude necessary to seek out unclaimed land in the Pee Dee Basin.

ENGLISH TRAVELER MEETS GRITS, A BEAR, AND HOSPITABLE PLANTERS

Near Georgetown, the anonymous traveler stopped at a small tavern and asked for punch, but the tavern keeper could offer only "a little bumboe, which is rum, sugar, and water, and some hominy and milk, and potatoes." He described hominy as a sort of meal "much resembling our oat meal in England, made of their Indian corn." He also commented that the potatoes were not like English ones. They were three or four pounds in weight and "they eat, when baked, much like a roasted chestnut."[32]

The gentleman traveler found Georgetown to be a pleasant town with a great many more houses than inhabitants. He expressed the opinion that inhabitants would soon be forthcoming because of the perceived Indian threat to the south. On February 7, 1734, he set out with friends in a large canoe with an intent to view lands on the Waccamaw River. "The same night we reached Mr. Gordon's on P.D., where we slept; it is about ten miles from Georgetown." James Gordon had purchased two tracts totaling 650 acres on the northwest side of the Pee Dee from William Waties in January 1734. The next morning Gordon accompanied the visitors to the Waccamaw where "Major Pauly" joined the group. The Englishman noted that the gentlemen of the country were exceedingly civil to strangers "so that a man, if he knows but the nature of the country, may go from one plantation to another for a year or two, and keep his horse, and never cost him a farthing, and the gentlemen will be always glad of his company."[33]

Unfortunately for the travelers, there were no plantations in the vicinity when they stopped for the night. They camped on a bluff where they found two half barrels of pitch. Since it was very cold, they set fire to the pitch for warmth and "dressed some salt beef and rice for our suppers." The next day, they came to some vacant land, but it proved to be "mostly pine barren, and that is but very indifferent, and not fit for any thing but tar and turpentine. . . ."[34]

Two days later they finally found some land worth claiming on "a beautiful bluff on P.D. side." Here they found plenty of good oak and hickory, valuable pine, and cypress swamp, which would be suitable for growing rice. Having a surveyor along, one gentleman decided to "run out" a claim. While the surveyor worked, several men in the group decided to take the canoe farther up river to look for more suitable land, leaving the writer and several others with only one bottle of punch and a biscuit apiece. When the boat did not return for two days, the party nearly starved.

After the sojourners' return, the provisions on the boat were also exhausted, but at least there were guns on board, and the group managed to survive by shooting some crows and woodpeckers.[35] The next morning they set out for some serious deer hunting. After having no luck all day, they were returning to camp when they saw a wolf chasing a deer and managed to kill them both. With meat on hand, they decided to proceed farther up river.[36]

"The next bluff we came to was the bluff on which Kingstown is to be settled," reported the traveler. He considered settling in a township a great advantage because of the ten-year exemption from taxes or quit rents. He noted, "The land hereabouts is, for the generality very good, and for the most part high champaign land, and is not subject to overflow . . ."[37]

The next night the group camped at Bear Bluff about thirty miles above the township.[38] "I think this tract is much the finest on all the river; and, I believe, if we had each of us a warrant, we should have fell out about the choice of it. . . ." That night a wolf stole a quarter of their venison before they shot him coming back for a second quarter. On the voyage home, they killed a bear at Kingston Bluff, which they barbecued for supper.[39]

The rest of the trip back to Georgetown was relatively uneventful. The Englishman proceeded to return to Charleston by horseback. He had to swim his horse across a creek after falling in when the horse stepped on a stump, which broke. Having lost his pocket book, he at last arrived at an inn, soaking wet with no money for lodging or for the ferry across the Santee the next day.

"As fortune would have it," he said, "there accidentally came in three country planters, who proposed playing a game of whisk [whist—an early form of bridge]." The young man recalled the proverb, "Nothing venture, nothing have," and proceeded to play until two o'clock in the morning "in which I made shift to win two pounds, seventeen shillings, and six pence." This was sufficient to see him to Charleston where he rejoined his friends and undoubtedly secured additional funds.[40]

KINGSTON TOWNSHIP IS SLOW TO DEVELOP

Despite the complimentary account of the gentleman traveler, the township of Kingston got off to a slow start. As the traveler noted, there was a wide strip of well-drained and fertile soil between the Little Pee Dee and the Waccamaw near the town site. Similar good land was found on the small creeks reaching back into the interior, but the bulk of the township was made up of a plain so level that drainage was bad and much of the soil was hardly practicable for settlement. In a petition of 1744, Robert Jordan stated that the five hundred and fifty acres of his former warrant had "proved so barren, that he cannot by labour nor Industry Get a Living thereby" and asked for other land.[41]

Fewer Kingston settlers appear in the colonial records than those of any other South Carolina district. Prior to 1736, between four and five thousand acres were taken up, but in 1736 over seventeen thousand acres appear in the records. It is evident that non-residents claimed a large proportion of the land. The militia returns of 1757 list a company of only eighty-six men with fifty-seven male slaves. A

Methodist Bishop Francis Asbury crossed the Pee Dee River and visited Kingston in 1785.
Portrait by John Paradise. Courtesy World Methodist Council, Lake Junaluska, North Carolina.

population of about four hundred total would probably yield a similar number of males meeting the age requirements for militia service.[42]

There is evidence that some Scots-Irish Presbyterians who originally planned to settle in Williamsburg Township moved on to Kingston when they found that most of the Williamsburg land was claimed. The Williamsburgers protested to the provincial council that nearly sixty families of their countrymen had to go elsewhere.[43] The Reverend John Baxter of Cainhoy served a Presbyterian congregation at Kingston occasionally, and in 1756, William Donaldson, a minister ordained in Pennsylvania, accepted a call to the congregation there.[44] When Donaldson died in 1759, the *South Carolina Gazette* advertised his estate consisting of seven hundred acres on the Waccamaw River, ten slaves, and the year's indigo crop.[45]

The Methodist circuit rider, Francis Asbury, crossed the Pee Dee at Euhaney—Yauhannah—Ferry and visited Kingston in 1785. He returned to the area in 1791 but did not hold services on either visit. On December 24, 1795, he preached at Kingston "in an old Presbyterian meeting house, now repaired for the use of the Methodists." Asbury went on to say, "I spent the evening with W. Rogers, formerly of Bristol, where our wants were richly supplied: thus, sometimes we abound and at other times suffer want; and we may balance the one with the other."[46]

There was evidently a village at Kingston by 1768 because the *Gazette* described a murder that occurred there. John McDougal, justice of the peace and tavern keeper, and Joseph Jordon "conducted an extensive quarrel," which included displays of horsewhip, sword, and knife. McDougal was wounded in the hand but eventually pursued Jordan to a smith's shop and there killed him. The account of the murder mentioned that a Negro belonging to Hunter's schooner saw part of the affair, suggesting that schooners could navigate the Waccamaw River as far as Kingston.[47]

Although water transportation was a definite advantage, the poor drainage and lack of large quantities of land suitable for agriculture meant that Kingston Township was slow to develop. The lower Waccamaw River, however, became an extremely prosperous area through the cultivation of rice. The continuous tidal swampland between the Waccamaw and the Pee Dee was ideally suited to rice culture, and it soon became one of the wealthiest regions of the nation.[48]

RIVER WATERS AND THE SWEAT OF SLAVES GENERATE WEALTH FROM RICE CULTIVATION

Rice culture required that the fields be flooded periodically, so location on a waterway or swamp was essential. In 1685 Captain John Thurber, a New England sea captain, brought some rice seed from Madagascar to Dr. Henry Woodward, a leader in Charleston. The treasurer of the East India Company provided another strain of the commodity to South Carolina in 1696.[49] It took about seventy-five years to develop the tidal culture of rice fully, but even in its earlier phases of cultivation, rice headed the list of staples by 1705. Production accelerated rapidly. Although records are fragmentary, estimates of rice exports jumped from approximately 2000 barrels in 1700 to over 15,000 barrels by 1715. By 1730 the total was 48,155 barrels.[50]

The Brown's Ferry Vessel was raised from the Black River and now rests at the Rice Museum in Georgetown.
Artist rendering by Danny McLaughlin. Courtesy Virginia Skinner.

Georgetown District at the mouth of the Yadkin-Pee Dee Basin was the leading rice-producing area in antebellum America, and the Waccamaw plantations were the most productive in Georgetown District. By the middle of the eighteenth century, the labor of slaves on rice plantations in the South Carolina low country afforded their masters the highest per capita income in the American colonies. In 1810, slaves made up eighty-eight percent of the population, and by 1840, Georgetown District produced almost half the total rice grown in America.[51]

African slaves supplied both the technical knowledge and the labor for growing the staple. Rice was plentiful along the West African coast, especially in the Senegal-Gambia region, which supplied nearly twenty percent of the slaves imported into South Carolina. Although Europeans contributed engineering and management skills, striking continuities between African and Afro-Carolinian methods of planting, hoeing, winnowing, and pounding—de-husking—rice persisted. There would have been little successful rice culture in South Carolina without the strength and skills of enslaved Africans.[52]

Slaves also acted both as boat captains and oarsmen for river craft. The oarsmen kept time to improvised songs sung in the antiphonal, or call and response, pattern. An Englishman described how "these chants break with their pleasant melody the calm stillness of the evening . . . and our crew with measured stroke keep time to the music of their own choruses." Welcome Beese, a former slave remembered one such song:

Oh, where Mausser William?
Sing "Glory in my soul!"
One day gone—another come!
Sing "Glory in my soul!"

We'll broke bread together!
Sing "Glory in my soul!"
Pender meddlesome—meddle everybody!
Sing "Glory in my soul!"[53]

The extent to which slaves worked as masters of vessels and as boat builders angered some white workers. A group of white boatmen complained to the provincial council in 1744 that slaves should not be employed as masters or patroons of periaugers or coasting vessels. Andrew Ruck of Charleston and several other shipwrights stated that "the great number of negro Men chiefly Employed in Ship Carpenters work is the reason that the Petitioner and white men of their Trade can meet with little or no encouragement in the Province, and that their familys are reduced to poverty. . . . " John Daniel, John Yarworth, George Hasket, and John Scott, shipwrights, protested Ruck's petition, however, saying the use of slaves was beneficial to his majesty's ships. The Council took no action. Slaves continued to act as masters of vessels and to build boats to transport naval stores, rice, and other products.[54]

In many ways, pine trees (or naval stores), rice, and rivers shaped the development of the Pee Dee Basin in the coastal region. Profitable products and convenient transportation to market stimulated settlement along the rivers. Another important factor was the institution of slavery. While the usefulness of slave labor became increasingly apparent, the population balance shifted so that by 1730, about two thirds of the population was African American.[55]

It is not surprising that the provincial government sought additional whites to populate the colony. The township at Kingston did not prove successful at first, but Williamsburg Township on Black River soon proved the worth of recruiting settlers through the township system. Its success would encourage other colonists to move into the inland Pee Dee Basin in the decades of the 1730s and 1740s.

The Black River from the landing at Kingstree. *Suzanne Linder.*

CHAPTER 5

Williamsburg Township on Black River

*"We were much oppressed with
fear on divers other accounts,
especially of being massacred
by the Indians, or bit by
snakes,
or torn by wild beasts, or of
being lost and perishing in the
woods."*
Robert Witherspoon
commenting on his family's
pioneer home in South Carolina.

Years before the survey of Williamsburg Township was completed in the spring of 1732, an unnamed explorer laboriously rowed his periauger from Winyah Bay up the sinuous channel of the Wee Nee—Black River. He traveled for about a hundred miles to a point where a large tree on the northeast bank resembled the white pine, a tree native to New England. By law, it was reserved for the king because of its usefulness in making masts for the Royal Navy. As the law required, the explorer marked the tree with a broad arrow and reported his action to the royal governor along with wonderful tales about the country surrounding the tree. The explorer was a pioneer who helped establish the settlement pattern for the Pee Dee and its tributaries. Soon colonists would follow, making their way by boat up the rivers to establish homes in the wilderness.[1]

IMMIGRANTS SETTLE IN NEW TOWNSHIPS

Shortly after the 1732 survey, Scots who had temporarily lived in Ireland began to arrive. On October 27, 1732, the *Happy Return* docked in Charleston with eighty-five passengers.[2] A colony of forty Scots-Irish under the leadership of Roger Gordon settled near King's Tree, the spot marked years before by the unnamed explorer. Included were the families of Roger Gordon, Edward Plowden, Robert Ervin, James Armstrong, David Johnson, Adam McDonald, William James, Archibald Hamilton, David Wilson, and John Scott. They all came by boat as far as possible, then made their way through the nearly impenetrable wilderness along Black River to the place of settlement.[3]

THE WITHERSPOONS WITHSTAND WEATHER, WILD BEASTS, AND PEE DEE PROFANITY

The provincial government offered transportation, basic tools, and staple foods to encourage immigrants to settle in the townships. A group of "Irish Protestants" received supplies from the township fund near the end of 1733.[4] Members of the Witherspoon family were likely part of this group. Noted for piety, integrity, intelligence, and a high sense of duty, members of the family suffered persecution in Scotland because they were zealous adherents to the Reformed Protestant Church of Scotland. John Witherspoon, a descendant of church founder John Knox, went to Ireland in 1695 in search of greater religious freedom. In the 1730s he and his seven children with their families made their way at different times to Williamsburg Township. The story of the experiences and hardships of the Witherspoons offers a detailed look at what it was like to settle the frontier of South Carolina on the Black River, a tributary of the Great Pee Dee, in the 1730s.

David Wilson, who married Mary Witherspoon, William James married to Elizabeth Witherspoon, and Gavin Witherspoon, a bachelor at that time, were among the first to immigrate. Additional members of the family arrived in 1734. Robert Witherspoon, who was a young boy, sailed with his parents, grandparents, and others on a ship called *The Good Intent*. Janet Witherspoon, Robert's grandmother—and mother of the earlier immigrants, Mary, Elizabeth, and Gavin—died on board ship. Robert said, "We were sorely tossed at sea with storms, which caused our ship to spring a leak, our pumps were kept incessantly at work day and night for many days together and our mariners seemed many times at their wits' end. But it pleased God to bring us all safe to land except my grandmother, about the first of December."[5]

The Witherspoons were in Charleston for about a month and found the people there kind. Robert's little sister, Sarah, probably about two, died there and was the first person buried in the Scots Meeting House yard. Sometime after Christmas, the immigrants boarded an open boat with tools, one year's provisions, and one grinding mill for each family. Provisions included Indian corn, rice, wheat flour, beef, pork, rum, and salt. Each male over sixteen received one axe, one broad hoe, and one narrow hoe. The supplies were provided under the township program. It also provided transportation to Williamsburg Township.[6]

The devout Witherspoons were almost as distressed by the "profane and blasphemous oaths" of the patroon and his boatmen as they were by the inclement weather they were exposed to day and night. The passengers disembarked at Potato Ferry, twenty miles or more up river from Georgetown,[7] while the boat continued to the King's Tree with the goods and provisions. The women and children took refuge in Samuel Commander's barn while the men went up river to build dirt houses or "potato houses" for a temporary shelter. They also borrowed a few horses and got what help they could to bring their families overland about twenty miles. It was frosty and the woods were full of water when they set out on the last of January. Tradition says they sent men ahead to cut notches on trees and construct log bridges across streams and swamps to ease the way for the women and children. When the leaders were out of sight, the ones who followed would shout to find out which way to go and would get the response, "Follow the bleezes!"[8]

Part of the group stopped at neighbors' cabins, and the rest went to William and Mary Witherspoon James' home. Robert recalled, "Their little cabins were as full that night as they could hold, and the next day every one made the best they could to their own places."[9]

The Black River. *Emily Garner.*

On February 1, 1735, Robert and his family reached the Bluff, three miles below the King's Tree. They found nothing but wilderness and a small dirt hut. The guide who brought them there left immediately, and when their fire went out, Robert's father, James Witherspoon, made his way through the swamp until he came to a branch and followed it to the cabin of the earlier settler, Roger Gordon.

"We watched him as far as the trees would let us see," Robert recalled, "and returned to our dolorous hut, expecting never to see him or any human being more." Fortunately, however, his father returned with fire, for with evening coming on, the wolves began to howl on all sides. "We then feared being devoured by wild beasts, as we had neither gun nor dog, nor even a door to our house, howbeit we set to and gathered fuel and made a good fire and so we passed the first night."[10]

The next day a thundercloud brought wind, lightning, and a pouring rain. Robert recalled, "The rain quickly penetrated through the poles of the hut and brought down the sand with which it was covered and which for a while seemed to cover us alive." The lightning and thunder seemed awful to six-year-old Robert, his older brother, David, and his younger brother, John. "I do not remember to have seen a much severer gust than that was. I believe we all sincerely wished to be again at Belfast," Robert said. But the storm soon passed, and the evening brought clearing skies and warmer temperatures.[11]

The immigrants had to go to the King's Tree landing to bring their goods from the boats. They were obliged to carry clothing, beds, chests, provisions, tools, pots, and bowls on their backs. The first thing James Witherspoon brought from the boat was his gun, "one of Queen Anne's muskets."[12]

Finding the way was a major problem for there were few roads or paths. The colonists used swamps and branches as guides at first. Three people were lost in the forest. Later some of the men gained enough knowledge of the woods to be able to blaze paths from place to place by cutting notches on trees.[13]

When a large opossum—an animal unfamiliar to Europeans—passed by the door, Elizabeth cried out, "There was a great bear!" She and her children took refuge behind some barrels and a chest, while James got his gun and shot the opossum "about the hinder parts, which caused him to grin in a frightful manner." Since the musket was loaded with swan shot, it did not kill the animal, and James finally ventured out and killed it with a pole.

Even more frightening was the appearance of Indians, who came to hunt in the spring "in great numbers like the Egyptian locusts." Although the Indians did not harm the settlers, Robert said, "We were much oppressed with fear on divers other accounts, especially of being massacred by the Indians, or bit by snakes, or torn by wild beasts, or of being lost and perishing in the woods."[14]

Although the time for planting was short, all who could "wrought diligently" and cleared and planted as long as the season would permit. Thus, the settlers were able to make provisions for another year. One advantage was that stock could forage in the woods and did not require feeding.[15]

FLAX AND INDIGO

In 1736, the Assembly passed an act that provided a bounty for growing flax and doubled the existing bounty on hemp. For "every hundred weight of water-rotted, well-cured and clean-dressed hemp," it promised four pounds. Fifty shillings would be paid for every hundred pounds weight of water-rotted, well-cured and clean-dressed flax.[16]

A former Georgia schoolmaster, John Dobell, wrote in Charleston in 1748 that the economy of Williamsburg was flourishing, "by whose Ingenious Industry our Market is often supply'd with abundance of Barrelled Butter and Flour. . . with Cheese tallow Bacon etc. Not to mention Linnen Cloth [from Flax] which they make in that perfection that our Governor has deign'd to wear it in Shirts himself."[17]

In addition to flax and hemp, farmers of Williamsburg Township grew corn, rice, and livestock, but the real money crop for Williamsburg in the 1740s was indigo, a plant that produced a rich, blue dye. King George's War[18] interrupted England's trade with the French and Spanish West Indies, traditional sources of the finest indigo. This created a potential market in Carolina. Eliza Lucas, a young girl of seventeen, is credited with reviving indigo in South Carolina.[19] She reported a successful crop in 1744. Later she and her husband, Charles Pinckney, gave samples of seed to other planters. Parliament offered a bounty or subsidy in 1749 to encourage the industry.[20]

A substantial investment was necessary for indigo production because it required a set of vats, sometimes made of wood, and sometimes brick. A good water supply was also essential. An expert of

In the common method of indigo production shown here, indigo plants produced a rich, blue dye. This method required a substantial investment. *Artist rendering by Darby Erd based on a contemporary drawing by Henry Mouzon, Jr.*

the period observed, "The French do always observe to place their indigo works near a river, where the water is clear and soft."[21]

Williamsburg residents were probably growing indigo before 1751.[22] The Scots, industrious though they were, knew nothing of indigo production. It is possible that some of their slaves came from parts of Africa where indigo grew. The slaves improvised vats by digging holes about thirty feet square at the top, shaped downward to resemble half of a broken inverted pyramid, and lining them with a water-proof composition of sand and pitch. They first dug one pit, and then they dug a deeper one beside it. From the bottom of this second pit, a line of wooden pipe drained the water-filled indigo into casks that stood in a third pit below.[23] There is a tradition that says the technique of lining indigo pits belonged to African slaves and that they jealously guarded the secret to keep it from their masters. A slave who possessed this special skill was valuable.[24] The leaves and stems of the bush fermented in the first vat. The liquid then drained into a second vat where the indigo oxidized and began to precipitate out of solution. It was necessary to beat or agitate the solution at this point, and timing was crucial. At the precisely correct moment, the excess water was drained and the remainder was put into a third vat to settle. Workers placed the wet indigo in linen bags, which they suspended to drain completely the remaining water. Then they spread the indigo in little boxes three feet by two feet by three inches deep to dry and harden. The whole process required considerable knowledge and skill if quality indigo was to result.[25]

Processing indigo was unpleasant. The fermenting leaves created an acrid stench, and the glucose released during fermentation attracted mosquitoes. Malaria was a frequent and often fatal illness.

Medical theory of the period associated the disease with "putrid effluvia" of coastal swamps, which was exacerbated by indigo vats. Although the role of the mosquito in spreading malaria was unknown at that time, indigo producers placed the vats as far from their homes as possible because of the stench.[26]

To supervise indigo processing, the farmer would have to walk a considerable distance. The conscientious Presbyterians of Williamsburg were strict about keeping the Sabbath—so much so that they made their small sons go into the fields and shut their bird and rabbit traps on Saturday evening. There is a tradition that one beautiful Sunday afternoon when an elder was strolling by his indigo vats, it happened that the precise moment to drain off the water had arrived. The good elder's foot accidentally struck the peg that controlled the drainage, and the crop was saved. The Session of Elders investigated but decided that accidents could happen and declined to take action on the matter.[27]

WILLIAMSBURG PROSPERS THROUGH RIVER ACCESS

Indigo brought wealth to the Williamsburg Township. James Witherspoon moved his family to "Thorntree" in 1749 where he built a comfortable two-story house. The house is still standing. It is not surprising that the living room is decorated with wide, intricately carved molding since James Witherspoon initially made his living by making reeds for looms. His wife Elizabeth finally had a beautiful and comfortable home, far removed from the mud hut where the family first lived. At his death in 1769, James Witherspoon's personal estate was worth £5028.0.6. The inventory included fourteen slaves but it did not include real estate. Witherspoon also owned his home and 300 acres on the Black River. He was a successful and prosperous yeoman farmer.[28]

In addition to the determination of the Scots-Irish settlers who "wrought diligently" at whatever they attempted, the township had other advantages for growing indigo. In many places, the soil was loose, dry, and moderately rich, and the Black River with its many branches provided a water supply as well as an avenue to ship the product to market. Cultivation of a money crop created a demand for transportation and labor. The total number of slaves in the township was more than six hundred by 1757. Henry Laurens, a prominent Charleston merchant, wrote: "We shall have a great deal offered to us from such Persons as deal with us for Slaves from Williamsburgh Township which affords in general the best Indigo."[29] Settlers solved the transportation problem by clearing the river. Robert Finlay received two hundred bushels of corn from the provincial government in 1737 as a payment for his clearing the river for large boats up to the town.[30]

Freeing the river from obstruction became so vital that the provincial legislature passed many acts for clearing Black River. The Acts of 1738 and 1753 made provisions for "cleansing, clearing and making navigable Black river" so it might accommodate boats, barges, periaugers, lighters, and other vessels.

The 1738 act for clearing the river addressed the problem of absentee owners. After 1735, the provincial government had opened the land previously reserved for immigrants to residents of the colony. The result was that half the land in Williamsburg taken up from 1734 to 1737 was by non-residents. Of the other half, one fourth of the total acreage can be identified with bona-fide settlers,

Settler James Witherspoon moved his family to "Thorntree" in 1749 and built a house that still stands. *Emily Garner.*

and the remaining fourth is doubtful. The Williamsburg Scots protested to the royal commissioner that all the good lands were taken up by "Gentlemen" residing in other parts of the province. They also complained that nearly sixty families of Scots who came over were forced to go elsewhere.[31] This may have been an exaggeration, for although much of the land surrounding the town and near the river was spoken for, there was other less desirable land available. Access to water transportation was evidently significant.[32]

THE CHURCH WAS THE CORNERSTONE OF TOWNSHIP STRUCTURE

The Scots also believed that religion was important. There was a meetinghouse for dissenters at Black Mingo, a tributary of Black River, which was completed about 1726.[33] This was, however, too far from the King's Tree settlement for convenience. On July 2, 1736, the following formed the Williamsburg Presbyterian Congregation: John Witherspoon, John Fleming, William James, David Wilson, James

Bradley, Robert Wilson, John Porter, David Pressley, Robert Ervin, William Pressley, John Henderson, William Frierson, Thomas Frierson, William Syms, David Allen, John James, James McClelland, and David Witherspoon. The first minister was the Reverend Mr. Robert Heron of Ireland, who served three years and returned to his native land in 1740.[34]

The congregation decided to call John Willison of Scotland, author of the "Mother's Catechism," "A Practical Treatise on the Lord's Supper," and "Discourses on the Atonement." An anecdote involving Gavin Witherspoon exemplifies the settlers' dedication to religion.

> Witherspoon: Wull, we must have a minister.
> Wull, Mister Witherspoon, wha wull ye git to be your minister?
> Witherspoon: Wull, wha but Mister Willison o' Dundee?
> But the minister must have a muckle sight o' money for his living.
> Witherspoon: And that we must gie him.
> And how much , Mr. Witherspoon, wull ye gie?
> Witherspoon: Ten pounds.
> But, Mr. Witherspoon, whar'll ye git the ten pounds?
> Witherspoon: Why if wus comes to wus, I ien can sell my cow.[35]

John Willison declined to come to the Black River frontier. Instead, John Rae arrived in 1743. A "high church" Presbyterian, he observed the ritual of the Church of Scotland and required his congregation to fast and pray on Saturday, listen to his four-hour sermon on Sunday, and spend Monday in thanksgiving that they had heard such a wonderful discourse. He served the congregation eighteen years until his death in 1761.[36]

Charles Woodmason, an Anglican cleric who was usually very critical of "dissenters," called John Rae "a learned Sensible and Good Man." Woodmason attended the auction of the Reverend's goods and books after his death. On that occasion, he found the widow "not so Nice." Woodmason said, "She courted the Writer of this to her Embrace, and wanted to Engage Him with Her on the Couch in the Study. . . . " Given the difficulties of survival in the colonial backcountry, Rachel Rae must have felt somewhat desperate. Unfortunately, Woodmason confessed to his diary that a fall and a kick from a horse had left him unsuited for "nuptial rites."[37]

The church played a key role in the stability of the Williamsburg settlement. The nearest court was at Charleston. The elders of the church served as a local tribunal. They called witnesses and sought confessions for drunkenness, cursing, swearing, and other acts they considered immoral.[38]

The religious background and the services provided by the church shaped the attitudes of the people and gave structure to the district. The strict Calvinist work ethic contributed to the fact that the settlers "wrought diligently" and succeeded in coping with all adversity and carving out a prosperous township in the wilderness. The family and the church were the foundation of the society, and these two factors were so interrelated as to produce a sturdy lot of secure people.[39]

The Williamsburg settlers emphasized religion and educated their children at home. British law required schoolmasters to have a license from the Lord Bishop of London, so they had to be communicants of the Anglican church. Because of their strong opposition to the established religion, Williamsburgers chose not to open a school. Legal documents of the colonial period, however, indicate that there was a high degree of literacy.[40]

ILLITERACY, ILLEGITIMACY, AND LAWLESSNESS IN THE BACKCOUNTRY

This was not the case in all parts of the backcountry. Charles Woodmason found much to criticize when he traveled across South Carolina as an itinerant Anglican minister. Before the organization of parishes in the back country, he noted swarms of orphans and other "pauper vagrant vagabond children" who joined groups of bandits and freebooters to survive. Woodmason protested against "Gamesters, Prostitutes, Filchers, Racers, Fidlers and all the refuse of Mankind." He claimed that in the weddings he performed, more than ninety percent of the brides were pregnant. He also estimated that about ninety percent of the people had "a filthy Distemper," presumably venereal disease. At militia musters or vendues—auctions—he noted fighting, brawling, gouging and quarreling.[41]

Woodmason also criticized the justices of the peace who provided the only law enforcement in the backcountry prior to 1768. He observed one magistrate who judged "in favor of Him that had the Majority of Swearers When, alas! the Truth laid quite the other Way; And the Right Claimant lost his Debt, and had a Load of Costs for to pay into the Bargain."[42]

In contrast to the lawlessness in many backcountry settlements, the discipline provided by the Presbyterian Church contributed to the success and prosperity of Williamsburg. The industrious Scots-Irish forged a cohesive community characterized by high standards of conduct and education and remarkable vigor. They faced a wilderness characterized by swamps and sand, wild animals, and frightening Native Americans. Yet within a period of about fifteen years, they had established a prosperous society, built churches, and educated their children. They adjusted to physical, economic, social, and political conditions in such a way as to make an effective unit in South Carolina life. Williamsburg has justly been called "the most successful township in Governor Johnson's scheme."[43]

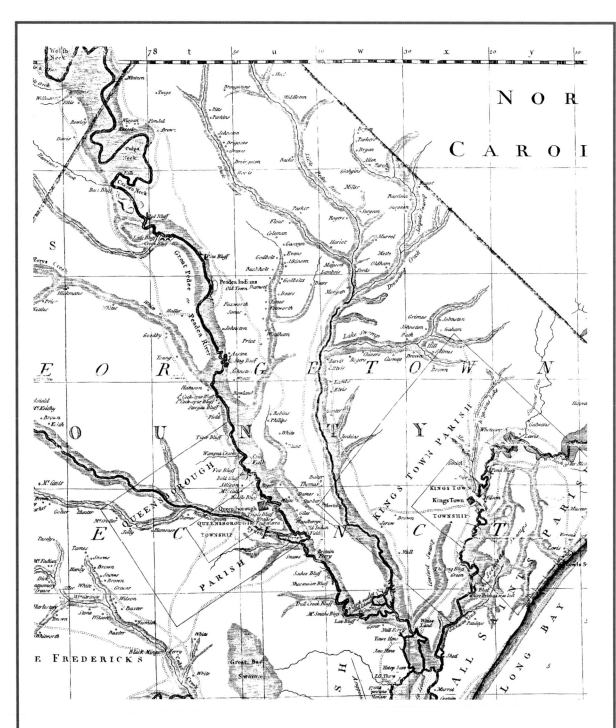

An early map showing Queensboro Township. *John Stuart-William Faden Map, 1780. Courtesy South Carolina Department of Archives and History.*

CHAPTER 6

Queensboro and the Welsh Tract

*The proclamation "strictly enjoins and commands
all persons whatsoever except Such as are Intitled
Under the said order appropriating the said Tract
To the Welch and Pennsilvanians forthwith to remove
themselves, their families, goods and chattels . . . ."*
The governor's council issuing support of Welsh demands to uphold their grant.

The name "Queensboro Township" evokes images of tree-lined avenues, manicured lawns, and white picket fences. In actuality the first settlers found forests of huge cypress trees hung with Spanish moss, treacherous swamps sheltering alligators, wolves, panthers, and an abundance of game like deer and wild turkey. Despite hardships colonists braved the wilderness, enticed by the promise of free land and the ten years of tax exemptions offered under the township system.

JAMES GORDON FOSTERS GROWTH OF QUEENSBORO

Surveyed in 1733, Queensboro Township was located on both sides of the Great Pee Dee. Its center point and town were on the west bank three or four miles above the mouth of Lynches River. This location later became part of lower Florence County near the town of Johnsonville.[1]

Because owners did not have to pay taxes on land in the townships for the first ten years, the exempt areas were attractive to land speculators. South Carolina designed its land policies primarily to try to insure accurate claims. Holding land for speculation was discouraged but was difficult to control. There were three steps to ownership.

First, a person applied to the governor and council for a warrant for a given number of acres. New settlers were entitled to a "headright" of fifty acres for each person in the household, including indentured servants or slaves. Indentured servants could receive warrants for themselves when they completed their servitude. Second, the warrant was taken to the surveyor general who issued a precept ordering a deputy surveyor to survey the land and prepare two copies of the plat, one for the surveyor general and one for the secretary of the province. Third, the secretary presented the plat to the governor's council, and it issued a grant. Although receipt of the warrant was intended only as a first step, for many it served as a valid claim. Warrants were bought and sold almost like deeds.[2]

James Gordon, an attorney in South Carolina who wanted to sponsor a settlement, applied to the provincial government in 1733 to help bring one hundred families to settle in Queensboro. The Commons House opined that the northern townships needed no encouragement and refused Gordon's request. In 1734 he unilaterally imported twenty-seven persons for whom he was entitled to claim fifty acres each. He freed them from indentures in 1735, and they were eligible for another fifty acres each for their own use.

Gordon applied for a bounty for those who came as indentured servants and twenty-one others who arrived from Pennsylvania. The bounty for each settler was eight bushels of corn and a peck of salt—less than the usual offering—but because most of the settlers were not foreign, they did not precisely meet the terms of the allocation for townships. Gordon acted as justice of the peace and captain of the militia.[3]

At least thirty-six plats appear in the records for 1735 in Queensboro Township. They range in size from 1000 acres to the 50-acre "headright." James Hepburne, John McDonald, James McPherson, John McQueen, William Maire, and Robert Glass received 50 acres each. At least one single woman, Mary Brickell, was among the 1735 pioneers, and she received two 50-acre plats. Other women soon followed.[4] In 1737 the plats of Mrs. Elizabeth Righton and Mrs. Catherine Ravine appeared along with those of David Dalbiace, Thomas Goodman, Hercules Coyte [Coit], and James and Patrick Dannielle. These 1737 surveys included a half-acre town lot in addition to acreage outside the town.[5]

UNSCRUPULOUS LAND CLAIMANTS INHIBIT TOWNSHIP DEVELOPMENT

Although lots were surveyed, the town never really developed. Claiming a lot would suggest the person intended to settle there. Some of the landholders who secured acreage without town lots evidently did not. For instance, Maurice Lewis and James Abercrombie, who respectively had 1500 and 1400 acres surveyed in 1735 and 1736, were residents of Charleston. Lewis was judge of the Vice Admiralty Court while Abercrombie was attorney general. Captain Thomas Hening, who had 1100 acres surveyed in 1736, made his home in Georgetown. James Gordon held plats for 3000 acres in Queensboro, owned property on the Pee Dee near Georgetown, and may have divided his time between his Georgetown and Queensboro holdings. John Hammerton, secretary of the province, held 4000 acres. It appeared that men of wealth and power were taking advantage of the township plan.[6]

Robert Wright, chief justice of the province, received a plat for 2000 acres in 1736. Alexander Skeene, a member of the council, had a 1000-acre plat in 1735 and another, undated, for similar acreage. The council had previously designated Wright and Skeene to "mark out three Townships, pursuant to his Majesty's instructions," obviously affording them an advantage when it came to claiming land.[7]

Because transactions regarding land had to take place in Charleston, many people who actually settled in the back country lived on the land for several years before they completed the steps to ownership. Jacob Buckholt, a native of Prussia, received two plats in Queensboro, one for 300 acres and another for 250 acres, in January, 1735. It was not until September 16, 1738, that the

Council finally issued grants for his land. Jeremiah Fickling received a grant at the same time for a plat for 450 acres surveyed in May, 1736.[8]

Queensboro Township was on the lower Pee Dee in a region of many large swamps.[9] It was better adapted to large plantations than small farms. Those able to secure large acreage claimed most of the high ground. Over a dozen holdings consisted of 1000 acres or more. This situation contributed to the fact that the town did not develop.[10]

WELSH SETTLERS GRANTED RICH LAND ADJACENT TO RIVER

Some of the settlers James Gordon helped to locate in Queensboro were from Pennsylvania. Perhaps they sent good reports of opportunities in South Carolina to friends and relatives, or perhaps Maurice Lewis, a native of Angelsea, Wales, and an influential Charleston attorney and judge, influenced other Welshmen to immigrate. Lewis represented the Welsh who settled on the Pee Dee.[11]

In August of 1736 David Lewis, Samuel Wilds, and Daniel James, representing a group of Welsh Baptists living in Newcastle County, Pennsylvania, later part of Delaware, petitioned the South Carolina provincial council stating that they had found the land of the Pee Dee valley suited for growing hemp, flax, wheat, barley, and other crops. They requested ten thousand acres in northeast Queensboro Township and all the land above for eight miles on each side of the river as far as the junction of its two main branches.[12]

The Council agreed and directed surveyor John Ouldfield "to admeasure and lay out, for the Welch families that were to be imported to this Province a tract of land, containing in the whole 173,840 acres, situated and being in Craven County." Ten thousand acres was to be taken from Queensboro Township on the north side of the Pee Dee.[13]

This grant gave the Welsh settlers privileges over a large territory, covering more than one hundred miles adjacent to the river and including the rich alluvial bottomlands and valuable lands next to the swamp. With such land and access to water transportation available, the Welsh were not slow to populate the area. They were hardy folk with experience in America. In addition they were part of a church organization, which gave structure to their community.[14]

The Welsh Tract Baptist Meeting called Pencader Hundred in Newcastle County dismissed the following members to South Carolina in November 1735: Abel Morgan, teaching elder, James James, ruling elder, Thomas Evan, deacon, Daniel James, Samuel Wilds, John Harry, John Harry, Jr., Thomas Harry, Jeremiah Rowell, Richard Barrow, Thomas Money, Nathaniel Evan, Mary James, Annie Evan, Sarah James, Mary Wilds, Elizabeth Harry, Margaret Harry, Eleanor Jenkin, Sarah Harry, Margaret Williams, Mary Rowell, and Sarah Barrow. Most of these names appear on Pee Dee plats within the next several years.[15]

A few of the Welsh group settled in Queensboro. Thomas Evans and the widow and children of Samuel Wilds had surveys made there near the mouth of Catfish Creek in 1737. Thomas James, Griffith Jones, and Evan, John, and David Harry did likewise in 1738.[16] Although there was still more land available in Queensboro, the other Welsh immigrants evidently preferred land farther north.[17]

Pee Dee River from a bluff at Welsh Neck. The blue barrel is a floating buoy marker. *Suzanne Linder.*

THE WELSH NECK

Between Crooked Creek and Red Bluff there was a great bend in the river. The soil on the east side of the Pee Dee in this location of about five square miles was a rich silt loam. In the 1730s the area was less subject to floods than it was later after settlers cleared the valley upstream. It was convenient to the river for water transportation, and the adjacent swamps provided forage for cattle. Because many of the Welsh settled there, it became known as the Welsh Neck. Among those who had plats surveyed in 1738 were William and Abel James, Thomas Evans, James Rogers, William Terrel, Daniel Devonald, and John Jones.[18] Additional surveys in the Welsh Tract in 1738 that cannot be pinpointed within the Welsh Neck are those of Richard Barrow, Griffith John, Hasker, Jacob, and John Newberry, and Thomas Harry.[19] By 1745 settlers had claimed about 25,000 acres. Few holdings were over five hundred acres. Most of the Welsh lived in or near the Welsh Neck. Other settlers included people of English, Scottish, and French Huguenot extraction.[20]

Some settlers had evidently preceded the Welsh to the area. John Thompson had bought land from the Cheraw Indians, including about forty cleared "old fields." The Welsh complained to the government, alleging that Thompson was inciting the Indians to disturb them.[21] Thompson appeared before the council, denied he had promoted any misunderstanding, and said he had bought the land legally from the Indians. He agreed to try to quiet the Indian disturbances both in the Welsh Neck and in the Williamsburg settlement. The Council paid him £105 to surrender his deed and gave him warrants for a thousand acres of land besides. The government then proceeded to pass an act "To restrain and prevent the purchasing Lands from Indians."[22] Francis Young, James Gillespie, and Thomas Elerby (Ellerbe) also had claims in the Welsh Neck area that preceded the Welsh.

Ellerbe petitioned the provincial council, saying he and his family of eleven persons came from Virginia about 1737. Francis Young and his son-in-law, James Gillespie, likewise petitioned the council to be allowed to claim land where they had settled in the Welsh Tract.[23]

Gillespie was an authorized Indian trader and deputy surveyor of the province. There is a tradition that he was associated with Christopher Gadsden, a leading Charleston merchant, in boating on the Pee Dee many years before the Revolution, and was the first person who ever brought a boat to Cheraw. Gillespie owned 1280 acres on the Pee Dee near the mouth of Thompson's Creek at Cheraw. He was dead by 1757 when creditors sued his widow, Mary Young Gillespie, and the provost marshall sold the land to Christopher Gadsden. The survey shows a small building on Thompson's Creek that might have been a store. In 1761 Gadsden published an announcement in the *South Carolina Gazette* indicating that he was closing his stores and warning people not to trust his Dutch servant lad who "lately attended at his stores at the Charraws and George-Town, the said servant being run away from him."[24]

Despite these predecessors, the council was generally supportive of the Welsh demands and in 1739 issued a proclamation which "Strictly enjoins and commands all persons whatsoever except Such as are Intitled under the said order appropriating the said Tract to the Welch and Pennsilvanians forthwith to remove themselves, their families, goods and chattels . . ."[25] The council refused a request, however, to secure lands for Welsh settlers solely on the basis of warrants. Thirty Welsh settlers petitioned the Council saying ". . . some of us had our lands run out, and the Plots put into the Surveyor-General's office four years ago, and as we are so poor that we cannot get money to pay the charge of surveying and granting it, has discouraged many from coming over." Although the request for skipping steps two and three was denied (see page 59), the Council did consent to extend the time for the Welsh monopoly until 1745.[26]

Christopher Gadsden. *Rembrant Peale. Courtesy Independence National Historical Park, Philadelphia.*

Undoubtedly, it was difficult to establish a farm in the wilderness. One of the quickest ways to get wealth was to raise stock. Traditionally in the wilderness, the first inhabitants are hunters, the next herdsmen, and finally farmers. The first settlers found large numbers of wild horses and cattle in the Carolina forest. They caught and domesticated some, but others foraged freely in the woods. To capture the wild stock, settlers built a pen in the fork of two streams and drove the animals into it. It was customary to brand or notch the ears of stock for identification.[27]

THE WELSH NECK BAPTIST CHURCH DOMINATES THE PROSPEROUS SOCIETY

The Welsh participated in stock raising and soon established a thriving community dominated by the Welsh Neck Baptist Church. In January 1738 the following men and the wives of each constituted a church: Philip, Abel, and Daniel James; Daniel Devonald; Thomas Evans; John and David Harry; Samuel Wilds; Griffith, David, and Thomas Jones. Philip James, son of James James, the original leader of the immigrants, became the first pastor, although he was not officially ordained until 1743.[28]

Ministers of the Welsh Neck Baptist Church were planters as well as clergymen. At his death in 1753, Philip James owned one slave, books valued at £4, two beds, a table and six chairs, pewter plates, a variety of cutlery, and various tools. The total value of his estate was £599.17.[29]

Robert Williams, who was ordained at Welsh Neck in 1752, became one of the wealthiest men in the area. After a disagreement with church members, he left the church and was excommunicated in 1761. He owned two boats, one flat, and three canoes worth altogether £940.10. The inventory of his estate also mentions "tar oakham and corking Irons." Pine tar and oakum, a fiber made from hemp or flax, were used to caulk or waterproof the hull of a boat. Skilled workers pounded oakum into the cracks between the planks, then coated the surface with tar or pitch.[30]

Williams owned seventy slaves who produced indigo, hemp, and flax among other crops. He also owned gristmill and sawmill utensils and brick molds. The total value of his personal estate in 1768, excluding real estate, was £24,347.[31]

Nicholas Bedgegood followed Williams as pastor of the Welsh Neck Church. His plantation, Cheraw Bluff, contained 350 acres, and when he died in 1774, he owned fifteen slaves. His house contained walnut and cypress desks, pine and mahogany tables, fire dogs, art prints, china, decanters, and pewter. His library was worth £300, while his entire personal estate was worth £6098.8.[32]

Evan Pugh, born in Matachin, Pennsylvania, of Welsh parents, came to the Pee Dee to study for the ministry with Bedgegood. Pugh became minister of the Welsh Neck Baptist Church in 1766. Although of an ethnic background similar to the original Welsh Neck settlers, he arrived by a different

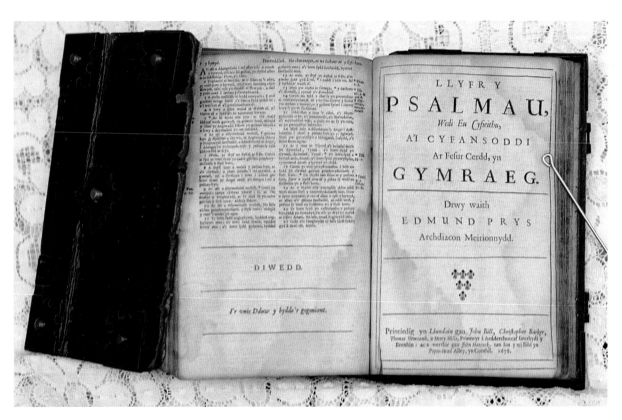

A Welsh Bible (1678) used by South Carolina Welsh Baptists in the eighteenth century. *Suzanne Linder. Courtesy Darlington County Historical Commission.*

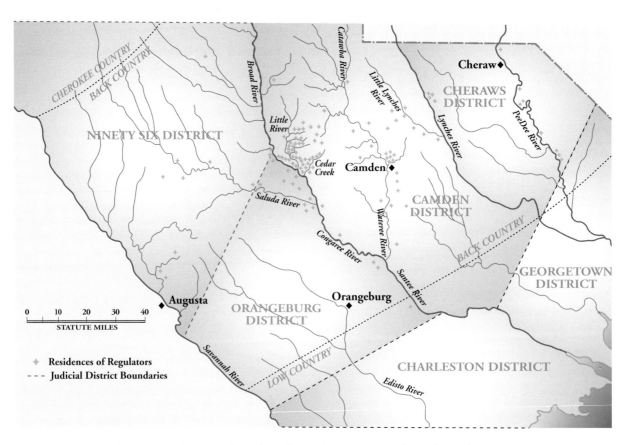

Vigilante groups known as "Regulators" spread out over several South Carolina regions.
Map by Tim Belshaw from sources in endnote 36.

route. In the 1750s he traveled down the Shenandoah Valley to the Yadkin River in North Carolina, where he left the Quaker faith to become a Baptist. He decided to move down river to the Welsh Neck to study for the Baptist ministry. He served the Welsh Neck Church for only a short time but preached at nearby Cashaway Baptist Church and its offshoots from 1767 until his death in 1802. During that time he became a prosperous planter. He grew rice, corn, flax, indigo, and other crops and by 1790 could afford seventeen slaves.[33]

The Welsh Neck ministers were in many ways typical of the back country planter class that developed before the Revolution. Frontier planters provided a variety of essential services to their less prosperous neighbors and thus rose to wealth and power within the framework of an economy based on the family or household as the fundamental unit of social order.[34]

THE REGULATOR MOVEMENT SEEKS ORDER

In the 1760s in the South Carolina backcountry, the social order was threatened by growing lawlessness exemplified by outlaw bands that plundered at random. Because the only courts were at Charleston, the costs of transportation and prosecution would often be more than the value of goods stolen or debts incurred. This situation prompted local citizens of the Pee Dee and elsewhere in the backcountry to organize vigilante groups known as Regulators.

Leaders in the organization on the Pee Dee included Claudius Pegues, George Hicks, Alexander Mackintosh, Philip Pledger and Gideon Gibson, all substantial planters. The Regulator movement, however, also included yeomen, merchants, ferry operators, and aspiring planters—people who shared an interest in making the backcountry safe for profitable agriculture and prompt collection of debts.[35]

In July 1768 Gideon Gibson led a group of Regulators who captured Joseph Holland, an anti-Regulator militia captain. Constable George Thomson, a coastal militia captain, delivered a warrant at Mars Bluff ordering Holland's release. The incident became violent, and Regulators administered fifty lashes to two of Thomson's party. This provoked the Charleston authorities to send Provost Marshal Roger Pinckney with about twenty-five men to take charge of the situation and arrest Gideon Gibson. When Pinckney called on the local militiamen for aid, it became apparent they were on the side of the Regulators. They refused to help capture Gibson and restated their need for courts located within a convenient distance.

After the confrontation with the provost marshal in 1768, the provincial government agreed to provide courts and representation in the backcountry. The Parish of St. David, established in 1768, elected Claudius Pegues as its first representative to the assembly.[36]

It is possible Evan Pugh lasted only about a year as pastor of the Welsh Neck Church because he attended Regulator meetings.[37] Pugh was a true frontiersman and man of many abilities. He had lived in the Shenandoah and Yadkin valleys where Indian attack was a constant danger. It was not unusual for Pugh to travel alone and sleep in the wilderness. He worked as a schoolmaster at one time, and he studied surveying with George Washington.[38]

THE CHURCH: MINISTRY AND JUDGMENT

Evan Pugh had some knowledge of medicine and often treated the members of his community. The tradition of the minister-physician was not uncommon in America. There were few physicians in proportion to the population in the eighteenth century, and of those, almost none chose to locate on the frontier. Pugh visited the sick, bled people, and administered "physicks" such as calomel, senna, jalap, or castor oil. Pugh treated his own colds with horehound. He also suffered from periodic bouts of "aigue," which was probably malaria, a disease that posed a constant problem for the colonists. They knew there was a greater danger of contracting aigue in swampy areas, but they had no idea that the mosquito was the carrier.[39]

Pugh noted in his diary a receipt for bitters. It consisted of saffron, orange peels, and logwood in a solution of equal parts of rum and water. Although it would not cure malaria, the concoction probably made the patient feel better temporarily. He also recommended ash bark for snakebite and "alim complain roots . . . to be sent from Philadelphia." One of Pugh's remedies may actually have been effective for some types of warts. It was impossible then to differentiate between malignant and benign growths. He said, "To cure a cancer wart, take the ashes of Ashwood, make a strong lye and bile the lye away to a salt or sulpher put a little of it on the wart after you have cut away the wart even

General Nathanael Greene surveyed rivers of the Pee Dee region as transportation routes.
Portrait by Charles Wilson Peale. Courtesy Independence National Historical Park, Philadelphia.

to the skin." Strong language undoubtedly offended his religious sensibilities, so he included in the instructions, "Say 'Temper!' as you see the wart die."[40]

Besides helping its members with physical ills, the church also provided a stabilizing influence on the community by supervising morals and settling disputes. Walton Downes was suspended, "having behaved in a very disorderly manner." He was found guilty of not filling his place in the church, spending his time in idleness, drinking to excess, and acting in contempt of the church's authority. Samuel Reredon was suspended for obscene conversation, unmarried couples were often reprimanded for "illicit conversations," and a woman with the colorful name of "Delight Walker" was excluded for adultery. Church policy discouraged the celebration of Christmas because it was "too generally devoted to pursuits unworthy of rational beings, and to prevent as much as possible, this prostitution of time, we will, when convenient, observe it as a day of praise and thanksgiving to God."[41]

The importance of river transportation is apparent in a church pronouncement that "if any member *travels up or down the river on a Sabbath-day* without an absolute necessity (of which the church shall be the judge) such member shall be censured." The Cashaway Baptist Church, an off-shoot of the Welsh Neck organization, said "no member shall at any time work his boat up or down the rivers on the Sabbath day without lawful reason nor shall any member charge hire for his boat on the Sabbath day when not worked and no member hired to in Boats shall charge for or work on the Sabbath." Church rules indicated that travel by boat was a regular occurrence and sometimes a necessity. It was the most practical means of transporting heavy goods.[42]

THE RIVER'S EVOLUTION AIDS REVOLUTION

When the Revolutionary War began, the river took on even greater importance. Both the river as a transportation route and boats carrying supplies played an important role in the war effort. Pee Dee boats were of special interest to General Nathanael Greene, who surveyed southern rivers with a view to using shallow-draft boats to transport supplies from Virginia to the army. Although this plan was not put into operation, the knowledge gained from the surveys was vital to the army's operations in early 1781. Another objective was to move the army as quickly as possible from place to place.[43]

George Washington, commander in chief of the Continental Army, wrote to Greene on November 8, 1780, "I intirely approve of your plan for forming a flying Army." He also advised, "I would recommend the building a number of flat bottomed Boats of as large a construction as can be conveniently transported on Carriages." Washington explained that the use of portable boats to cross rivers that would otherwise be impassable would furnish the means to take advantage of the enemy's situation.[44]

On his way to Charlotte, North Carolina, to take command of the patriot army in the South, Greene stopped at Salisbury. He sent instructions to General Edward Stevens, an officer of the Virginia militia: "I am induced to believe that the Yadkin [River] may be made subservient to the Business of Transportation of Stores from Virginia." Greene asked Stevens to appoint "a good and intelligent officer" with three privates to go up the Yadkin as high as Hughes Creek to explore the depth, current, rocks, and other obstructions. From Hughes Creek, the officer was to ride across country through Bethania to the upper Saura Town and report the distance and condition of the roads. At Saura Town, the officer should meet a similar party exploring the Dan River and obtain the report on the Dan. Greene continued, "I also wish the officer to make enquiry respecting the Transportation that may be had from the Yadkin to the Catawba River, and whether the Transportation cannot be performed with Batteaus down that River."[45]

Greene stated his intention to construct boats "of a peculiar kind. . . that will carry Forty or Fifty Barrels and yet draw little more Water than a common Canoe half loaded." The officer should keep that intention in mind when making his survey. Greene realized that transportation on the upper part of the rivers would be difficult, "But," he said, "water transportation is such an amazing saving of expence that small difficulties should not discourage the attempt." He pointed out that wagons and forage were not available by land transport[46] and expressed the hope that the rivers Dan, Yadkin, and Catawba would prove navigable by batteaus and thus would enable the army to receive supplies from Virginia with a minimum use of overland routes.[47]

RIVER BOATS FACILITATE MOVEMENT OF TROOPS AND SUPPLIES

On December 15, 1780, Greene wrote to Colonel Nicholas Long that to facilitate the movement of troops and the collection of provisions, boats were to be built on the Pee Dee River.[48] In late December Greene moved his camp to the Pee Dee in the vicinity of Hicks Creek, opposite Cheraw.[49] Food and forage were available in the Cheraws District, and there was at least one boatyard, that of Stephen Parker, between Hicks Creek and the North Carolina line. On January 16, Greene requested a party of fifty men to report to Parker's landing "about seven miles above camp" to take the orders of Morgan Brown and "man the boats."[50]

Greene had split his army, sending General Daniel Morgan and a detachment of six hundred Continentals to the western part of South Carolina where a body of militia would join him. "The object of this detachment," said Greene, "is to give protection to that part of the country and spirit up the people, to annoy the enemy in that quarter; collect the provisions and forage out of the way of the enemy. . . ."[51]

Greene used his time at the Cheraws to write endless appeals to the governors and legislatures of the southern states asking for more men and supplies, particularly wagons, horses, forage, clothing, flour, and salt. By inviting officers new to his command to dine with him in turns, he made friends and was able to learn their opinions and habits. He tightened discipline and worked to improve sanitation and hospital facilities. He called his station a "camp of repose," but for Greene himself, it was a time of intense preparation.[52]

Greene appointed a local citizen, Morgan Brown, "Superintendant [sic] of the boat department; & the business of transportation upon the Pedee, under the direction of the Quarter Master General." Brown was to collect boats at specified locations and hold them in readiness to bring in supplies or aid the army in its movements. On January 2, 1781, Greene authorized Brown to engage a number of "Batteau men" to navigate the boats. Men from the militia were preferable, but if they were not available, he was to hire others by the month.[53] By January 26 boat operations were in progress, for Greene wrote to Lieutenant Colonel Henry Lee, ". . . we cannot spare a boat from this quarter without starving the army; the whole being employed in collecting provisions and forage."[54]

While Brown's assignment was to gather and organize already existing boats, others actually built boats to Greene's specifications. Greene authorized payment in provisions equal to $5775 to William Ramsey and $2900 to William Covington for their services in building boats at the Cheraws. Others who received similar payments were William Williams, $1840; Humfrey Rodgers, $750; William Mask, $2585; William Frazier, $1050; Elisha Parker [Stephen Parker's father], $750; William Ratlif, $1250; and William Ratlif, Jr., $841. The payments were in provisions equal to the listed amounts in Continental dollars. The officer in charge stated, "The want of money in the Military Chest obliges the General to adopt this mode of satisfying these people whose services were important and indispensably necessary. You will act in behalf of the public and see that strict justice is done. . . ."[55]

Greene offered to share some boats with Daniel Morgan. He warned Morgan that Carolina rivers were subject to sudden and swift swells that might block a strategic retreat. He noted that the Pee Dee had risen twenty-five feet in thirty hours during the week of January 19, 1781. Greene said, "I am preparing boats to move always with the army. Would one or two be of use to you? They will be put upon four wheels and may be moved with little more difficulty than a loaded waggon." Morgan, however, met the British at Cowpens before Greene's letter could be delivered.[56]

News of Morgan's victory at Cowpens took nearly a week to reach Greene's camp on the Pee Dee.[57] Amid the great rejoicing, Greene made preparations to move. His objective was to reunite his army and prevent British General Charles Cornwallis from joining Benedict Arnold, who had established a British post at Portsmouth, Virginia. The route lay across western North Carolina to the Dan River in western Virginia.[58] In this "race to the Dan," Greene's reconnaissance of the terrain and the rivers and the arrangements he had made to ferry his army across those rivers proved decisive.

On February 1, 1781, Greene's aide, Colonel Lewis Morris, Jr., wrote to Colonel Thaddeus Kosciuszko, "You will order such of the boats as are finished to follow the army immediately and such as are not finished you will deliver to the charge of Colonel Wade[59]. . . The artificers you will order to join the army as soon as possible, they are much wanted."[60]

When Morgan's troops reached the Yadkin, heavy rains had made the Trading Ford impassable by foot. Thanks to the boats, the Americans got across the river just as the British advance guard approached the west bank. Of course, the Americans had all the boats on the east side. To get across, Cornwallis had to make a long detour to the north, thus affording Greene some precious time.[61]

When the Americans reached the Dan River, boats were available again to take them across just ahead of the British. The Dan could not be forded, and the boats were all on the north bank, so Cornwallis turned back towards Hillsboro, North Carolina. Nathanael Greene was able to gather reinforcements and return on his own terms to meet Cornwallis at Guilford Court House on March 15, 1781. Both sides claimed victory because the Americans withdrew, but the British sustained heavier losses.[62] The fact that Greene was able to pick the time and place for the battle was undoubtedly an asset. This advantage was in large part made possible by Greene's careful reconnaissance of transportation routes and his preparations for the use of boats.

The river also provided cover for "Swamp Fox" Francis Marion, the main hero of the Revolution for the Pee Dee region. Small of stature but wiry and tough, Marion grew up in the Georgetown vicinity and spent much of his youth riding and hunting in the forests. He drank no alcohol but instead adopted a habit practiced by ancient Roman soldiers of mixing vinegar with his ration of water. Vinegar has the potential to kill some germs, so this probably helped protect him from digestive diseases that plagued colonial armies.

Francis Marion—the "Swamp Fox"—offering sweet potatoes to British prisoners. *William D. Washington. Courtesy South Caroliniana Library.*

Marion's high personal honor and insistence on fair treatment of all combined with his astute military decision-making made him a favorite among his troops. His men came primarily from the plantations and small farms in the Pee Dee region. They were hearty outdoorsmen to whom riding hard and shooting straight were second-nature. Marion's guerrilla-style tactics utilized their talents to best advantage. They could strike the enemy and then quickly disappear into the swamp.[63]

Although Marion used many of the rivers and swamps of eastern Carolina, it is believed that his famous hideout was Snow's Island at the intersection of Lynches River and the Pee Dee.[64] The exact point of Marion's secret camp has been the center of an archaeological investigation led by the University of South Carolina. The mystery has yet to be solved, but archaeologist Steven Smith pinpointed an area across the creek from Snow's Island, which has proven to be a large eighteenth-century site.[65] The findings are consistent with what is known about Marion's camp, but more investigation is necessary to determine if the site was actually the lair of the elusive Swamp Fox.[66]

BOATS, FERRIES, AND CLEARING THE RIVER

Boat building continued on the Pee Dee after the Revolution. Achilles Knight, who married Stephen Parker's daughter Elizabeth, was also a boatwright. He bought land on Marks Creek adjoining Stephen Parker, Jr., in 1801.[67] Knight died in 1809. At the sale of his estate, Elisha Parker,[68] son of Stephen, bought several boat-building tools such as one mallet and four caulking irons, a lot of spoke timber, twenty-four pounds of iron, one lot of planes, one square, one pair of compasses, one half-inch screw auger and a foot adze. When Stephen Parker died in 1821, he gave his son-in-law, Cannon Weaver, the use of the boatyard for fifteen years, after which time it was to revert to his estate.[69]

Stephen Parker's father, Elisha Parker, owned land in the Pee Dee area as early as 1765.[70] He established a ferry over the Pee Dee just below the North Carolina line. Stephen Parker operated the ferry as well as a tavern at the site in 1788. The court ordered that William Pouncey be permitted to retail "spiritous liquors" there by the quart for one year beginning in March 1789.[71]

Because settlement progressed simultaneously along both sides of rivers, ferries were essential. In 1747 the legislature noted that since the upper settlements on the Pee Dee, Waccamaw, and Black rivers were extensive and remote from each other, it would be convenient to divide the same into several districts under commissioners to supervise roads, cleanse waterways, and establish ferries.[72]

Five districts were established, and the commissioners who were appointed were to meet at least twice each year on Easter Monday and the first Monday in August. They had responsibility for keeping open roads and waterways and had the authority "to contract with any person or persons to attend and keep such ferry or ferries, at any rates or prices for the transportation of men, horses, cattle and carriages, not exceeding the rates . . . now in force in this Province."[73]

Later the Commons House licensed ferries individually. In 1765 John Murray received permission to establish a ferry for the convenience of inhabitants of Black Mingo, Pee Dee, and parts adjacent at Mars Bluff, located just north of Queensboro Township. Fees were one shilling and three pence for a single person or a horse, two shillings and six pence for a horse and chair or horse and cart, five shillings for a four wheeled carriage, and one shilling per head for hogs, sheep, and neat cattle.[74]

James James became a licensed ferry keeper in 1768 in the Welsh Tract located on the northeast side of the Pee Dee opposite Cedar Creek on the southwest side. Fees were slightly higher at that time. A horse and chair or horse and cart cost five shillings; a four-wheeled carriage with five horses, twenty shillings; neat cattle, "ferried or swam," one shilling and three pence; for calves, sheep, or hogs, "ferried or swam," seven pence half penny. All ministers of the gospel, persons going to and from divine service and musters of militias, and all persons in time of alarm, or messengers on service of the government in addition to free Indians in amity with the government were exempt from payment. The law further provided that if any person should be unreasonably delayed, James James would have to pay the person ten pounds plus an additional five pounds for every hour afterwards.[75]

A tavern or "ordinary" often accompanied a ferry site to provide travelers with refreshment and lodging. More than merely inns, however, taverns were important in the structure of the community. Complaining about the breaking of the Sabbath, minister Charles Woodmason noted that:

> Magistrates have their Sittings—Militia Officers their Musters—Merchants their Vendues—Planters their Sales, all on Saturdays: Is there any Shooting, Dancing, Revelling, Drinking Matches carrying on? It is all begun on Saturday, and as all these Meetings and Transactions are executed at taverns, Not

a Saturday in the Year, but some one or other of them (and at more than one Tavern) are statedly repeatedly carried on—So that at these rendezvous there is more Company of a Saturday, than in the Church on Sunday. . . . [76]

Drinking and carousing were common activities in the taverns, but patrons also "ate, slept, sang, danced, smoked, made love, played various games (on which they often bet), fought, conducted club meetings, watched traveling exhibitors, sent and received mail, held political discussions and celebrations, and did business with their neighbors, with peddlers, and with itinerant craftsmen."[77] Although it appears women were often unwelcome participants in tavern activities,[78] the legislature did grant ferry licenses to women. Frances Port received a license in 1778 for Port's Ferry, located on the Pee Dee about two miles above the mouth of Lynches River, and Elizabeth Bishop took over the ferry at Cheraw in 1796.[79]

In addition to regulating ferries, the legislature made provisions for clearing rivers and streams. Although commissioners had operated on the Black River since 1738, a specific act to provide for the Great Pee Dee was not passed until 1784. Of course, commissioners could have operated under the act to establish roads and ferries mentioned above, but clearing the river did not seem to be a major priority.

In 1784, however, Benjamin Hicks, Sr., George Hicks, Thomas Powe, William Kershaw, and William Pegues were authorized to draw orders on the treasury for no more than three hundred pounds sterling to contract with workmen to remove obstructions in the Great Pee Dee. The next year, William McCotery, James Greir, Francis Greaves, John Irvin, Hugh Giles, Henry Davis, and Archibald Odum were added as commissioners and given further powers to assess lands and also to assess male inhabitants between sixteen to fifty who lived within six miles of the river from Euhany to the Warhee Bluff and within ten miles of the river from the bluff upwards. In later years, all males from sixteen to fifty were liable to work on the river for six days a year under the direction of the commissioners.[80]

Concern for keeping the river navigable increased with time. When land was cleared upstream, more silt likely accumulated in the lower portion of the river, and increased flooding caused trees and brush along the banks to topple and obstruct navigation.

EDUCATION: A CONSISTENT CONCERN IN THE PEE DEE

In addition to working on roads and keeping the river navigable, the Pee Dee colonists also cooperated in providing education. The Welsh Neck Baptists believed in the importance of an educated clergy.[81] They also wanted education for their young people.

On December 13, 1777, members of the community met at the Welsh Neck Baptist Church to promote learning. The outgrowth of this meeting was the St. David's Society, an organization with the avowed purpose of erecting a seminary of learning in the Cheraws District. St. David was the patron saint of Wales, and St. David's Parish, named in his honor, was an official political and religious division that was conterminous with Cheraws District. The district included the present-day counties of Chesterfield, Marlboro, Darlington, and parts of Lee—east of Lynches River—and northern Florence.

The society met a second time at the home of Benjamin Williamson, a planter on the west side of the Pee Dee. The minutes stated: "As the endowing and establishing Publick schools and other

ST. DAVID'S PARISH

In April of 1768 the bill creating St. David's Parish passed. With its passage, the quest for law and order in the Pee Dee took a significant step forward, for the parish was not only a religious entity but also an instrument of local government. The settlers chose the name of St. David, patron saint of the Welsh, because of the preponderance of settlers of Welsh extraction. Anglican priest Charles Woodmason wrote the petition, and the act noted that "the inhabitants residing on Pedee river . . . have represented many inconveniences which they are under for want of having a parish laid out and established. . . ."[1]

St. David's Church and parish represented the established Church of England and served as the first local government in the Pee Dee area. In the years prior to 1768, the wilderness of the backcountry provided a safe haven for outlaw gangs, and lawlessness was rampant. There were no courts of law within a hundred miles, and law enforcement was almost non-existent. Although it had limited powers and duties, the parish was the basic unit of local government in South Carolina and provided a framework for the citizens to address the problems in their society.

St. David's Church held its first meeting on April 12, 1773. Located in Cheraw at the head of navigation of the Pee Dee, the church architecture was typical of Anglican churches of the period.[2]

The Provincial Assembly appointed Claudius Pegues, Philip Pledger, Alexander Mackintosh, George Hicks, Thomas Lide, James James, and Thomas Ellerbe as church commissioners. James and Mackintosh declined to serve.[3]

Because there was a scarcity of ordained ministers, St. David's had no resident Anglican rector, but the vestry accomplished many things. It supplied relief to the poor, helped homeless children, and organized elections. The people of the parish unanimously elected Claudius Pegues to the South Carolina House of Assembly in 1768. Pegues was one of the wealthiest and most influential planters in the backcountry.[4] Although the Parish contained dissenters as well as Anglicans, both groups saw the practical utility of using the established church as a catalyst for the organization and growth of their community in the wilderness.

After the war, the Americans reorganized their government, and St. David's Parish split in 1785 to form the counties of Chesterfield, Darlington, and Marlboro. St. David's Church still stands as a monument to the prosperity of Pee Dee planters who made their fortunes shipping their products down the river.[5]

The Pegues Place, home of Claudius Pegues, built about 1760, was the site of the signing of a cartel for exchange of prisoners in the Revolution. *Suzanne Linder. Courtesy William Pegues.*

semenaries of learning has in all Countries and in all ages been attended with the most salutary effects . . . what benevolent mind . . . wou'd not deplore the great want of this necessary qualification in our youth. . . ." The members went on to express the responsibility they felt for educating leaders for the new republic they hoped to see established, provided the patriots won the Revolutionary War.[82]

Members of the organization backed up their worthy aims with pledges of nearly £9000. Because of the severe partisan fighting in the vicinity, it was not until after the Revolution that the school actually opened. Several early masters were graduates of Rhode Island College, which became Brown University after 1804, because the Welsh Baptists naturally sought graduates of a Baptist institution as their instructors. It is possible that they chose not to establish a school before the Revolution because of the British law that required schoolmasters to be communicants of the Anglican Church. Not all teachers came from Rhode Island, however. Enoch Hanford, a Yale graduate, left St. David's Academy to become one of two faculty members of South Carolina College, later the state university, when it opened in 1805.[83]

By 1800 early settlers of the Pee Dee had transformed a wilderness into a comfortable and orderly society. They had survived dangers from the elements, from Indians, from outlaw bands, and from war. The Revolution was especially devastating because it pitted neighbor against neighbor—a civil conflict that, more than actual battles with the British, was responsible for the destruction and disruption of Pee Dee society.[84]

PROSPERITY SPRINGS FORTH FROM THE RIVER'S BOUNTY

In 1800 Pee Dee settlers had prosperous farms, strong churches, adequate courts and law enforcement, and an educational institution that would rival any in the region. Homes of planters that have survived to the present day—the ca. 1760 Pegues Place, home of Claudius Pegues, and the 1790s Drury Robertson home show a comfortable lifestyle. On his Ragtown Plantation, Baron Frederick C. H. B. von Poellnitz, former chamberlain of Frederick the Great of Prussia, built an impressive house, which included running water provided by a flume from a nearby stream. He experimented with scientific agriculture and corresponded with George Washington on the subject.[85]

Throughout the eighteenth century, the Pee Dee River served as the main artery nourishing the development of society. It was a landmark and a highway guiding settlers through the uncharted forest. It provided an inexpensive way to transport heavy goods to market and bring back manufactured goods not available locally. It drew to its shores resourceful boatmen and boat builders whose talents supplied the army of Nathanael Greene in 1781. It gave settlers an incentive to clear the wilderness in Queensboro and the Welsh Tract and develop trading centers. The river also contributed to a regional identity that persists to the present day.

The Yadkin River was settled quickly in the mid-eighteenth century. Caldwell County, North Carolina, near Scenic Byway 268. *Suzanne Linder.*

CHAPTER 7

Yadkin Pioneers

*"Inhabitants flock in here daily, mostly from Pennsylvania and
other parts of America, who are overstocked with people and some
directly from Europe, they commonly seat themselves toward the West
And have got near the mountains."*
North Carolina Governor Gabriel Johnston in the North Carolina Colonial Records, IV, 1073–1074.

In contrast to the gradual settlement of the Pee Dee, the settlement of the Yadkin valley resembled the swift and sometimes precipitous movement of the river's headwaters. In 1745 scarcely any white inhabitants lived on the upper reaches of the Yadkin, but by the fall of 1748 sufficient settlers had arrived to warrant the formation of Anson County. It centered on the Pee Dee portion of the river just above the South Carolina line and extended westward indefinitely. By 1755, residents had established Salisbury as the seat of the new county of Rowan, and the Moravian Brethren had purchased and begun to develop a large tract of land they named Wachovia.[1]

The earliest colonists near the upper Yadkin settled there sometime in the 1740s. The Clark family, who lived on the Cape Fear River, recorded that a family or possibly a company of emigrants went to new homes west of the Yadkin as early as 1746 to join families who were already living there.[2] Christopher Gist, friend of George Washington and Indian agent, had a home on the Yadkin near present-day Wilkesboro, North Carolina, as early as 1744.[3]

THE GRANVILLE DISTRICT

The Granville District included the tier of counties from the town of Bath, North Carolina, northward to the Virginia line, east to the Atlantic, and west for an indefinite distance.[4] This area originated because John Carteret, Baron Carteret of Hawnes, who was one of the proprietors of Carolina, declined to sell his share when the crown canceled the proprietary charter in 1729. After much negotiation, both parties agreed to a new charter in 1744. It gave the original proprietor's great grandson, John Granville (Earl Granville), an area equal to one eighth of the total original territory of Carolina.

In 1746 Matthew Rowan, who became acting governor of North Carolina in 1753, estimated that there were not more than one hundred fighting men in the entire western part of the province between Virginia and South Carolina. By 1751, he believed there were at least three thousand fighting men in the same territory.[5] Gabriel Johnston, governor at that time, reported, "Inhabitants flock in here daily, mostly from Pennsylvania and other parts of America, who are overstocked with people and some directly from Europe, they commonly seat themselves toward the West and have got near the mountains."[6]

The rapid population growth in the Yadkin region was largely because of the influx of Scots-Irish and Germans[7] from Pennsylvania and the Shenandoah Valley of Virginia. Many immigrants landed in Maryland, Delaware, or Pennsylvania but were forced to move into western Pennsylvania and later into the Shenandoah Valley because of population pressure, soil depletion, and the high cost of new land. When more immigrants arrived, land values rose, and attacks by Indians increased. Families or groups of kin moved on to North Carolina and into the Yadkin region.[8]

Many of those who moved to unsettled areas were second- or third-generation Americans. Movement of families often occurred immediately after the death of the father or family patriarch. The sons might have wished to leave sooner, but only by waiting for their inheritance could they afford to move and purchase land in a new location.[9]

Three North Carolina governors who recruited immigrants from the north may have had a particular interest in the Scots-Irish. Gabriel Johnston, governor from 1734 to 1751, was a native of Scotland. The two governors who followed Johnston, Matthew Rowan and Arthur Dobbs, were from Northern Ireland. Dobbs associated himself with the agent of Granville, Henry McCulloh.[10]

In 1745 McCulloh, a wealthy gentleman of Scots-Irish background, acquired 100,000 acres of land on the Yadkin River and its branches for speculation. After obtaining the land from Granville, McCulloh's agents recruited settlers for the area. In 1761 Henry Eustace McCulloh, son of the owner, came to America to act as land agent.[11] In 1744 the population of the Granville District was estimated at 30,000 whites. Of the sixty-mile-wide strip of land, which included almost half of North Carolina, 1,093,779 acres—largely in the coastal area—had been patented. Granville set the attractive price of £8.4.0 Virginia currency per 640 acres, plus £7.9.0 in fees, and reserved the moderate annual quitrent of four shillings proclamation money per hundred acres. Between 1748 and 1763, when the proprietor's land office was active, almost two million acres were sold, mostly in tracts of 300 to 500 acres.[12] McCulloh recruited buyers for his land by "hawking it about in small quantities thro' all the back parts of the Province and quite thro' America even to Boston."[13]

Large numbers of Scots-Irish and Germans from Pennsylvania responded and set out on the long trek. They followed the ancient Indian trading path, which Joshua Fry and Peter Jefferson, father of Thomas, called "The Great Wagon Road from the Yadkin River through Virginia to Philadelphia distant 435 Miles" on their 1755 map. Fry and Jefferson were official commissioners for the extension of the southern boundary of Virginia beyond the Blue Ridge. The wagon road they mapped began at the Schuylkill River Ferry opposite Philadelphia and ran west through Lancaster to Harris' Ferry of the Susquehanna River, then through York to cross the Potomac at Williams' Ferry. It then traversed the Shenandoah Valley through Winchester, Stephensburg, Strasburg, and Staunton. After crossing the James River at Looney's Ferry, it turned almost due south to the site of Roanoke, then east through the Staunton River Gap of the Blue Ridge and south close to the Blue Ridge across the Blackwater, Pigg, Irvine, and Dan rivers to the Moravian settlement at Wachovia. It later extended through Salisbury and continued through the Catawba Valley to Pine Tree (Camden), South Carolina, then west and south where (beyond the Congaree) one fork went to Charleston and the other to Ninety-Six and Augusta.[14]

The Scots-Irish who traveled the Great Wagon Road to the upper Yadkin valley in the 1740s and 1750s were very different from their countrymen who immigrated to Williamsburg Township in the

1730s. Robert Witherspoon of Williamsburg recalled how his mother mistook an opossum for a bear and his father was unable to kill the animal with his musket.[15] In sharp contrast, the Yadkin settlers were usually second-generation pioneers, people who had grown up on the borders of civilization and learned woodcraft and survival skills from an early age.

The settlers of the Yadkin were Americans, a breed apart from those who thought of some far-away land as home. Psychologically as well as physically, they could subsist without traditional law and order, religious institutions, and even minimal comforts. Their versatility enabled them to kill a bear, write a poem or a song, preach a sermon, mend a gun, make a moccasin or a boat, teach school, dress their own wounds, or till the soil as need be.[16] Yet in the Yadkin region, the accouterments of civilization such as courts, churches, and artisans followed shortly after settlement.[17]

Knowledge of woodcraft and marksmanship were valuable talents for both the men and women who established homesteads in the wilderness, often miles from their nearest neighbor. Wild game, nuts, and fruits could provide food for a family until crops could be harvested. Frontier men and women sometimes had to use a rifle for protection from hostile persons or wild beasts. As late as 1764 numerous Yadkin hunters received bounties for killing wolves, panthers, and "catts." On the bounty list, Scots-Irish names predominate.[18]

Evidence that the Scots-Irish slightly preceded the Germans in settling the land west of the Yadkin is provided by the fact that Scots-Irish families claimed most of the land composed of Cecil clay, a soil especially suited to the production of corn, wheat, oats, rye, clover and grasses—the chief crops of the first settlers. German pioneers generally took up land composed of Appling loam, a soil considerably less productive. Efficient and experienced in agriculture, German farmers would likely have chosen the most productive soil had it still been available when they arrived. The general German immigration did not begin until after 1752.[19]

MORAVIANS SEEK RELIGIOUS FREEDOM IN THE GRANVILLE DISTRICT

In 1752 Bishop August Gottlieb Spangenberg of the *Unitas Fratrum,* or United Brethren Church, explored western North Carolina in search of a location for a colony. The *Unitas Fratrum* was a pietist sect of central Europe that traced its origin to the followers of John Hus. The brethren had left the Margravite of Moravia[20] and established the village of Herrnhut, where Nicholaus Ludwig, Count von Zinzendorf, had led a revival of the religion. Persecution in the German states, however, forced the Moravians to seek a new home where they would be free to practice their religion as they chose. In 1749 after a personal campaign by Count von Zinzendorf, the British parliament passed a bill formally recognizing the *Unitas Fratrum* as an ancient Protestant Episcopal church. This opened the way for colonization on crown lands in America.[21]

The Moravians were looking for two things: a location that would permit them to practice their religion and raise their families in relative security and an area with good economic prospects. One bishop expressed the first criterion thus: "We dont want extraordinary Priviledges, if only we can live together as Brethren, without interfering with others & without being disturbed by them." He especially wished to keep the children from being exposed to "the foolish and sinful ways of the World."

Moravian Bishop August Gottlieb Spangenberg led settlers to western North Carolina in 1752 in search of territory suitable for settlement. *Portrait by John Valentine Haidt. Courtesy the Moravian Archives in Bethlehem, Pennsylvania.*

The brethren did not expect instant riches. "It is more often like mining works," said a Moravian, "one must invest for a long time, then one can begin to extract something. But the difference is that in a mine the yield is uncertain, and in a human colony, so to speak, it is quite certain."[22]

The Granville District in North Carolina was one of the few places that could offer a large tract of isolated land. The Earl of Granville was delighted to negotiate with Zinzendorf for a sale of approximately 100,000 acres in a single block slightly more than twelve miles square and to accept a quitrent of three shillings per hundred acres in addition to the purchase price.[23]

Although he was born and educated in Germany, Bishop Spangenberg had spent much of his adult life in America. In 1752 he was in Bethlehem, Pennsylvania, where he received instructions to go to North Carolina and select land for another Moravian colony.[24]

The warrant provided by Earl Granville specified that the Moravians could choose land on a navigable river. Spangenberg was disappointed when his guides said, "First show us a navigable river in this part of Carolina." The bishop noted that the Yadkin was "a large river, but on account of its terrible falls and numerous rocks useless for commerce."[25]

After hundreds of miles of travel and getting lost in the mountains in snow, the bishop and his party located a site for a settlement on Muddy Creek, about ten miles from the Yadkin River on the upper road to Pennsylvania and about twenty miles from the Virginia line. The total tract of land extended to within two or three miles of the Yadkin.[26] Between that point and the navigable portion of the Pee Dee lay the narrows where the river fell 91 feet in four miles for a rate of 22.75 feet per mile. These rapids and others created an effective barrier to navigation.[27]

Spangenberg went on to say, "A road is being built from here to a Landing [three miles below present-day Fayetteville], to which goods can be brought in boats from Cape Fear, and then be hauled further into the country." He estimated the distance to the landing on the Cape Fear River to be 150 miles. It was 350 miles to Edenton and 19 miles to the nearest mill. Despite the long distances, the bishop found countless springs and numerous fine creeks suitable for building mills. "There is good pasturage for cattle, and the canes growing along the creeks will help out for a couple of winters until the meadows are in shape." He warned that the settlers would need "a good, true, untiring, trustworthy forester and hunter, for the wolves and bears must be exterminated if cattle raising is to succeed."[28]

The fact that the Moravian brethren chose to settle on nearby creeks rather than directly on the Yadkin River was typical of the settlement pattern of the region. Since Piedmont rivers were not significant as transportation routes, pioneers built their homes along the upper reaches of the numerous creeks. Each farm usually included a freshwater spring, while the creek provided water for the animals and possibly water power for a sawmill or gristmill.[29]

In other ways, however, the Moravians were atypical. Their society was a theocracy with the church directing a communal living arrangement that included religious, personal, and economic considerations. The economic organization, the *Oeconomy*, did not abolish private property since members could keep whatever resources they brought with them when they entered. Life in Wachovia, however, resembled life in a company town. The church owned all factors of production except labor. The members provided labor in return for food, housing, clothing, medical care, and education—which began with day care for toddlers.[30]

With careful planning and cooperative work, the brethren were able to build a thriving settlement in a remarkably short time. The church chose the first residents according to their ability to contribute to carving a community out of the wilderness. Fifteen unmarried men, including a cook, a mill-wright and carpenter, a cooper, shoemaker, woodcutter, farmer, pastor, and physician made the journey to North Carolina in October 1753. Church leaders designated Johannes Lischer to study the road and the countryside so that he could become a regular messenger to the sponsoring congregation in Bethlehem, Pennsylvania.[31]

After a long and difficult journey, the Moravians reached the Wachovia Tract and found an uninhabited cabin where they could all take shelter. They prepared a ritual called a Lovefeast, which included sharing bread and coffee. Brother Gottlob Konigsdorfer, leader of the Single Brethren, began singing:

We hold arrival Lovefeast here,
In Carolina land,
A company of Brethren true,
A little Pilgrim Band,
Called by the Lord to be of those
Who through the whole world go,
To bear Him witness everywhere,
And naught but Jesus know.

The texts for the day were "I know where thou dwellest, even in a desert place," and "Be ye of the same mind one with another." A brother wrote in the group journal, "While we held our Lovefeast the

Thyatira Presbyterian Church, founded by Yadkin pioneers near Salisbury in 1755. *Suzanne Linder.*

wolves howled loudly, but all was well with us, and our hearts were full of thanksgiving to the Saviour Who had so graciously guided and led us."[32]

With faith and hard work, the single brothers planted crops, cleared land, and built houses so that others soon came to join them. Before the end of the following year they had a carpenter shop, a flour mill, a pottery, cooperage works, a tannery, a blacksmith shop, and a shoe shop.[33] Their physician, Dr. Hans Martin Kalberlahn, had a thriving practice. People traveled over a hundred miles to get medicine and advice from him. Others came to trade with the productive Moravians, and Brother Jacob Loesch, the *Vorsteher*—or business manager—made a trip to the Cape Fear port of Wilmington. He confirmed Bishop Spangenberg's assertion that large boats traveled up the river to a storehouse located 140 miles, not 150 as Spangenberg said, from Wachovia—one hundred miles by a good road, then forty miles more through the forest to the settlement. The brethren were looking for opportunities to trade on a larger scale than merely with neighbors. In 1761, Charleston merchant Henry Laurens visited Wachovia. As a result, the Moravian trade wagons began trips to Charleston in the fall of that year.[34]

TRADE WITH CHARLESTON INCREASES

The Moravians were not the first in western North Carolina to begin trade with the South Carolina port city. Their neighbors in Salisbury had developed a brisk trade with Charleston merchants as early as the fall of 1756. In March 1756, Governor Dobbs ordered that a road be built from Salisbury to Charleston. Merchants William Glen and Charles Stevenson of Charleston named Thomas Bashford and John Cathey attorneys for the purpose of collecting their debts in the community.[35] By 1765 a British army officer passing through the South Carolina low country noted the extensive trade with the back country and remarked, "the produce of considerable part of North Carolina, comes down to Charlestown in waggons, drawn with four horses, two abreast—perhaps at the distance of three hundred miles. . . . "[36]

ROWAN COUNTY

The opportunity for trade was one of many factors that drew settlers into western North Carolina. On April 3, 1753, 348 inhabitants of the frontier portion of Anson County petitioned the General Assembly to establish a new county. The General Assembly divided Anson County by a line that began where the Anson line crossed the Granville District line and continued in a direct line north to Virginia. The southern boundary was to follow the Granville line, and the western boundary was indefinite. The new county was named for Matthew Rowan, acting governor at the time.[37]

In the spring of 1753, the court of Rowan met for the first time and authorized construction of a courthouse. The following year, the court minutes stated that "James Carter, Esquire, his lordship's deputy-surveyor, produced a warrant for six hundred and forty acres of land for the use of the inhabitants of this county &c. and for the use of the prison courthouse and stocks &c. . . . "[38] On February 11, 1755,

William Churton and Richard Vigers, agents for Lord Granville, made a formal grant to James Carter and Hugh Forster, trustees, for 635 acres of land for a township by the name of Salisbury.[39] Governor Arthur Dobbs passed through the town in the summer of 1755. He remarked, "The Town is but just laid out, the Court House built and 7 or 8 log Houses erected."

Through his association with Henry McCulloh the land speculator, Governor Dobbs owned land on Rocky River, a tributary of the Yadkin. He commented, "There are at present 75 families on my Lands. I viewed betwixt 30 and 40 of them, and except two there was not less than from 5 or 6 to 10 children in each family." Dobbs noted that they were barefooted and wore only shifts in the warm weather. "They are a Colony from Ireland removed from Pennsylvania, of what we call Scotch Irish . . . Besides these there are 22 families of Germans or Swiss, who are all an industrious people." In addition to livestock, the governor observed corn, wheat, barley, rye, oats, flax, cotton, hemp, and indigo.[40]

Of the river at Salisbury, Dobbs said, "The Yadkin here is a large beautiful river where is a ferry. It is near 300 yards over, it was at this time fordable scarce coming to the horses bellies."[41] Three men had petitioned the first Rowan County court for a license to keep a ferry over the Yadkin: Benjamin Rounsavill at the Trading Ford, Edward Hughes at the Shallow Ford, and Isaac Feree at an unnamed location.[42]

SETTLERS FEAR INDIAN ATTACKS AND SEEK REFUGE AT BETHABARA

One of the purposes of the governor's visit to the Yadkin country was to select a site for a fort that would provide protection from the Indians.[43] From 1754 to 1758 numerous Indian attacks occurred in the Shenandoah Valley of Virginia and in western North Carolina. The number of taxable[44] persons in Rowan County declined from 1,531 in 1756 to fewer than 800 three years later because settlers moved east seeking safety.[45]

Some refugees came to the Moravian settlement, Bethabara. On July 22, 1755, the Moravian scribe recorded, "A so-called Dunkard[46] or Bearded Man came to the smithy. He has just come from New River with his entire family, fearing to remain there longer because of the Indians, who are wandering about." The man told stories of murder and torture and reported that other settlers were also leaving their homes.[47]

That night, Henry Benner, or Banner, a non-Moravian neighbor who had been searching for strayed horses, stopped by the settlement on his way home. About four in the morning he returned "almost frantic." When he had reached his home he had found his wife and four children gone and his house robbed. The brethren prayed for the family during their morning prayers. "This was the first time that at morning prayer we have used the trumpets," recorded the scribe, "which the last company brought with them from Pennsylvania." At the close of the service they continued to sound the trumpets and fired a gun as well. "As the trumpets began again we heard a call, ran thither, and found Mr. Benner's wife and four children; one child she carried on her back, another little one was in the arms of an older child." Mrs. Benner explained that the dogs had become very restless, and when she went to see what was wrong, stones flew by her head. She took the children and fled. Somehow, they found their way to Bethabara although they had never been there.[48]

In July 1756 the Benners, a Dunkard, the younger Guest[49] with his wife and mother-in-law, and others requested asylum in the Moravian settlement. The brethren were exempt from military service

Music played an important part in Moravian village life. *Courtesy Old Salem.*

by act of Parliament, but they offered to contribute money to the defense of the colony and organized for their own defense. After much prayer and deliberation, they decided to build a stockade around the village and to give asylum to those who requested it.[50]

By July 23, 1756, the stockade was complete, and for the next four years it served as a place of refuge for settlers in the vicinity. In response to Governor Dobbs' instructions, Captain Hugh Waddell, a militia officer, supervised the building of "Fort Dobbs," a stronghold located near Fourth Creek about two miles north of present-day Statesville.[51]

The Indian conflict, which was a part of the French and Indian War in America and the Seven Years War in Europe, continued intermittently in western North Carolina through 1761. In May of 1759 the Assembly authorized Governor Dobbs to call out the militia of Anson, Rowan, and Orange counties. Settlers again came to Bethabara for protection. One man "arrived in great consternation, bringing with him a little child that he had found alone in a house." On May 8 the Moravian scribe recorded, "There is great fear all through the land."[52]

The tension continued throughout 1759. On February 27, 1760, Indians attacked Fort Dobbs, but the small garrison under Hugh Waddell defended the fort successfully. The Moravian scribe recorded news of the encounter and added, without further comment, "Some hours later a beautiful rainbow formed over Bethabara." On March 9 a man pierced through with an arrow arrived and

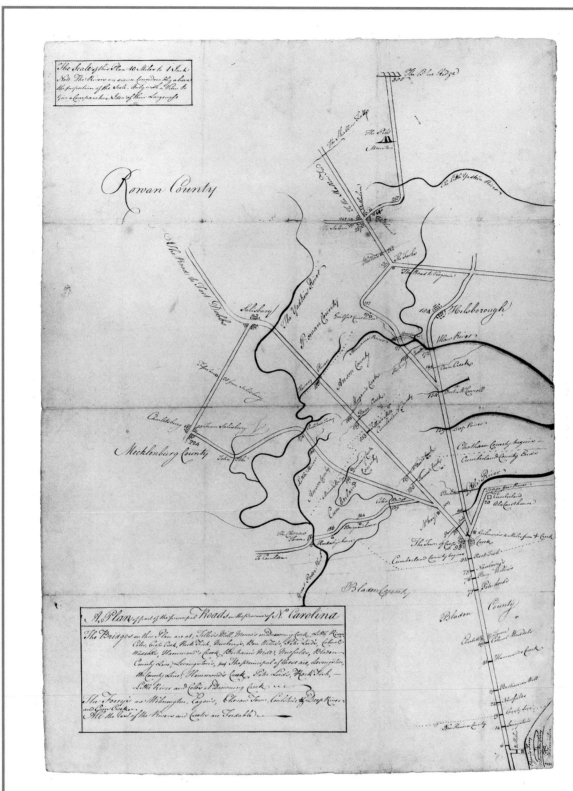

Good trade routes drew settlers into western North Carolina areas such as Rowan County, established in 1753. *Courtesy Clements Library, University of Michigan.*

related how his two companions had been killed by Indians. With the expert care of the Moravian physician, Dr. Jacob Bonn, the man recovered.

The next day about fifty more refugees came to Bethabara, and the Moravians doubled their watch. The Indians were so close the settlers could see the smoke from their campfires. Later through a Cherokee diplomat called Attakullakulla, or the "Little Carpenter," who had tried to keep the peace with the English, the Moravians heard that a strong party of the overhill Cherokee had been in North Carolina, where they had lost one of their chiefs. After they went home, they said they "had been to a great town, where there were a great many people, where a great bell rang often, and during the night time after time a horn was blown, so that they feared to attack the town, and had taken no prisoners." The bell the Moravians used to call the brethren to prayer and the trumpet they used in worship services and, among other things, to speed the reapers to the fields had proved to be unforeseen protection.[53] Another visitor to Bethabara confirmed the story. Aaron Price of Charleston said that the Indians called the Moravian neighborhood, "Dutchi," and said that the Dutchi were a dreadful people, very large and very smart because they had seen into their forts.[54]

By Easter of 1760 four hundred soldiers had arrived at Bethabara to secure the town. After the British won victories in Canada, they sent troops south to subdue the Cherokee. Lieutenant-Colonel Archibald Montgomerie with 1,200 Highlanders and 350 South Carolinians attacked the Native Americans in April 1760 but failed to secure a decisive victory. In 1761 Lieutenant-Colonel James Grant with 2,250 regulars and militia destroyed fifteen Cherokee towns and all growing crops. Attakullakulla, always faithful to the English, was then able to negotiate peace. The treaty of December 18, 1761, marked the end of the Cherokee War.[55]

SALISBURY THRIVES AFTER INDIAN CONFLICT IS RESOLVED

Security from Indian attack encouraged additional settlers to seek homes on the frontier. Benjamin Franklin estimated in 1763 that 10,000 families had emigrated from Pennsylvania to North Carolina in the previous few years. The population of Rowan County almost quadrupled from 1754 to 1770.[56]

Located at the intersection of two great thoroughfares, the Great Wagon Road from Pennsylvania running north and south and the Trading Path from Fort Henry (Petersburg, Virginia) westward to the Cherokee towns, Salisbury became a thriving commercial center. By 1762 the town could boast thirty-five homes, inns, or shops. In fact more than half the buildings in Salisbury were taverns and inns. With so many families passing through in search of new homes, shrewd hostelers became wealthy by frontier standards.[57]

Elizabeth Gillespie is an example of an innkeeper who prospered. Indians killed and scalped her husband, Robert Gillespie, the former business partner of Thomas Bashford, in 1759. The widow bought part of lot number two in the north square in June 1760 and operated an inn, probably one built in 1755 by John Ryle, former owner of the property. Mrs. Gillespie bought the remainder of Ryle's lot in 1762. Meanwhile she had acquired lot number eleven in the north square and a 275-acre tract adjoining the town land on the north. The extent and location of her purchases indicate that her husband must have left her comfortable financially and that she was a shrewd, capable businesswoman.[58]

In addition to numerous inns, Rowan County in 1759 included a total of 124 artisans who could provide services such as spinning, weaving, tailoring, shoemaking, tanning, saddle making, and blacksmithing. Among these were carpenters, millwrights, joiners, brickmakers and bricklayers, coopers, turners, wheelwrights, wagonmakers, potters, hatters, and gunsmiths. Of the 124 artisans, seventeen or 13.71 percent were Moravian.[59]

Earlier historiography indicated that settlers on the southern frontier were self-sufficient and produced everything they used because the rural nature of their surroundings made it difficult for craftspeople to survive outside major cities like Williamsburg, Annapolis, or Charleston.[60] Close examination of the Rowan County court records and the Moravian records, however, has shown that artisans were among the first settlers. Prior to 1790 the artisans mentioned above were joined, among others, by fullers and dyers, glovemakers, tinsmiths, locksmiths, clockmakers, silversmiths, and jewelers. A significant number of women participated in trades, particularly in clothing and textiles.[61]

At least one slave woman, a "certain Mulattoe Girl named Ester," became apprenticed to Joseph Hickman to learn the art of weaving.[62] There may have been other slave artisans whose names do not appear in the records. In 1756, however, Governor Dobbs reported to the Board of Trade that Rowan County had only fifty-four slaves out of a total population of 1,170.[63] Politician John Frohock was possibly the largest slaveholder in 1768 with a total of thirty-eight. Most other slave owners had four or fewer, and even the Moravian congregation owned a small number, some of whom they admitted to the brotherhood.[64] By 1790 slaves still made up less than twenty percent of the population of western North Carolina.[65]

The fact that there were craftspeople in the backcountry both free and slave who produced not only necessities but also luxuries supports the allegation that the traditional view of the frontier as a series of zones progressing westward from the coast, each in a different stage of development, does not apply to North Carolina. The western part of the colony was settled mainly from the north rather than the east, and urban settlements developed alongside the first rural settlements. In the case of the Moravian tract, it was both urban and rural almost from the beginning.[66] As mentioned above, the Moravians had no monopoly on artisans in Rowan County.

THE REGULATORS CALL FOR CHANGE

Discontent among backcountry settlers became apparent in the 1760s with the activities of the Regulators. In South Carolina the principal complaint had been the lack of courts and justice in the backcountry. The problem in North Carolina was not the lack of courts but rather dissatisfaction with public officials appointed by the royal governor from among his friends. Many officials received no salary but instead met expenses by charging fees. Clerks, judges, and sheriffs, who were often outsiders, did not hesitate to charge more than was legal for their services. Another cause for dissatisfaction was that representatives of the eastern seaboard generally ruled the colonial Assembly. The poll tax fell on rich and poor alike, but on the frontier, where much business was conducted by barter, paying taxes in currency was difficult .[67]

Fireplace of the stone house completed by Michael Braun in 1766 in Rowan County. *Suzanne Linder.*
Used with permission of the Rowan Museum, Inc.

Two of the colonial leaders most hated by the Regulators were John Frohock of Rowan County and Edmund Fanning of Orange County. Frohock was a member of the Assembly, clerk, justice of the peace, member of the county court, and colonel in the militia. Fanning, a New York native and close friend of Governor William Tryon, was a lawyer, register, superior court judge, colonel in the militia, assemblyman from Orange, and later borough representative from Hillsboro. He reputedly hated the common people, and they detested him.[68] Rednap Howell, "poet of the Regulation," criticized Frohock and Fanning in a satirical ballad that was handed down orally for many years.[69]

To a modern audience, the demands of the Regulators seem quite reasonable. They petitioned the Assembly to exclude lawyers and clerks from the Assembly, to tax all according to wealth, to pay clerks by salary instead of permitting fees, and to examine what had been done with taxes collected in 1767. When nothing was done, most Rowan citizens refused to pay taxes. In 1770 the situation became so serious that there was no sheriff in Rowan. Finally in May 1771, open conflict broke out. Governor William Tryon and his troops defeated a large group of Regulators at Alamance Creek. Several Regulator leaders were brutally executed, and shortly thereafter, a number of former Regulators left Rowan County. Many followed Daniel Boone into Kentucky.[70]

THE REVOLUTION REACHES ROWAN

Despite the exodus of the Regulators, Rowan was the largest county in the state in both acreage and population by the time of the Revolution. At the outbreak of the war, North Carolina was divided into six military districts. Griffith Rutherford was brigadier general of the Salisbury District. In July of 1776 he led an expedition to subdue the Cherokees. Virginia, South Carolina, and Georgia also sent troops to enter Indian territory simultaneously from different directions. The Native Americans offered little resistance, but the colonial troops burned their villages and destroyed their crops, after which the Cherokee no longer posed a threat to the colonists.[71]

Loyalists, however, were a problem to those supporting the American cause. Tory leader Samuel Bryan, who lived in the forks of the Yadkin, raised eight hundred troops in support of the British. In the summer of 1780 Elizabeth Gillespie Steele wrote to her brother-in-law in Pennsylvania: "We have been surrounded by Tory Insurrections, one party in the forks of Cataba have been defeated with considerable loss. Another from the forks of Yadkin have been pursued but not overtaken."[72] Patriots led by South Carolina General Thomas Sumter finally defeated Bryan and his Tories along with British regulars at Hanging Rock on August 6, 1780.[73]

In January 1781, General Nathanael Greene met Daniel Morgan at Sherrill's Ford on the Catawba and proceeded to Salisbury in advance of his forces. He had dispatched his aides to different parts of the retreating army. Greene was wet from rain and exhausted. An army physician observed that he appeared to be fatigued, to which Greene replied, "Yes, fatigued, hungry, alone, and penniless!" Elizabeth Gillespie Steele welcomed him at her tavern, fed him a warm meal, then brought him a bag of coins. Encouraged by her kindness, Greene went to a picture of King George hanging on the tavern wall. He turned the King's image to the wall and wrote on the back, "O, George, Hide thy face and mourn."[74]

British General Cornwallis and his army followed the Americans to Salisbury. Elizabeth Steele wrote to Ephraim Steele, "In Feb. last the British were so kind as to pay us a visit, at a time when my little family were ill with the small pox, in which my little youngest grand daughter died, the rest have all happily recovered." She continued that the British plundered all horses, dry cattle, horse forage, liquors and family provisions, but, "I escaped well with my house and furniture and milch cow, some in this country were stript of all these things. It comforts me to think that the enemy will probably never return."[75]

YADKIN PIONEERS ENJOY PEACE AND PROSPERITY

A German pastor wrote in 1789 "it is still a very prevalent belief here in this region that peace is not absolutely certain." The pastor was Arnold Rochen, a Lutheran who had recently immigrated and lived near Abbotts Creek, a tributary of the Yadkin. He found the neighborhood to be prosperous. The elders of his congregations brought flour, corn, hams, sausages, dried fruits, chickens, turkeys, geese, and other food. "In fact," wrote Rochen, "we have up to the present time not paid out a cent in our household for such things." He said that anyone willing to work could easily obtain a plantation and "poor people generally are not to be seen here at all." People often married early and had big families. "Thirteen or fourteen children, which usually all live, are not infrequent in these families." Rochen reported that most people were contented. When he asked one of his parishioners how he was faring, the man replied, "If we were to complain God would have to punish us; we lack nothing necessary . . . Since we already have a surplus so soon after the war, we will rapidly become wealthy, if God grants us peace."[76]

In spite of the abundance of necessities, "Luxury is unknown here," the pastor reported. "All the necessities are made at home, both utensils as well as clothing. The women are quite experienced in the weaving and working of linen, and skilled in the utilization of wool, and especially of cotton, which thrives here unusually well . . . Likewise the women are very adept in the dyeing of wool."[77]

The community continued to prosper and to develop trade with the coast. In the nineteenth century, influenced by the national interest in internal improvements, leaders in both North and South Carolina attempted to improve navigation and connect the Yadkin and Pee Dee without success.

The Yadkin River was important in the settlement of western North Carolina in the eighteenth century, not as an avenue of transportation but as a landmark and geographical feature that provided attractive home sites along its many tributaries. It did not provide an impassable barrier because it was usually fordable. In addition, ferries provided a convenient means of crossing. Most settlers reached the Yadkin valley by way of the Great Wagon Road through the Shenandoah Valley of Virginia. The Moravian towns of Bethabara and Salem as well as Salisbury, the county seat of Rowan, developed almost as rapidly as the countryside was settled. In the period from 1745 to 1755, settlers poured into the Yadkin region. After diminishing a little during the French and Indian War, the influx of new citizens continued. Not only farmers but also craftspeople and artisans entered the community.

Settlers populated the Yadkin basin only slightly later than the Pee Dee region. The settlement patterns make it apparent why the upper and lower parts of the river have different names and why the different names initiated by Native Americans before Europeans arrived persist to the present day. The slow and gentle Pee Dee and the swiftly flowing Yadkin maintained their individual identities.

By hard labor, a crew of fifteen or twenty men could propel a pole boat loaded with several tons of cargo at a rate of ten miles a day (re-enactment). *James Huff. Courtesy Santee Cooper.*

CHAPTER 8

A Technological Turning Point

"Wanted to Hire: Fifty or more Labourers,
to work on Pee Dee river . . . one dollar per day. . . ."
Winyah Intelligencer, May 8, 1819

The advent of the nineteenth century marked a turning point in the history of the Yadkin-Pee Dee River. The growth of technology enabled people to assume a greater degree of control over the waterway. Construction of dams made crops in rich bottom lands more secure by offering protection from freshets, and the availability of the cotton gin promoted a profitable money crop. Because increased production created a need for better transportation to markets, citizens supported a program to clear the river of obstructions and deepen the channel to make the route for new types of vessels operated by horsepower or steam more reliable. Fervor for internal improvements swept the nation as settlers of frontier areas demanded adequate transportation and eastern merchants wished to expand their trade. In the period from 1800 to 1825 the importance of the Pee Dee as an avenue of transportation increased significantly, and residents of the Yadkin Valley made serious attempts to make the Yadkin navigable as well.

OPENING THE YADKIN AND PEE DEE FOR STEAMBOAT TRAVEL

From about 1820 steamboats could provide transportation for both passengers and freight at a considerable savings over land transportation. Enterprising North Carolinians wanted to open the Yadkin to steamboat navigation to take advantage of the tremendous opportunities that merchants and planters of the Pee Dee enjoyed. For a time it appeared they might succeed in connecting the Yadkin and the Pee Dee by means of canals around the falls, but railroads and plank roads intervened before the problems and expense of building canals could be solved.

An early canal that was somewhat successful led from the town of Sneedsborough in Anson County, North Carolina, just above the South Carolina line, through Whortleberry Creek to the Pee Dee River. Sneedsborough, chartered in 1795, was above the falls on the Pee Dee. It was, however, near Parker's Ferry and Marks Creek where Stephen Parker and Achilles Knight operated a boatyard. It was one of many landings on the Pee Dee that flourished after cotton became the principal export.[1]

There was an increasing demand for cotton in the closing years of the eighteenth century. After the Revolution, Pee Dee indigo planters faced new foreign competition and the loss of the lucrative British bounty. In addition, traditional markets for surplus corn and wheat also softened.[2] The demand for cotton by British manufacturers, however, increased along with technological improvements in cotton spinning and weaving. The Charleston newspaper *City Gazette and Daily Advertiser*, which had close associations with the Pee Dee through its editors John E.McIver and David Rogerson Williams, lamented the neglect of South Carolina's cotton culture in 1787. A year later a writer in the same paper declared that back country men were "very anxious to get the machines for ginning, carding and spinning cotton."[3]

COTTON PRODUCTION INCREASES WITH WHITNEY'S GIN

Although other gins were available, the most efficient was Eli Whitney's. Whitney, a Yale graduate, completed his invention in 1793.[4] Using one of the early hand gins, a worker could clean about 5 pounds of cotton a week. Whitney's gin increased production to about 50 pounds a day. South Carolina's cotton exports rose from 9,840 pounds in 1790 to over 6,425,000 pounds in 1800.[5] By 1811, the upcountry alone exported over 30 million pounds of cotton.[6]

Because short-staple cotton required no large capital outlay, Charleston historian David Ramsay stated in 1809 that individuals or white families without slaves could grow the crop profitably. Ramsay continued, "it appears. . . that the clear profits on one crop planted in cotton. . . will purchase the fee simple of the land. Two, three, or four will in like manner pay for the Negroes who make it."[7]

The increase of production created a need for larger watercraft on the Pee Dee, first to transport heavy bags of about 300 pounds and later to transport 320-pound bales that were both bulky and heavy.[8] As a finished product, indigo was so compact and expensive that a planter might send his entire crop to market in a periauger or dugout made on his plantation. A crop of cotton, on the other hand, required a much larger craft, and yeomen farmers who could not afford to own a boat could pay freight charges more readily than they could transport their cotton by wagon over extremely poor roads.

By 1810, the prosperity of the cotton producers caused a significant increase both in the need for transportation to the coast and the demand for manufactured goods to supply the comforts of life. The War of 1812 and the restrictions on commerce that accompanied it delayed development of transportation, but the arrival of peace in 1815 brought a great rise in cotton prices and a renewed interest in more efficient means of moving freight.[9]

Leaders in the national government shared this interest. Henry Clay, senator from Kentucky, supported federal funding of roads and canals. When the Second Bank of the United States paid the government $1.5 million for its exclusive privileges, Senator John C. Calhoun of South Carolina in 1817 induced Congress to pass the Bonus Bill under which the bank money would be parceled out to the states. President James Madison vetoed the bill because he believed spending federal funds for internal improvements in individual states would violate the strict interpretation of the Constitution. The states, therefore, had to provide for their own internal improvements at that time.[10]

MOSES ROGERS, STEAMBOAT CAPTAIN

One of the most renowned steamboat captains to traverse the rivers made his final voyage on the Pee Dee. Moses Rogers, an accomplished and enterprising commander, was born in New London, Connecticut. He died in Georgetown at the early age of forty-two and was buried in the port city. The story of Moses Rogers is yet another small piece of history that has a special connection to the Pee Dee.

Rogers was interested in ships and water travel from boyhood. He learned to sail as a youth and commanded his first vessel at the age of twenty-one. Rogers experimented with various types of watercraft and took out patents in 1814 and 1815 for a horse-powered ferryboat, which served several ferry lines in New York harbor and other places.[1] Although he is credited with commanding the *Fulton*, the first steamboat on the Hudson, the *Phoenix*, the first steamboat on the Delaware, the *Eagle*, the first steamboat on the Chesapeake, and the first steamboat between Charleston and Savannah, his crowning achievement was his involvement with the *Savannah*, the first steamboat to cross the Atlantic.[2]

In 1818, Rogers participated in the birth of the steamship *Savannah*. He supervised the building of the vessel's engines, the construction of the paddle wheels, and the installation of the machinery. He also had the ingenious idea of constructing the *Savannah's* wheels so they could be removed and placed on board in case weather required the sole use of sails.[3]

The *Savannah* set sail on May 25, 1819, and arrived in Liverpool twenty-nine days and eleven hours later. Although sails supplemented the steam power, the *Savannah's* journey demonstrated the feasibility of transatlantic steam navigation. The *Savannah* safely continued on to Stockholm and St. Petersburg and finally back to the United States. The "great experiment" had been a success at the hands of Moses Rogers.[4]

Shortly after Rogers' return to Savannah, a group of Southerners who wanted to establish a steamboat service on the Pee Dee river approached him. Joined by longtime friend and Nantucket shipmaster Daniel Elkins, Rogers supervised the building of the steamer *Pee Dee* and helped to develop a thriving passenger and freight business on the South Carolina river.[5]

On November 6, 1821, Rogers set sail from Cheraw as captain of the *Pee Dee* on what would be his last voyage. By the time the steamboat reached Georgetown a few days later, the captain was quite ill. Although attended by the best doctors, Rogers succumbed to a fever on October 15, 1821.[6]

A friend wrote to the captain's wife that his passing was "deeply deplored" at Georgetown and predicted that at Cheraw "where he was more generally known, his loss will be severely felt." The friend continued that although "he had not been but a little time among us . . . his manners were of that attractive kind, his conduct in every instance so correct and his heart so kind, open, liberal and feeling that all who knew him loved him."[7]

In 1818 South Carolina launched the most ambitious program of domestic improvement undertaken by the state government prior to the twentieth century. With an annual budget of only $250,000 dollars, South Carolina committed itself to spend a million dollars on internal improvements over a period of years. Within a decade, an additional amount of nearly $900,000 had been added. Of this amount, the majority was for the construction of canals around the major obstructions in the Broad, Congaree, Saluda, and Wateree rivers. Some $217,788, however, went toward improvement of navigation of rivers below the fall line. The Pee Dee benefited directly from this allocation.[11]

David Rogerson Williams, owner of several plantations in the Society Hill area, became a leader in opening navigation on the Pee Dee. Williams depended on water transportation to market his crops and manufactured goods and to procure goods for his store at Society Hill.[12] In 1816, as governor of South Carolina, he was in a position to exert his influence to promote improvement of rivers. He called for "commencing on a large scale, works of internal improvement." The next year his successor, Governor Andrew Pickens, recommended that the surplus in the state treasury be applied to such a program.[13]

The legislature hired John Wilson, a graduate of the University of Edinburgh, as civil and military engineer for $4,000 per year and appropriated $50,000 to begin the work. In 1818 Wilson presented a report and asked that a million dollars be devoted to an extensive program of internal improvement. With the leadership of Representative Joel R. Poinsett, the General Assembly pledged the requested amount and instructed the engineer to proceed with improving the navigation of rivers, cutting canals, and building turnpike roads.[14]

In his report of 1818 Wilson stated that the Pee Dee was navigable for boats drawing four feet of water from Winyah Bay to Long Bluff (Society Hill). He said that the logs and driftwood that had accumulated in the river could easily be removed. Between Society Hill and Cheraw he observed three rapids "where the water falls over loose stones and rocks, and at times is not more than two feet deep." Above Cheraw to the North Carolina line were several ledges of rock extending across the river that obstructed navigation. "The water here is represented never to fall below two feet."[15] At Parker's Ferry at the North Carolina line the water was so shallow that the stagecoach could sometimes ford the river. There was a large rock with a mark to indicate the water level. When the water was below the mark, the river could be forded at that point.[16]

Wilson reported that several tributaries of the Pee Dee were also navigable but in need of improvement. Logs and driftwood obstructed the mouth of Lynches Creek to about three miles up the creek, he said, but added that the removal of these logs might open navigation for boats drawing three or four feet to the confluence of Big and Little Lynches Creek—a distance of eighty-two miles by land. In addition, each of the branches might be rendered navigable ten or twelve miles above the confluence.[17]

Black Creek enters the Pee Dee about ninety miles from Winyah Bay and flows near the town of Darlington. Because the inhabitants of Darlington District had cleared the creek for twenty miles from its mouth for boats drawing five feet, the state engineer thought it could be opened fifteen miles higher up to the bridge on the road leading from Camden to Society Hill.[18]

The Waccamaw River was navigable from Winyah Bay to North Carolina, between seventy and eighty miles. One sand bar and some logs were the only problems. "There is never less than five feet water in any part of the Waccamaw, within this state, and in times of freshets, the river rises twelve and fourteen feet," reported Wilson.

For about eighty miles from its confluence with the Great Pee Dee to the North Carolina line, the Little Pee Dee was navigable for boats drawing three feet of water, the only obstruction being the accumulation of logs. The Lumber River was navigable from its confluence with the Little Pee Dee to Lumberton, North Carolina—about thirty-seven miles. Boats carrying forty or fifty barrels of rice could navigate the Black River to Kingstree—forty-five miles in a direct line from Winyah Bay—and smaller craft could continue to Lowry's bridge, twelve miles above Kingstree. Wilson thought Black River might be opened twenty-five miles farther.[19]

WILLIAMS CLEARS THE UPPER PEE DEE

As the main artery of transportation, the Great Pee Dee would receive the first efforts. In April 1819 Wilson forwarded machinery and other implements to Society Hill to "fit up" boats and flats to begin clearing obstructions from the river.[20] David Rogerson Williams was in charge. On May 8, 1819, Williams advertised in the Georgetown newspaper, "Wanted to Hire: Fifty or more Labourers, to work on Pee Dee river. . . one dollar per day. . . and their food consisting of corn meal, bacon, and molasses found them; also a reasonable allowance of whiskey."[21]

On October 20, 1819, Williams made a report to the civil engineer. He stated that he had purchased two boats, fitted them with machinery suitable for raising and removing logs, stumps, and snags forming obstructions to navigation, and had them operating by June 4. He had rented two additional boats similarly fitted and had them operating by July 10. On August 4 he added one set of flats "with machinery similar to that employed on the Congaree river." The greatest number of hands employed at any one time was sixty. Two captains and two mates alternated with each other in supervising the work so that only one captain or superintendent and one mate or "white coxswain" were on duty at a time.

Williams was concerned about the health of the workers. He noted that he had taken every precaution to provide a "regular and temperate course" including proper preparation of food, a liberal use of lime in keeping the boats cleansed with white wash, and a constant use of hoarhound tea, "of which, all were made to drink freely." Only once was a physician called, "although the superintendents were constantly enjoined to do so, when a case should seem to require one."[22]

Between June and October the crew was able to clear about a hundred and thirty miles from Chatham (Cheraw) to Cooper's Bluff, or six miles more than half the distance from Chatham to Georgetown. "This extent," observed Williams, "embraces all the falls or rapids and sand bars of the Pedee over which there is the least depth of water below Chatham." Williams recommended clearing the lower part of the river at a later date, but he noted that it was deeper and although obstructed was still navigable by steamboats directed by skillful pilots. The total cost of clearing the upper river was figured meticulously to $9803.075. Williams conscientiously employed the workers on rainy days in preparing oakum for the future use of public boats and flats.[23]

Near the end of 1819 legislators decided that the projected internal improvements were beyond the ability of one man to superintend. The General Assembly established a board of public works

David Rogerson Williams.
*Courtesy South Caroliniana
Library.*

composed of five commissioners. The first board, elected by the General Assembly in December 1819, was composed of John Wilson, Joel Poinsett, David Rogerson Williams, W. R. Davie, and Thomas Baker. Williams declined to serve and was replaced by Abram Blanding, who, in February 1820, became commissioner of roads, rivers, and canals. In 1822 a single superintendent of public works, with Abram Blanding appointed to that office, superseded the board. Blanding served through 1828 when an excess of two million dollars resulted in two thousand miles of navigable streams.[24] In 1820 under Blanding's leadership, the work progressed on the Pee Dee. David R. Williams reported that on June 1 of that year the workmen returned to the Pee Dee with six boats manned with fifty-five hands and commanded by John Barnett, superintendent. The workers cleared a channel from Chatham to Georgetown,[25] and Williams prepared to transfer the equipment to the Waccamaw and Black Creek. He stated that the net cost of clearing the entire Pee Dee was $15,000.[26]

NEW IDEAS IMPROVE RIVER NAVIGATION

Work continued on the Pee Dee and its tributaries during the decade of the 1820s, and new methods developed with experience. David R. Williams strengthened the levees he had built earlier along the river bank to protect his plantations from floods. He also erected jetties in the river to divert the current away from vulnerable sites near these levees. Williams said, "I was ridiculed by old and young . . . when I first attempted to dam out the inundations of the Pee Dee." He said it almost kept him out of Congress because it was thought any man who believed he could keep the freshets from his low grounds was too big a fool to be elected. "Now," he said, "there is nearly as much swamp land reclaimed from freshets in South Carolina as on the Mississippi."[27]

David Gregg, a boat owner and proprietor of a store at Society Hill, also had a personal interest in river navigation. He accepted a contract to improve the channel of the Pee Dee. Gregg invented a machine to cut a channel through a sand bar. It consisted of two flats placed about ten or twelve feet apart and secured by timber crossing them at each end. Between them, Gregg placed a water wheel ten feet in diameter and about ten feet long. The arms of the wheel extended a little beyond the paddles and were pointed "with iron in the shape of a bull tongue plough." Gregg moored the flats at the head of the shoal and by a chain and capstan allowed the flats to move across the shoal and then pulled them back up. "While the flats are passing slowly down, the wheel is lowered into the water till the iron arms strike the bottom, and being set in rapid motion by the water of the river passing between the flats, the gravel and clay are torn up and carried by the wheel and current into the deep water below." This apparatus could cut a channel to four feet or deeper by increasing the diameter of the wheel. A jetty was necessary to funnel the water into the channel to provide sufficient power to operate the wheel and carry off the debris. Afterwards, the strong current provided by the jetty would help keep the channel clear.[28]

FLATS, COTTON BOXES AND POLE BOATS

Navigation increased after the state became involved in the improvement of the Pee Dee and its tributaries. When planters needed larger boats for transporting cotton they adapted and enlarged existing types to develop boats that served their needs. Flats that had been in use in the eighteenth century were similar to rafts with shallow sides added. Because ordinary plantation carpenters could construct them, planters used them as their principal cargo craft in the creeks and canals of rice fields and to transport cotton down a creek to a landing on the river. A typical flat, forty-five to fifty feet long and fifteen feet in the beam, might be decked over in part to protect the cargo. Flats could make downriver trips, but their barge-like shape prevented them from returning against the current. "Cotton boxes" were a type of flat specifically developed for hauling bulk cotton. They therefore had high sides to accommodate the fleecy cargo. At the end of the trip down river they were usually broken down and sold for lumber. Cotton boxes were roughly built and slightly larger than the average flat. They were sixty feet long or more and twenty-five feet wide. Sweeps at bow and stern enabled boatmen to steer the craft. David

Rogerson Williams said in 1819, "An immense amount of produce has heretofore been annually carried down in large flats, constructed only for the voyage, always very hazardous, and resorted to in consequence of the previous high freights and scarcity of boats."[29]

Pole boats sometimes had a small keel for better balancing and steering and a pointed or rounded bow and stern to reduce resistance in the water. Plank ways along each gunwale provided walking space for the crewmen, who were divided into gangs for starboard and port and perhaps into shifts alternating work and rest. Each poleman in the gang would in turn walk to the bow, secure his pole against the bottom of the stream, bear against its upper end with his shoulder, and walk from bow to stern, thus forcing the boat forward. The captain or coxswain would guide the boat with the rudder. A crew of fifteen or twenty men could pole a boat with several tons of cargo upstream at the rate of about ten miles a day by hard labor.[30]

Shallow draft was essential for Pee Dee pole boats, which could be from thirty to seventy feet long. Most did not have keels because without them they could move sideways when necessary to avoid an obstruction in the river. On the downriver trip with a full load, boat hands used poles on each side of the boat and sweeps at bow and stern if the water was deep. A coxswain needed to be familiar with every foot of river bottom to steer the boat clear of snags and shoals.

On the arduous return against the current, boatmen used ash poles from ten to sixteen feet long to shove the craft forward.[31] In some places the current was so swift they had to "warp up." This involved running strong lines to the bank and moving the boat forward by windlass. In a process called "hooking," boat hands used iron grapnels to snag overhanging trees and pull the vessel forward. "Jamming" referred to thrusting poles outward on the river bank to guide the boat.[32]

Operating a pole boat required considerable skill and knowledge of the river. The crews of pole boats were usually slaves, who were frequently in sole charge of their boats. David Gregg McIntosh, grandson of David Gregg, recalled that both his father and his grandfather owned pole boats. He said, "I recall my Father's having one built, chiefly with Negro hands,[33] of very considerable size, (capable of carrying several hundred bales of cotton, stored in her hold, and piled in the middle of the deck)."[34]

The hands were under the control of a coxswain, who held the rudder and directed the movements of the boat. The polemen kept together by "some vocal music which was peculiarly their own." The crew of the McIntosh boat addressed their coxswain as "Cap'n Sam," but David Gregg McIntosh called him "Daddy Sam." Although a slave, Sam was a carpenter by trade and was the chief builder of the boat he commanded. "My Father had the utmost confidence in him and he well deserved it. He had in his control on these trips cargoes, worth thousands of dollars, and I never heard that he was ever in the slightest degree unfaithful to his trust."[35]

Cleland Belin, a successful planter and businessman at Willtown in Williamsburg County, sent his crops to market by boat from Black Mingo Creek to Black River and thus to Georgetown. Belin held in high esteem his slave who was in charge of transporting the crops. In the cemetery adjoining the lovely little white church known as "Belin's Black Mingo Baptist Church" is the following epitaph: "Sacred to the memory of Bill, a strictly honest and faithful servant of Cleland Belin." The inscription goes on to say that Bill was often entrusted with the care of produce and merchandize to the value of many thousands of dollars without loss or damage. He died October 7, 1854, at age thirty-five, an approved member of the church. "Well done, thou good and faithful servant. Enter thou into Joy of thy Lord."[36]

The slave Bill was obviously respected by his master. He and David McIntosh's slave Sam provide examples of the responsibility and autonomy that boat captains possessed. It was customary for planters to send their crops to market in charge of slaves. Sometimes the planter met the boat at Georgetown,

Belin's Black Mingo Baptist Church. The church is no longer standing. *Carl Julien. Courtesy South Caroliniana Library.*

Abram Blanding. *Courtesy South Caroliniana Library.*

but in other cases, the slaves took their cargo to a factor and returned to the plantation unaccompanied. It is possible that slaves with boating experience in Africa were able to continue that line of work in America. West Africa near the Gulf of Guinea, where many slaves originated, is an area of many rivers.

Bright Williamson, who lived on Black Creek in Darlington County, conducted a mercantile business and operated a line of pole boats from Williamson's Bridge to Georgetown. The account books for his store in 1804 and 1805 show that he carried a wide variety of goods from farm implements to cloth such as India cotton and cambric; to groceries that could not be grown locally such as nutmeg, salt, pepper, sugar, and coffee; to spirits such as brandy and "Meadarea" wine.[37]

Thomas Harllee had a similar operation on the Little Pee Dee. He made boats and flats. After building boats for a time, he established a store near where the modern road from Little Rock, South Carolina, to Lumberton, North Carolina, crosses the Little Pee Dee and supplied his store with goods brought by pole boat from Georgetown.[38]

There were numerous pole boats in operation. In his letter to the state engineer in 1819, David R. Williams reported that in addition to many flats, "One team boat, and about thirty poling boats, navigated this river last winter." The teamboat was a specialized craft, similar to a steam boat in paddle-wheel type construction, but it utilized mules as motive power. Williams stated, "For the conveyance of persons [usually as ferries], they have been used with success elsewhere; but to Mr. David Gregg, a merchant at Society Hill, is justly due the modification of the principle which renders them useful as vessels of burthen." Williams took pride in the fact that he introduced mules as work animals in the South, so he was undoubtedly glad to find another use for them.[39]

Eight mules provided power for the teamboat, which five men navigated. The mules, walking in a circle on deck, turned a gear system that turned the paddle wheels. The boat could carry three hundred bales of cotton and complete a trip from Society Hill to Georgetown in fifteen days at a cost of seventy-five cents per bale. Transporting three hundred bales by land required thirty wagons, one hundred twenty horses, and at least thirty men for about eight days.

Abram Blanding noted, "Estimating the expense of the mules at fifty cents a day, and the value of the labour of the men at seventy-five cents, the cost of transporting three hundred bales of cotton by the team boat amounts to one hundred and sixteen dollars and twenty-five cents. The same estimate gives six hundred and fifty dollars as the cost of land carriage." He continued that previous to the improvement of the river, a boat carrying three hundred bales of cotton required fifteen men to pole it up and the trip was never performed in less than twenty days. According to Blanding's calculations, teamboat transportation saved $2,175, without considering that the extra manpower required for land transportation could be employed in agriculture and thus increases production. Blanding also asserted that the saving was equally great on the return cargo because less expensive transportation would decrease the price of consumer goods.[40]

STEAMBOATS ARRIVE ON THE PEE DEE

The first steamboat began operation on the Pee Dee late in 1819. The Georgetown *Winyah Intelligencer* reported on October 8, 1819, "A beautiful steam Boat called the 'Pee Dee' intended for the navigation of the Pee Dee from this place to Chatham [Cheraw], S. C. was launched at Charleston on the 26th. She may be expected at this place shortly."

The steamboat reached Georgetown on Wednesday, December 17, along with two tow boats. The tow boats were lighters to provide the shallow draft necessary to navigate the river. By distributing the freight over a larger area, the water displacement was appreciably smaller, thus making it possible to traverse shallow water while utilizing the full motive power of the steamboat.

The local newspaper remarked, "The boat is considered a very superior one and affords handsome accommodations for passengers. This is the first boat of the kind that has ever appeared at this place, and little doubt is entertained but she will handsomely remunerate the patriotic citizens by whom she was built, and greatly facilitate the communication between this place and the up country."[41]

Opening the navigation of the Pee Dee to Cheraw produced a rapid growth of the community. The report of the Board of Public Works for 1821 noted that during the last season, which was only the second of its existence, the goods received and sold at Cheraw amounted to about $200,000. According to the best estimates of the merchants of the place, the exports were as follows: cotton—9,500 bales, tallow—10,000 pounds, bees wax—5,000 pounds, flax seed—2,000 bushels, flour—1,000 barrels, corn—30,000 bushels, in addition to "considerable Bacon, Lard, &c."

The report continued that in the last eighteen months about fifty new buildings had been erected in Cheraw, and ten more were in process. The population had increased from 35 to 450 inhabitants. "All that is required to give this place the whole trade of the country on the Yadkin, extending one hundred and fifty miles into North Carolina, is a perfect Steam Boat navigation to Georgetown."[42]

THE YADKIN NAVIGATION COMPANY

North Carolinians were also interested in extending the trade of the Yadkin country. Archibald DeBow Murphey, representative of Orange County in the North Carolina senate from 1812 to 1818, took the lead in promoting internal improvements in the state. Murphey was chairman of the joint committee of the legislature on inland navigation in 1816 and of the committee on internal improvements from 1817 through 1819. His comprehensive plan included deepening inlets along the coast, clearing river channels, building locks, and connecting the Catawba and the Yadkin rivers with the Cape Fear by canal to funnel commerce to Wilmington, North Carolina, at the mouth of the Cape Fear.[43]

In his report to Hamilton Fulton, the British engineer the North Carolina legislature hired to implement internal improvements, Murphey estimated that six million acres of land lay along the Yadkin and its tributaries. He said that one third of the white population of the state lived on the river and that the export value of cotton, tobacco, wheat, and other crops grown there would total 2 million dollars. Murphey believed that the Yadkin could be made navigable for boats of ten tons burden from Wilkesboro, North Carolina, to the narrows. The falls at the narrows might be bypassed either by canal, turnpike road, or railway. From the mouth of the Uwharrie below the narrows to the South Carolina line, he said that "there are no very serious obstacles to its navigation."[44] In July 1818 the North Carolina General Assembly appropriated $25,000 and chartered the Yadkin Navigation Company with an authorized capital of $250,000. Archibald Murphey was president of the company. An advertisement appeared in the *Winyah Intelligencer* of Georgetown on February 24, 1819, stating, "Frederick Randle of Sneedsborough announces plans to improve navigation on Pee Dee and Yadkin from the South Carolina line to Blue Ridge. Installment of $10 per share is required to be paid by March 1." Randle, treasurer of the company, advertised in the Salisbury *Western Carolinian* that the fifth and sixth installments on shares were due in 1821.[45]

Along with plans for the Yadkin, new interest in Sneedsboro developed. Many of those who invested in the Yadkin Navigation Company also invested in a company formed to buy the town from its owner, William Johnson of Anson County, for $38,410. Murphey wrote to his friend Thomas Ruffin, offering him shares in the company. Murphey said, "It will be the great Town of the Pedee, and a little encouragement would give it a Cotton and Tobacco Trade better than this place enjoys. . . . Our

A BARON IN THE PEE DEE

An early celebrity in the Pee Dee, Baron Frederick C. H. B. von Poellnitz continues to be an intriguing figure. Poellnitz lived in the Pee Dee for less than ten years, but the story of how he came to own Marlboro County swampland is the subject of fascination.

According to Henry Poellnitz Johnston, a descendant, the baron was born in Germany and became imperial baron and chamberlain of Frederick the Great, king of Prussia. After declaring he "could no longer conceal the desire to be counted among the free men of America," Poellnitz and his young third wife, Lady Anne Stuart, moved to Edenton, North Carolina, on July 25, 1782, and soon thereafter to New York.[8]

After his arrival in New York and no later than 1785, Baron Poellnitz acquired an estate called Minto. There he broadened his interest in agriculture and agricultural experimentation. Minto was described as "the most highly cultivated country place near the city" with "a greater variety of the choicest fruit trees and flowering shrubs than perhaps any other place in the state," and the "richest soil of any estate on Manhattan Island."[9]

One of the baron's inventions was a threshing machine, which appeared in a 1788 New York parade celebrating ratification of the United States Constitution. Among his other contributions are several varieties of grass, plows, and other farm tools. Poellnitz also suggested to George Washington a prototype of what would eventually become the United States Department of Agriculture.[10]

Despite his many achievements, South Carolinians remember Poellnitz for the property that brought him to the Pee Dee. In 1790 Poellnitz left the valuable acreage (now in New York City) that was Minto and purchased 2,991 acres of Pee Dee River swampland for £5000.[11] Poellnitz had never even seen the Pee Dee land.

From the baron's viewpoint, the southern climate and growing season may have been better suited for his farming and agricultural experimentation.[12] North Carolina writer Inglis Fletcher suggested in her novel *The Wicked Lady*, that the amorous escapades of Lady Anne Stuart embarrassed the baron and prompted him to leave her in New York and retreat to the country. At any rate, he did not bring her to Marlboro County. His children were by his second wife, Charlotte de Bondelli, a lady of the Swiss nobility.[13]

The Poellnitz name is no longer found in Marlboro County, but the baron's descendants may still be counted as leaders in the Pee Dee. Mary Ann Carloss, granddaughter of Baron Poellnitz, married Light Townsend, a prominent cotton planter on the Pee Dee. Their descendants remain in the region today and carry the tale of the baron as part of their proud history.

A steamboat similar to this one began operating on the Pee Dee in 1819.
Courtesy Sarah G. Spruill, Cheraw Visitors Bureau.

Navigation Company, will make improvements there in Canaling and in a Bason, which will attract the Attention of all Persons, who see them." Richmond Pearson, a successful merchant and planter who lived in the forks of the Yadkin and South Yadkin, effected the navigation of the Yadkin to the narrows where he transferred his goods by land below Grassy Islands and thence by water to Sneedsboro.[46]

Murphey and some of the same investors also planned the town of Clinton to be located in the point where the South Yadkin joins the Yadkin. The stockholders believed their location was an ideal spot between the two rivers. They sold forty-six lots and carefully laid out the town, but the failure to make the river navigable along with the Panic of 1819 ruined the plan for the new town. A Salisbury newspaper satirically reported in May 1820 that a distressing fire had destroyed one third of the town, "but thanks to the foresight of the people in not building there, no houses, but a great many stumps fell victim to the all devouring element."[47]

All experiments prompted by the Yadkin navigation project were not failures. Peter Hairston, a planter who had served four terms in the state legislature, was acquainted with Archibald D. Murphey and his plans for the river. The hopes of river navigation encouraged Hairston to purchase Cooleemee Hill Plantation from Jesse A. Pearson in 1817. Before buying the 2,300-acre plantation, however, Hairston sent workers to experiment with growing cotton there. When they succeeded in producing a good crop, he went ahead with the purchase.[48] Although the experiment in producing cotton proved most successful, the Yadkin navigation project seemed doomed.

Nevertheless, the Yadkin company did considerable work on parts of the river. In 1819 and 1820 workers constructed a canal a mile long at Bean Shoals, which necessitated the building of a rock retaining wall about 1,200 feet long and 16 feet high. By August 1820, however, the contractor, Hiram Jennings, was in dire financial straits. He wrote to Murphey: "My situation at present is raley humiliatung . . . I have been going upon Creded, as long as, that, would doe, and I am unable to obtain, even provision, to feed my hands." Jennings went on to say that he was working on the head of the canal and was preparing to turn in the water. He insisted that with a small sum he should be able to complete improvements on the most difficult part of the river above the narrows.[49]

YADKIN IMPROVEMENTS UNSUCCESSFUL

Unfortunately, the money gave out before the Yadkin improvements could be completed. In 1822 Governor Gabriel Holmes stated, "By dividing our strength so much in attempting to effect everything at once, we have effected comparatively, nothing." In addition to trying to spread a relatively small amount of capital over multiple projects, conservative easterners were hesitant to support financing for projects that would immediately benefit the western part of the state. Richard Dobbs Spaight, Jr., declared that what prevented internal improvements from being successful in North Carolina was that "we have constantly attempted to do too much. In the legislature there was not only an eastern and western interest, but there was a Roanoke, a Cape Fear and a Neuse interest; and the result had been to prevent any thing being effectually done." By 1825, in spite of expenditures of more than $84,000, there was little progress.[50]

Despite the failure to make the Yadkin navigable, technological improvements made success possible in other endeavors. In the period from 1800 to 1825 the balance of power between mankind and the river gradually shifted toward mankind. Dams along the river bank with gates at strategic places to provide drainage gave greater security in planting crops. The cotton gin made it profitable to grow the staple to meet the needs of an expanding world-wide textile industry. Tributaries of the Yadkin-Pee Dee supplied water power for a few textile mills.

Engineers using slave labor cleared the Pee Dee of obstructions and devised a method of deepening the channel in shallow areas to prepare the way for larger watercraft. Teamboats held ascendance on the river for a short time until steamboats appeared and largely dominated freight transportation.

By the 1820s steamboats made regular runs from Cheraw to Georgetown and Charleston, stopping at plantation landings along the way. Some freight from the Yadkin region came overland to Cheraw to connect with a steamboat route. Dependable and relatively inexpensive transportation contributed to the tremendous growth of the cotton economy, an economy that would have a profound influence on the culture of the region in the antebellum period.

This house, built by Charles Irby near present-day Wallace, South Carolina, is typical of antebellum Pee Dee plantation homes. *Suzanne Linder. Courtesy Mr. and Mrs. Kenneth Rosser.*

CHAPTER 9

The Plantation Era

Way down upon the Pedee river
Far, far away
There's where my heart is turning ever
There's where the old folks stay.
Stephen Foster, in the first draft of "Old Folks at Home"

The piercing blast of the steamboat whistle, heard for miles around, came to signify progress, social interaction, and man's increased dominion over the river. As a relatively inexpensive way of getting goods to market, the steamboat created an unprecedented opportunity for economic expansion in the Pee Dee and contributed to the growth of the region's plantation system.

More specifically, steamboats offered a feasible solution to the age-old problem of getting commodities such as cotton, rice, and naval stores to market quickly and efficiently by linking the isolated plantations and backcountry farms of the Pee Dee to the centers of trade. The editor of the *Pee Dee Gazette* of Cheraw quoted a letter from a Wadesboro, North Carolina, man to his agent in Cheraw in 1836: "I think we are about to commence a new era of business in this section. Some of our merchants have received goods by the new steamboat Atlanta [Atalanta] *in nine days* from New York via Georgetown and Cheraw." Even after a trip of twenty-five miles by wagon from Cheraw to Wadesboro, the New York shipment beat the mail from Georgetown. This quote proved to be prophetic as the advent of steamships allowed river trade to flourish and planters to grow wealthy.[1]

The steamers with their speed and capacity greatly increased commerce. The *Pee Dee Gazette* wrote, "We take pleasure in copying an article from the *Charlotte Journal*. Although we have never had the pleasure of seeing Charlotte, we learn on the best authority that it is among the most decidedly respectable of our up country villages. One gentleman assures us that he got his supplies from the north by way of Georgetown and Cheraw in less than a month after they were ordered." In 1839 cotton from the North Carolina counties of Richmond, Anson, Montgomery, Union, Mecklenburg, Stanly, Cabarrus, Rowan, Lincoln, Catawba, Iredell, and Robeson passed through Cheraw. One newspaper writer said more cotton from North Carolina than South Carolina found a market at Cheraw. [2]

The plantations bordering the Pee Dee frequently served as "ports of call" where the steamers customarily stopped for supplies, repairs, and the exchange of goods and cargo. Large plantations had individual landings, and some stops were particularly for loading wood to stoke the boilers of the steamboats, such as Allison's Wood Landing in what is now Florence County near the town of Poston. A contemporary lady remembered that the laborers "would form a line, a sort of bucket brigade, and pass [the wood] quickly to the deck. Often there were women as well as men and they would sing, cut steps, and shout back and forth to the crew."[3]

In December 1850 the steamer *Wateree* sank in $11\frac{1}{2}$ feet of water at Allison's carrying 990 bales of cotton. The cause of the sinking was unknown, but the river was rising rapidly, and witnesses surmised that a drifting log must have struck the hull. No permanent obstructions were at that location because the landing was "frequented more or less by all the boats on the river to 'wood up.'" The crew managed to save about 700 bales of the cotton.[4]

PASSENGER TRAVEL ON STEAMBOATS

Although the main function of steamboats was the transportation of goods and produce, passengers were welcome. On October 4, 1839, one paper announced a quick trip from Charleston to Cheraw by means of the new steamboats *Swan* and *Anson*, stating "both boats have excellent accommodations for passengers and to carry much cotton, reshipped at Georgetown to New York."[5]

Duration of a trip could vary, and the time was not always quick. Edgar Welles Charles of Millwood Plantation in Darlington District boarded the steamer *Pee Dee* with his friend Peter Wilds at Cashaway in mid-January 1846 bound for Charleston.[6] They got aboard the boat on Thursday, but it did not depart until Friday about eleven o'clock. Passengers already on board included Dr. Henry Bacot and Peter Edwards of Society Hill, and John Julius Cannon and Robert Dickinson of Darlington. On Saturday at nine o'clock, the *Pee Dee* reached Georgetown, where the passengers spent the night and went to church on Sunday morning before resuming the journey at three o'clock. The route was through the inland passage. At one point a storm caused concern. Edgar Charles wrote to his wife, Jane, that the wind was so strong the passengers feared the boat would be blown into the marsh flats where they risked destruction of the operating mechanism and the possibility of having to throw cargo overboard to lighten the load. "After nearly a week's absence from home I am within one day of Charleston," wrote Charles. He continued, "If I had known this trip would have been so tedious I would have taken the stage."[7]

Steamboat passengers traveled in a style that was not always the most desirable. Nineteenth-century steam travel was a primitive affair with crowded quarters; decks sometimes shared with coops of chickens, live horses, mules, cows and other farm animals; and a dependence on fair weather and benevolent tides. Staterooms consisted of wooden benches along the wall with bedding provided by the passenger. Since steamboats usually stopped for the night, accommodations on shore were often available. White passengers, the captain, and the dining salon had space on the upper deck, while the lower deck provided room for cargo, fuel, and the crew.[8] Restrooms of the outhouse type were located over the paddle wheels, which afforded a constant flushing system as the wheel churned and sometimes splashed the participant. Travelers could not complain, however, as travel along the river had never been a comfortable, much less luxurious, affair.[9]

Even so, steamboat travel was not without its special amenities. The steamer captain would generally preside over a communal table covered with a white tablecloth. One traveler noted that breakfast was served in the dining salon and consisted of "a huge plate of bacon and an endless supply of the largest-ever-pancakes, brought hot from the galley to be smothered in local cane syrup." Much of the food served on board the steamboats came from the plantations they served.[10]

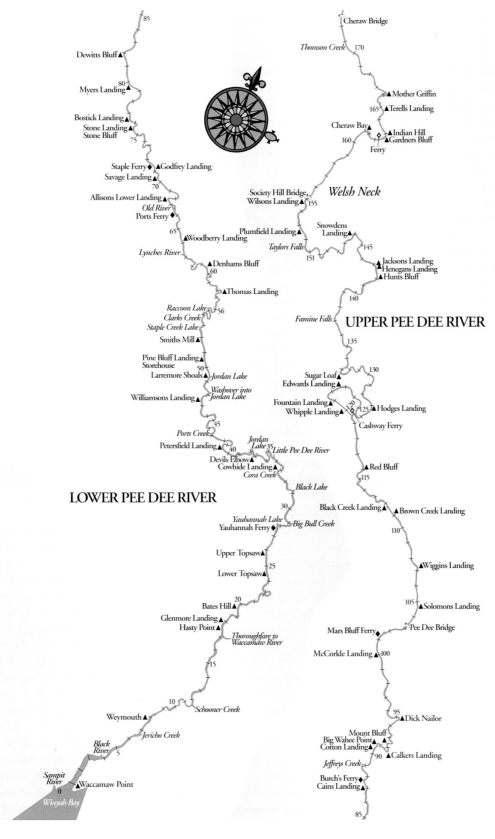

85

Dewitts Bluff▲

80
Myers Landing▲

Bostick Landing▲
Stone Landing▲
Stone Bluff
75

Staple Ferry◆ ▲Godfrey Landing
Savage Landing▲
70
Allisons Lower Landing▲
Old River
Ports Ferry◆

65
▲Woodberry Landing
Lynches River

▲Denhams Bluff
60

▲Thomas Landing

Raccoon Lake 56
Clarks Creek
Staple Creek Lake
Smiths Mill▲

Pine Bluff Landing▲
Storehouse 50
Larremore Shoals▲ *Jordan Lake*
Washover into
Jordan Lake
Williamsons Landing▲

45

Ports Creek
Petersfield Landing▲ 40
Jordan
Lake 35 *Little Pee Dee River*
Devils Elbow▲
Cowhide Landing▲
Cora Creek
Black Lake
30

Yauhannah Lake *Big Bull Creek*
Yauhannah Ferry◆

Upper Topsaw▲
25
Lower Topsaw▲

20
Bates Hill▲
Glenmore Landing▲
Hasty Point▲
Thoroughfare to
Waccamaw River
15

10
Weymouth▲ *Schooner Creek*
Jericho Creek
Black
River 5
Sampit
River 0
▲Waccamaw Point
Winyah Bay

LOWER PEE DEE RIVER

Cheraw Bridge

Thomson Creek 170

▲Mother Griffin
165 ▲Terells Landing
Cheraw Bay▲
160 ◇ ▲Indian Hill
▲Gardners Bluff
Ferry

Society Hill Bridge *Welsh Neck*
Wilsons Landing 155

Plumfield Landing▲ Snowdens
Landing▲
Taylors Falls 145
151
▲Jacksons Landing
▲Henegans Landing
▲Hunts Bluff
140

Famine Falls ## UPPER PEE DEE RIVER

135

Sugar Loaf▲ 130
Edwards Landing▲

Fountain Landing▲ 120
Whipple Landing▲ ◇ 125 ▲Hodges Landing

Cashway Ferry

▲Red Bluff
115

Black Creek Landing▲
▲Brown Creek Landing
110

▲Wiggins Landing

105
▲Solomons Landing

Mars Bluff Ferry◆ Pee Dee Bridge
McCorkle Landing▲ 100

95
▲Dick Nailor
Mount Bluff
Big Wahee Point▲ ▲
Cotton Landing▲
90 ▲Calkers Landing
Jeffreys Creek
Burch's Ferry◆
Cains Landing▲

85

Landings on the Pee Dee River. Map adapted by Tim Belshaw from a map by Reid Whitford, Corps of Engineers, 1889, donated to Marlborough Historical Museum by John L. Napier.

As the steamboat churned its way downstream the anticipation of people along the river grew. While the sound of the whistle alerted people on shore that the boat was approaching, the engine of each steamer made a certain distinctive rhythm as the boat traveled, and the natives would know which one was coming by its signature "voice." One steamboat sounded like, "One cuppa coffee and two big biscuits, One cuppa coffee and two big biscuits." Another steamer announced its arrival by chugging, "Going down de river black and dirty, All I need is soap and water."[11] Perhaps the steady "Hootenanny cha-cha, Hootenanny cha-cha" may have signaled the arrival of a new bonnet for the lady of the plantation, or new implements for running the farm. At the very least, the rhythmic sound moving steadily forward was the sound of progress to the hardworking men and women of the Pee Dee.

The ledgers of J. Eli Gregg of Mars Bluff near present day Florence, South Carolina, give an idea of items the steamboats carried. In addition to being president of the Merchants and Planters Steamboat Company, Gregg operated a general store, and his inventory included tools, locks, hinges, sheep shears, hammers, pots and pans, and grubbing hoes. A lady might wish to buy pink calico and thread to make a dress, a new leghorn bonnet, a corset, or a silk shawl with silk mitts to wear with the dress. A gentleman could purchase a Panama hat, a "super black Italian cravat," elastic suspenders, goatskin shoes, and a "Cabana Segar" to smoke on his way home. Drugs for sale included alum, cloves, calomel, pink root, jalap, quinine, and opium. Toothbrushes, combs in various styles, looking glasses, books, oil cloth, crockery, and carpeting helped make Gregg's inventory complete. It is not surprising that Mars Bluff was a frequent stop for steamboats and poleboats.[12]

Little mention of steamboat crewmen remains in the record, but what there is indicates that the crewmen were black, usually slaves but occasionally free blacks. The captains hired by steamboat companies were often strangers to the Pee Dee, so they hired (from their owners) black pilots—probably men with experience in taking complete charge of pole boats or flats for their masters. The pilots knew the hazards of the river and were key players in a successful trip. The pilot of the steamer *Richland* was "Simon," belonging to David Gregg of Society Hill. On the *Atalanta*, "Prince," a slave who was "trustworthy and distinguished for his vigilance and experience" was the pilot and a "freeman" was the engineer. The entire crew of a steamboat consisted of a captain, a first mate, an engineer, a pilot, a fireman, and about twelve deck hands.[13]

Farther up the river, farmers along the Yadkin were eager to take advantage of the benefits of steamboat transportation. Although the state of North Carolina did not promote water transportation as much as railroads and plank roads, the state did purchase stock in four "navigation companies" between 1848 and 1854.[14] One of the purchases was an investment of $5,000 in the Yadkin Navigation Company, which elected John A. Boyden and Tyre Glenn as directors in 1855. Peter Hairston, James C. Kerr, and H. C. Jones served on the board. The president of the Yadkin Navigation Company, John Boyden, also organized the Yadkin Steamboat Company to build a boat of light draft to run on the Yadkin River. By August 1855 sixty-three citizens had subscribed more than $10,000.[15]

Although steamers continued to work a small portion of the Yadkin until well after the Civil War, they never reached the same level of popularity enjoyed by the Pee Dee boats because the rocky falls cut off an important link in the chain of transportation. Nevertheless, newspapers reported limited steamboat activity on the Yadkin through the late 1800s. The steamer *Alice* was reportedly ready for excursions on the Yadkin in 1884. Charles F. Pierce ran the *Alice* to carry freight and passengers.[16] And in 1879 the *Christian Reid* under command of Frank Brown sailed from Wilkesboro to Salisbury carrying produce and passengers.[17]

Unfortunately the excitement created by the coming of the steamboat was often tempered by tragedy. There is no record of steamboat disasters on the Yadkin, but the same is not true of the Pee Dee. Earlier in the history of the steamboat on the lower river, accidents were not uncommon. The most dangerous accidents happened when a boiler exploded. In 1846 a burst boiler wrecked the *Osceola* at Cheraw.[18] The *Richland* suffered a similar fate in 1849 when an explosion killed fifteen people at Britton's Ferry. The steamer was in the middle of the river on a regular run from Cheraw to Georgetown with thirty people on board. Both boilers exploded, and the cotton on deck caught fire. Jacob Brock, the captain, was in the wheelhouse. He was seriously burned but recovered and went on to have his own boat built, which he named the *Darlington*. Brock later moved the *Darlington* to the St. John's River in Florida where he developed a hotel and his own line of steamboats. John Ferguson served as first mate on the *Darlington* and later became captain of the *Planter,* which operated on the Pee Dee.[19]

One of the worst steamboat disasters was the wreck of the *Robert Martin*. The *Marion Star* reported casualties on Tuesday, November 22, 1853 as follows:

> The steamboat *Robert Martin*, in her upward trip from Charleston, on Saturday last at Port's Ferry on Pee Dee River, burst her boiler while stopping to take in wood and discharge freight. Eleven persons were killed, six dangerously wounded, while only three escaped unimpeded. The boat is much injured as we have been informed, and much of the freight lost and damaged. She is in shallow water, having sunk on a sandbar. Of the course of the accident we cannot speak with any degree of certainty, though it is supposed by some that it was produced by permitting the water to get too low in the boiler and then pumping water in for the purpose of starting. Two or three of the bodies of the killed had not been found on Sunday."[20]

Steamboats were also likely to suffer damage from running aground or hitting logs and stumps when the river was low, or by running into foul weather. Pole boats and flats probably had a better chance of navigating the hazards of the river, but they often encountered problems in crossing Winyah Bay to reach the Sampit River and continue to Georgetown. The *Winyah Observer* reported in an obituary in 1846, "Our bay is a dangerous sheet of water in bad weather, and it should not be attempted to be crossed in other than large and good boats. The annual casualties should be a warning to strangers. . . ."[21]

Although steamers were faster and more fashionable, pole boats, flats, and lumber rafts continued in use. Whereas a steamboat might transport more than a thousand bales of cotton, a pole boat could carry several hundred. In November of 1842 Augustus La Coste's flat from Cheraw brought 203 bales of cotton to Georgetown, while Harllee's flat loaded 200 bales, and Williamson's flat transported 187 bales. In 1846 Cleland Belin's boat from Black Mingo brought 175 bales and James H. Macintosh's boat from Society Hill brought 360 bales of cotton and 200 bushels of corn, both to Eleazer Waterman, a Georgetown merchant. The pole boat *Pee Dee* from Mars Bluff brought 343 bales to Benjamin King.[22]

The Merchants and Planters Steam Boat Company of Cheraw operated the *Osceola* as well as other steamers, but the company also ran pole boats. On April 20, 1838, the directors voted to buy the pole boat *Bennettsville* from John McCollum for $800 and to hire seven boat hands and a coxswain to operate her. They also bought the pole boat *Elizabeth* from John F. Wilson for $1,000 on May 1, 1838, and hired a coxswain and six hands.[23]

HE DECIDED TO CHANGE THE NAME

By Miles Richards

A pleasant tradition has developed that the eminent American composer Stephen Collins Foster (1826–1864) from Pittsburgh, Pennsylvania, toured South Carolina in 1851, and that while visiting friends at a plantation near the Pee Dee River, he became quite entranced with the natural beauty of that waterway. Consequently, he declared that the Pee Dee would appear within the lyrics of his next song. Unfortunately, there is little historical basis to this story. After returning to Pennsylvania, he did compose a piece entitled, "Old Folks At Home." And the first line initially did read, "Way down upon the Pee Dee River." The music publisher, Firth, Pond, & Company, though, demanded that the name be changed to Suwannee River.

Stephen Foster certainly never made any sojourn to South Carolina. In fact, his travels within the American South were quite limited. While working in Cincinnati, Ohio, during the mid-1840s, Foster did take several short trips into nearby Kentucky. Furthermore, in the spring of 1852, the composer and his new bride, Jane McDowell Foster, made a honeymoon trip down the Ohio and Mississippi Rivers aboard a steamboat bound for New Orleans. This journey to Louisiana, therefore, was the only time he traveled farther south than Kentucky.

Of course many of Foster's popular musical compositions reflected distinctly southern themes. And the words of these "plantation melodies" were purported to be authentic African-American dialect. His tunes often utilized the pentatonic or five-note scale, typical of African music. Such works were composed mostly at the behest of various white minstrel show troupes. In their performances the troupers always wore black-face makeup. In late 1852 Edwin P. Christy, the founder of Christy's Minstrels, asked Foster to produce a new song for an upcoming national tour. Foster already possessed a melody he had written several years earlier, though without a satisfactory word score. The evolution of what became the final lyrics to "Old Folks At Home" may be traced within Foster's extant musical sketchbook.

In the original draft, he penned the phrase, "Way down upon de old plantation." Foster, though, was unhappy with this line and scratched it out. Upon the next page, he proceeded to write this quatrain:

> Way down upon de Pedee ribber,
> Far, far, away.
> Dere's where my heart is turning ebber
> Dere's where my brudders play.

Doubtless he was recalling another minstrel show song, "Old Pee Dee," which had been published in 1844 by an anonymous composer. Always the perfectionist, Foster resolved to use a more original geographical reference.

Accordingly, he sought assistance from his brother, Morrison Foster, a business agent for a local river freighting company. One morning in November 1852, the composer hurried into Morrison's office, situated on Third Street adjacent to Pittsburgh's city wharf along the Monongahela River. "What is a good Southern river name with two syllables?" he queried. Foster rejected his brother's suggestions of both the Yazoo and Pee Dee rivers. The brothers, therefore, began to peruse a comprehensive marine atlas of North America. At that point, he chose the Suwannee River that coursed through northern Florida. In his usual manner, Stephen hastily departed the office without further comment.

Foster was never an astute businessman. Consequently, after receiving his $500 commission from Christy in 1853, the composer gained no further royalties for "Old Folk;s At Home." The song became an immediate hit following its original performance by Christy's Minstrels at Mechanic's Hall in New York City. In January 1864, when a financially destitute Stephen Foster died in New York City's Bellevue Hospital, "Old Folks At Home" was still among his most popular tunes.[1]

In addition to agricultural products, the lumber and naval stores industries increased trade on the Pee Dee and its tributaries in the 1840s and 1850s. Captain Henry Buck came to South Carolina from Maine and set up steam saw mills on the Waccamaw River. Buck exported lumber to northern states as well as to the West Indies. Within three days in 1847, the Georgetown newspaper reported seven ships to and from Bucksville: the schooner *Michigan* with lumber for Barbados, the schooner *Mount*, bound for New York; the schooner *Richmond*, with lumber for Guadalupe; the *Egremet* for Bermuda; the brigs *E. L. Walton* and *William* for New York and New Bedford, and the bark *William M. Harris* for Boston.[24]

Three sawmills operated in Georgetown by the end of 1847, increasing the market for logs floated down the river in rafts lashed together and topped by a crude hut or tent for the crew. Lumber rafts might originate in the creeks and tributaries of the river. In 1850 T. R. Grier's raft of eighty sticks from Lynches Creek made the long trip, and nine rafts arrived in November 1853 from Lumberton, North Carolina, having floated down the Lumbee River to the Little Pee Dee and thus to the Great Pee Dee.[25] A receipt found in the papers of Jacob Rhodes of Lumberton reads, "Received Georgetown— July 1812 from Jacob Rhodes, Esq., by the hand of Pennywell Lamb two rafts of lumber in the water. Four dollars cash and 2 qts. Of rum for the hands. (Signed) John Arch Taylor." Whether that receipt covered the entire compensation is impossible to determine, but it is possible Rhodes received credit with the purchaser. Even if the receipt only paid for the hands, it seems hardly worth the long walk back to Lumberton. Lumber rafting helped supply the five sawmills that were operating in Georgetown by 1855 and producing 25,000,000 feet of lumber annually.[26]

Producers of naval stores also used the river. Tar, pitch, and resin were heavy commodities that brought handsome profits with export merchants or turpentine distilleries in Georgetown. Black Mingo Creek and Black River (tributaries of the Pee Dee) in upper Georgetown County had a naval stores industry.[27] The production of naval stores required a much smaller investment than rice or cotton planting. For tax purposes, the state of South Carolina assessed prime tide swamp rice land at $26 per acre, high land at $3 per acre, and pine barrens at 20 cents per acre.[28] This was an assessment, not an actual cost of the land, but it demonstrates the relative investment necessary to produce rice or cotton and naval stores. To harvest the sap of the pine tree, the worker needed only to remove the bark from a portion of the tree and cut ridges slanted downward and toward the center to direct the resin toward a hollow at the base of the cut. The worker then had to dip the resin every few days and transport the heavy kegs. It was hard work, but it did not require slaves or expensive implements, although some slave owners undoubtedly utilized their labor force in this way. The naval stores and lumber businesses enabled enterprising men with little capital to make a start economically.

It was also possible for a small farmer and his family to raise a few acres of cotton and gradually expand. Yeomen farmers who worked hard could sometimes move into the ranks of great planters. Large cotton planters in Marion County in 1860 included Colonel James Savage Gibson,[29] who produced 392 bales; S. E. McIntyre with 250 bales; James H. Jarrot with 225; and J. N. McCall with 200. These planters also produced from 600 to 3,500 pounds of rice, probably for their own consumption.[30]

In Marlboro, Ann Eliza and her son Lawrence D. Prince led the field with 430 bales of cotton in 1860. Owner of 221 slaves, Ann Eliza Prince was the daughter of Drury Robertson, a large landowner and community leader whose home still stands. She married first William Farr Ellerbe and second Clement Lampriere Prince.[31] The second largest cotton producer in Marlboro was Dr. William Crosland with 330 bales. The third was Light Townsend with 307. Other producers with more than 200 bales were John Wilson with 300, Samuel Wilds Evans with 296, John Witherspoon with 282, Dr. Alexander McLeod with 250, Samuel Sparks with 225, and Zachariah A. Drake with 210.[32]

The leading cotton producer in Darlington District was George Jay Washington McCall with 410 bales. He also led the district by producing 9,000 pounds of rice. Other cotton producers were Joseph Burch Nettles with 235, the estate of Chancellor George W. Dargan with 211, Edgar Welles Charles with 220, Benjamin F. Williamson with 215 (with the possible addition of 150 bales listed for the estate of B. Williamson), and Allen Evander McIver with 200.[33]

The Pee Dee cotton planter who owned the largest number slaves (328) also grew the largest crop in Chesterfield County with 353 bales. Colonel Allan Macfarlan of Westmoreland, Montrose, and Shandon plantations and Westmoreland mansion in Cheraw graduated from Princeton College, read law and was admitted to the bar, served in the South Carolina legislature, and was president of the Northeastern Railroad.[34] James C. Craig grew 270 bales of cotton, Zacheriah Ellerbee, 164, and Alexander McQueen, 130.[35]

Although cotton planters prospered, their wealth could seldom compare with that of the rice planters of the lower Pee Dee and its tributaries, the Waccamaw and Black rivers. The rich tide swamps of the Pee Dee delta provided prime rice fields. Rich silt washed down from lands upriver while the ocean tide pushed saltwater into Winyah Bay, thus pushing the fresh river water through the trunks or sluice gates into the rice fields regularly. Almost all land between the Pee Dee and the Waccamaw was rich, freshwater marsh, and the Black River had numerous horseshoe curves, well suited for building banks (or dikes) and planting rice. Planters in Georgetown District, where these three rivers come together near Winyah Bay, grew almost half the nation's rice in 1840. In 1850 the harvest was 46,765,040 pounds of rice out of a national total of 215,313,497 or about 22 percent. By 1860 the national total had declined to 187,167,032 while Georgetown District's total had grown to 55,805,385 or about 30 percent. Ninety-one planters who produced at least 100,000 pounds each accounted for 98 percent of the Georgetown total in 1850. By 1860 fourteen planters in the district produced more than 1 million pounds each. These were the rice barons of legendary wealth.

The estate of Joshua John Ward of Brookgreen on the Waccamaw, worked by 1,130 slaves, led the list with 4,441,000 pounds in 1860. Governor of South Carolina Robert F. W. Allston of Chicora Wood on the Pee Dee grew 1,500,000 pounds of rice, while his cousins William A. Alston and Charles Alston grew 1,450,000 and 1,100,000 respectively. John Hyrne Tucker of Willbrook and Litchfield produced 1,530,000 pounds, while John I. Middleton of Clermont harvested 1,860,000. Other planters who exceeded 1 million pounds were William Branford Shubrick Horry of Milldam; the estate of Ralph S. Izard at Weymouth, Hickory Hill and Milton; Andrew Johnstone of Annandale; Henry A. Middleton's estate at Weehaw and Kensington; Francis Simons Parker of Mansfield; William Bull Pringle of Pleasant Meadow; and John Harleston Read of Belle Rive.[36]

In Georgetown District in 1850, 18,253 persons were slaves and 201 were free persons of color. The total population was 20,647, indicating that nearly 90 percent of the people were of African descent.[37] As previously discussed, slaves from the rice-growing section of Africa contributed skills in cultivating and harvesting the crop.[38] Because of their high population concentration in Georgetown District, black people were able to preserve not only patterns of work but also elements of African culture and language, which have contributed to the rich cultural diversity of the entire Pee Dee region. How many people who grew up in the area refer to a tortoise as a "cooter" or a baby chick as a "biddy," without

DROWNING CREEK, LUMBER, OR LUMBEE?

The swift and treacherous branch of the Little Pee Dee River has been known by at least three names in recorded history. Whatever the name, however, the Pee Dee tributary is recognized as a significant feature of present-day Robeson County, North Carolina.

Colonial records from 1749 use the name "Drowning Creek" for the river that serves as one of the boundaries for Anson County. The name, suggestive of a dangerous reputation, was common for the next sixty years. The "Swamp Fox" Francis Marion had camps on Drowning Creek, and it was a place where Tories "lay out," to avoid serving in the military forces during the American Revolution.

In 1809 "Drowning Creek," by act of the North Carolina legislature, officially became the Lumber River between McFarlands Turnpike in Scotland County north of Wagram and the South Carolina line. Presumably the negative image presented to prospective settlers by the old name needed to be replaced by something more dynamic. Recitals of the act refer to the importance of the timber industry and the importance of the river in transporting the timber.

Another name for the river used by generations of people who lived along its banks is "Lumbee," an Indian word meaning "deep waters" or "dark waters." Native Americans of Robeson County adopted it as their official tribal name.

The origin of these Indians is as mysterious as the dark waters that share their name. The Lumbee people may be related to the Cherokee, the Tuscarora, and the eastern Sioux, or they may be descendants of John White's lost colony, who left Roanoke Island between 1587 and 1590.

The largest tribe east of the Mississippi River, the Lumbee Indians are the largest federally-unrecognized tribe in the United States. The outdoor drama *Strike at the Wind* portrays the story of the Lumbee and their folk hero, Henry Berry Lowrie. According to legend, Lowrie was eighteen years old when he witnessed the murder of his father and brother, who were shot by soldiers for refusing to serve the Confederacy as laborers at Fort Fisher on the coast of North Carolina. During the Civil War, Confederate officials denied the Lumbee the right to fight as soldiers but compelled them to suffer intolerable working conditions as forced labor. Henry Berry Lowrie sought to right the wrongs perpetrated on his people, and they hailed him as a symbol of the fight for justice and a voice of the oppressed. Law enforcement officials were never able to capture Lowrie. At one point they jailed his wife and asserted that they would hold her until Lowrie gave himself up. He sent word that unless they let his wife go, *their* wives would be in danger. They soon released her, enhancing Lowrie's reputation as a folk hero. More than 40,000 Lumbee currently live in Robeson and adjoining counties in southeastern North Carolina and northeastern South Carolina.

The poetry and prose of John Charles McNeill, born near the Lumber River in 1874, reflect the feelings of many who know the river:

> "She is a tortuous delicious flirt, but she does not deserve the punishment put on her by the geographers who have perverted her sweet Indian name of Lumbee into something that suggests choking sawdust, rotting slabs and shrill screams of the circular saw. Though she now be wedded to civilization she should not have been robbed of her maiden name."[2]

connecting the terms to the Malinke word, *kuta,* or the Bantu word, *bidibidi,* meaning "small yellow bird"? The use of the word "monkey" as a term for collapsing from excessive heat may derive from the Bantu word *dipungi* meaning "exhaustion" or "fatigue."[39] Elements of dance, music, visual arts, basketry, and religion that derive from African sources have become an integral part of local practice. As expertly stated by historian Charles Joyner, African American men and women played important, if unsung, roles in a momentous process of culture change. "For out of pride and compassion as well as anguish and injustice, out of African traditions as well as American circumstances, they created a new language, a new religion—indeed, a new culture—that not only allowed them to endure the collective tragedy of slavery, but to bequeath a notable and enduring heritage to generations to come."[40]

Although in the antebellum period most of the people in the Pee Dee region were slaves or whites who farmed on a small scale, the large plantation played an important part in shaping regional identity. It would be impossible to give details about all the important plantations, but a closer look at a rice plantation on the Pee Dee, a cotton plantation on Lynches River, and a cotton plantation on the Yadkin provide examples.

CHICORA WOOD PLANTATION ON THE PEE DEE

One of the most distinguished examples is the rice plantation known as Chicora Wood. Robert Francis Withers Allston, the proprietor, owned some 13,500 acres, which included other rice plantations such as Nightingale Hall, Exchange, Waterford, Guendalos, Pipe Down, and Rose Bank. He also owned land at the Warhees in Marion County, a farm at Morven on the Pee Dee above Cheraw, the Nathaniel Russell house in Charleston, and 590 slaves.

A graduate of the United States Military Academy at West Point, R. F. W. Allston ran his plantations as he did his life, with high principles and sound judgment. An overseer once said that Allston's tremendous success as a planter was due not to any special agricultural abilities but to his gift for organization. His plantations functioned in an orderly, systematic manner. Contrary to the belief of the overseer, Allston did have a gift for agriculture, and Chicora Wood rice won a silver medal at the Paris exposition in 1855.[41]

His capacity for delegating and organizing enabled Allston to find time to write scholarly articles for agricultural journals and to engage in public service. Among many other offices, he served as president of the South Carolina Senate and governor from 1856 to 1858.[42]

In so far as possible, Allston made Chicora Wood a self-sufficient entity. The plantation had its own rice mill, blacksmith's and carpenter's shops. The carpenters built the big flats and lighters needed to harvest the immense rice crops. "There was almost a fleet of rowboats, of all sizes . . . also canoes, or dugouts, made from cypress logs," remembered Elizabeth Allston Pringle, daughter of the governor. She remembered a dugout capable of carrying several 600-pound tierces of rice. Tierces were oversized barrels, usually constructed on the plantation.

Her father offered prizes such as pretty, bright-colored, calico frocks to the women or fine knives to the men as rewards for being the best ploughman, sower, or harvest hand for the year. He also offered incentives to his crews of boatmen (all slaves). They faced special challenges when the Union

The rich tide swamps of the Pee Dee delta provided prime rice fields. *Suzanne Linder from Springfield Plantation. Courtesy Dr. and Mrs. J. Howard Stokes, Jr.*

blockade closed the port of Georgetown. To market his rice, it was necessary to transport it to the railroad bridge at Mars Bluff or sometimes to Cheraw. He had two lighters built. They were decked over and secured from weather and carried from 150 to 200 tierces each. Each had a captain and a crew of eight men. When the freshet was up, the only way to propel such a heavy load upstream was by carrying a line ahead, making fast to a tree on the riverbank, and warping up by the capstan. Charles Allston, son of the governor, said that the crew were all able men who had plenty to eat and seemed to enjoy themselves. "I have often been with my father when the boats returned from a trip and the captain came to make his report;" he said, "it was worth listening to; the most minute account of the trip, with all its dangers and difficulties." The captain seldom had any complaint about his crew because they knew that any problem could send them back to fieldwork.

Eventually Allston established a depot at what later became Salters on the Black River near Kingstree for connection with the Northeastern Railroad. Charles Allston reported, ". . . here he put a very intelligent Negro, Sam Maham, in charge; he received the rice from the captains of the river-craft, and delivered it to the railroad on orders, and I have never heard a word of complaint against him."[43]

Chicora Wood Plantation home still stands on a bluff overlooking the Pee Dee. *Suzanne Linder.*
Courtesy Marcia and Jamie Constance.

After the death of Governor Allston, his widow planted rice until her death in 1896. The Allstons' daughter, Elizabeth Allston Pringle, ran Chicora Wood and neighboring White House plantation following her mother's death. Elizabeth Allston Pringle's accounts of her life as a rice planter are considered classics of life on a South Carolina rice plantation from the point of view of an owner who enjoyed the ultimate in luxury before the Civil War and then endured great hardships afterwards.[44]

Susan Lowndes Allston wrote of the home of her grandparents that the "house still stands on the bluff, and the rice fields were across the river, of which there is a fine view from the high piazza looking downstream. In freshet, the river is yellow from the turgid waters of upper South Carolina and from the clay soils of North Carolina. But sometimes, especially in the spring it is more silver than any other color."[45]

Chicora Wood passed out of the Allston family in 1921 with the death of Elizabeth Allston Pringle and has now been restored. Outbuildings like the rice mill, outdoor kitchen, barns, brick smokehouse, and schoolhouse used by the Allston children have been renovated and restored as well. Owners Jamie and Marcia Constance have placed a conservation easement on the property so it will remain undeveloped in perpetuity.[46]

A shipping barn at Chicora Wood Plantation on the Pee Dee. This rice plantation upriver from Winyah Bay is one of the most distinguished on the river. *Suzanne Linder. Courtesy Marcia and Jamie Constance.*

RED OAK WOODS PLANTATION ON LYNCHES RIVER

The story of Red Oak Woods Plantation, located on the bluffs of Lynches River in Kershaw County, is reminiscent of chivalrous gentlemen and the magnolia-scented swoon. Designed by Benjamin Latrobe, architect of the interior of the United States Capitol, the mansion rose three and one-half stories above the ground. It was an imposing structure with six brick columns and a large porch on the north front, and six Corinthian columns with a second story porch on the south facing Lynches River. Having inherited the property from a great-uncle around 1830, William Batts Horton ran the cotton plantation and experimented with the growing of tea, using plants he acquired in China.[47]

Horton's success as a planter was apparent throughout Red Oak Woods Mansion which boasted a fireplace in each room, a spiral staircase with a dome-shaped skylight, highly polished marble and granite floors, wallpaper ordered from France, oak parquet flooring in the dining room, and family portraits adorning the walls. Before the war, Red Oak Woods hosted grand balls, elaborate banquets, and summer barbecues. The invitations for the balls appeared in the local paper.[48]

Cooleemee Plantation on the Yadkin, home of the Hairston family. *Suzanne Linder. Courtesy Peter Hairston.*

The gardens and grounds of Red Oak Woods were just as spectacular as the main house and featured six giant red oak trees circling the lane. In the center of the red oaks was a fountain with water piped from an underground spring. The garden was one of the finest in this country and rivaled those in Europe. The grounds contained Jane Horton's teahouse near the river's edge, a kitchen, wine cellar, smokehouse, stables, carriage house, cotton house, two family cemeteries, and numerous barns.[49]

The garden was noteworthy because it ran to Lynches River where two bridges over the river connected it to the garden of the neighboring plantation, Red Oak Camp. A stream running through the garden also had a bridge supported by two bronze lions on each side.[50]

COOLEEMEE PLANTATION ON THE YADKIN

Cooleemee plantation, located in Davie County near Mocksville, North Carolina, offers a glimpse of the gracious living enjoyed by the cotton planters on the northern river. Still inhabited by descendants of Peter Hairston, who built Cooleemee, the house has been called a "time capsule." It has seen few changes, and many of the furnishings in place before the Civil War are still in use today. The house, an "Anglo-Grecian villa," matches a plan by architect William H. Ranlett, published in *Godey's Lady's Book* of January 1850. Peter Hairston's brother-in-law, J. E. B. Stuart, who was later to gain fame as a Confederate general, was studying at West Point in 1852 when he told a relative he was looking for a plan for his brother-in-law. Whether or not he sent a plan is unknown, but Peter Hairston completed the house at Cooleemee in 1856.[51]

Peter Hairston was influential in attempts to make the Yadkin navigable in the 1850s. Records show that he was sending tobacco to markets in Petersburg and Lynchburg, Virginia, a round trip by wagon of about a month. On September 2, 1850, he wrote to his brother in Virginia, "My house lately has been filled with engineers surveying the Plank Road and the River with the view of rendering it navigable . . . If these improvements are carried out it may make this part of the country worth living in. As it is, it is almost a misfortune to have any produce to send to market. The expense and trouble of getting it there is so great."[52]

Cooleemee covers over 1,900 acres of farm and forest land, and the mansion is one of thirty-one National Historic Landmarks in North Carolina. Judge Peter Wilson Hairston and his family have placed Cooleemee under conservation easement designed to protect 2.5 miles of the Yadkin from economic development and preserve the natural features of the river.[53] The easement, a project of The Land Trust for Central North Carolina, will ensure that future generations of Hairstons can continue to enjoy their legacy and will allow river enthusiasts and nature lovers to enjoy the unspoiled section of the river that borders Cooleemee.

RAILROADS CHALLENGE RIVER TRANSPORTATION

By 1830, the locomotive "Best Friend of Charleston" carried 141 people over six miles of track at twenty-five miles per hour. The line was completed in 1833 and was 136 miles long from Charleston to Hamburg making it the longest railroad in the world. Branch lines were added to Columbia and Camden, and by 1860 the state had nearly 1,000 miles of railroad connecting all the major towns.[54]

The old transportation route down the Pee Dee River and through the port of Georgetown faced a serious challenge with the completion of the Cheraw and Darlington Railroad. Chartered in 1849, the line actually began operation in 1856. It connected with the Wilmington and Manchester at Florence and thus diverted commerce to the port of Wilmington, North Carolina. In October 1857 the Northeastern Railroad began service between Charleston and Florence, thus giving patrons of the Cheraw and Darlington a choice of final destinations for their goods. The Northeastern, with the leadership of its president, Allan Macfarlan of Cheraw, was most successful. Between 1857 and 1864, gross revenues increased from $32,132 to $859,265. Although General William T. Sherman ordered his troops to destroy all trestles between Cheraw and Florence as well as the railroad shops in Cheraw, the line was back in operation by July 1865. Transportation by rail was the greatest challenge to the dominance of river traffic, and although steamboats continued in operation after the Civil War, they gradually declined in importance.[55]

COTTON FACTORIES IN THE PEE DEE WATERSHED

The railroad offered a choice of transportation for agricultural products as well as for the limited amount of manufactured goods that were available. Cotton factories, using slave and white labor, existed to spin and weave the cotton into cloth. General David Rogerson Williams operated a successful cotton mill near Society Hill in Darlington County on the waters of Cedar Creek. Williams was also instrumental in founding The Marlboro Yarn Factory on the upper waters of Crooked Creek, a Pee Dee tributary that joined the Pee Dee below Bennettsville. It manufactured yarn contracted for by companies in the North. Other investors in 1836 were John Taylor of Cheraw, John McQueen, and William T. Ellerbe of Marlboro. Meekin Townsend bought the factory in 1840, and it burned in 1852. The millpond is still known as "Burnt Factory Pond."[56]

In North Carolina, Walter Francis Leak and his brother Francis Terry Leak chartered the Richmond Manufacturing Company in 1833 near Rockingham on Falling Creek, a tributary of the Pee Dee.[57] On the Yadkin portion of the river, the Mocksville Cotton Factory was in operation by 1836, and the Yadkin Cotton Factory in Wilkes County was open by 1849. The Yadkin Manufacturing Company in 1838 and the Salisbury Manufacturing Company in 1841 conducted business in Rowan County, and the H. and F. Fries Cotton and Woolen Mills were located in Forsyth County in 1840. A list of exports from the port of Georgetown in the early 1840s included 100,000 yards of cotton cloth.[58]

Despite the limited success of mills at Society Hill and Bennettsville, most South Carolinians considered manufacturing to be an unworthy endeavor. In the review of factories in *Mill's Statistics for the State* in 1826, few operating mills were listed, but considerable cloth was woven for personal use. Several districts noted reasons for the lack of cotton factories. Georgetown reported that the "cultivation of rice and cotton in this district is too profitable to permit much attention to be given to manufactures." Marion District reported that "labor is too valuable in raising cotton to be devoted to manufacturing it into cloth."[59] This attitude against manufacturing prevailed in the South and was one of the reasons the Confederate states became embroiled in a war that they were unprepared economically to win.[60]

THE PEE DEE PARTICIPATES IN THE CIVIL WAR

As the war between the states began, the Pee Dee joined with the majority of the southern states in supporting secession. People of Chesterfield District took part in the first popular approval of secession in the state on November 15, 1860. Darlington claimed the first company of militia, the Darlington Guards, who mustered into service in Charleston on January 4, 1861.[61]

Through Georgetown, Pee Dee boats participated in naval warfare by trying to sink federal ships and run the blockade. The *Nina,* a steamer that had regularly run on the Waccamaw River, became a blockade runner in 1862.[62] The Mars Bluff navy yard also made a patriotic contribution to the Confederate war effort with the construction of the gunboat *Pedee.* The *Pedee* was a community project in that planters furnished labor, businessmen made contributions, and the women of the Pee Dee gathered jewelry and silver to pay for the boat's equipment.[63] The ladies of the region referred to the *Pedee* as "our boat."[64]

The old market in Cheraw provided patrons with an outlet for selling their goods. *Emily Garner.*

In Bennettsville, Union troops pitched their tents on the courthouse square.
Frank Leslie's Illustrated Newspaper, April 3, 1864.

The *Pedee* was schooner-rigged, had double propellers, and carried two three-inch rifle guns on pivot bow and stern and a nine-inch Dahlgren shell gun on pivot amidships. The launching of the *Pedee* in 1865 was the cause of great celebration, and crowds gathered from Marion, Williamsburg, Darlington, Chesterfield, Marlboro, and Georgetown to witness the christening of the new vessel. [65]

The launching was in sharp contrast to the actual duty of the gunboat since Sherman was advancing on land. The *Pedee* carried out its one assignment to protect General William J. Hardee's army crossing the river at Cheraw as it retreated from Sherman. The *Pedee* then returned to Mars Bluff and destruction at the hands of its own officers since the fall of the Confederacy was imminent, and the officers preferred destroying the vessel to having it fall into Union hands. Officers exploded the *Pedee* at ten o'clock Saturday night, March 15th or 18th, 1865.[66]

In September of 1925 during a dry spell, river levels dropped and exposed the vessel. The *Morning News Review* of September 15, 1925, described the sight:

> "The sunken ship lies just below the Atlantic Coast Line bridge. Its propellers and boiler are plainly visible as is a large portion of the deck. The propellers are of iron, or steel. . . . The old boiler is a tremendous affair. . . . Both the boiler and the propellers are in a good state of preservation."

To preserve the relic and protect it from souvenir hunters, salvage operators moved the propellers to the grounds of the Florence Public Library. Again in 1954 a low water level exposed the *Pedee,* and the Driftwood Company of Marion salvaged the remains and set them up on the farm of Calvin Yarborough, near U. S. Highway 301-76. Later the wreck was moved to the "South of the Border" tourist mecca on Interstate 95.[67]

SHERMAN CROSSES THE PEE DEE

The advance of General William T. Sherman and his army, which prompted the destruction of the gunboat *Pedee,* eventually culminated in the arrival of Union troops in Cheraw. The town was at the mercy of Union troops for four days as they waited to cross the river. Unwelcome soldiers plundered homes, sacked businesses, and started fires. Mrs. C. E. Jarrott remembered that it seemed the whole of Sherman's army was in Cheraw "with banners flying, bands playing and hundreds of cheering soldiers."[68]

As soon as Sherman was able to construct a pontoon bridge across the river, one branch of the Union army moved into North Carolina. Union troops were more lenient toward the residents of Richmond County than they had been in South Carolina. Richmond T. Long, a strong Unionist, had made a personal plea to Sherman that the county be spared. Nevertheless, certain essential structures and businesses were designated for destruction. At Rockingham, a primary objective was to burn Richmond Manufacturing Company because it had supplied cloth for Confederate uniforms and other uses by the army. Rebecca Jane Sanford Kelly witnessed the scene when she was a girl of nine. In her reminiscences she recalled that the guard stationed at her house asked her mother if she could use any of the cloth from the mill before the troops burned the building. Her mother replied, "It is not ours to take." Union officers let it be known when they would burn the mill so that people could watch and take warning. Soldiers made a game of tossing flaming torches back and forth across Falling Creek. After they torched the mill, flames continued far into the night.[69]

While one branch of the Union Army was moving into North Carolina, another branch under the command of Major General Frank P. Blair turned southeast towards Bennettsville. The Fourth Division, Fifteenth Army Corps, camped near Irby's plantation on March 6, 1865. Charles Irby had served in the state legislature and was state senator from 1858 to 1861. Tradition says that the Yankee soldiers broke into his wine cellar and after imbibing freely, one of the company played "Yankee Doodle" while several others danced on top of the piano, leaving imprints of the heels of their boots to remind later generations of their vandalism. When the party was over, they cut the blue velvet piano cover into saddle blankets and proceeded on to Bennettsville.[70]

In Bennettsville the Union troops pitched their tents on the courthouse square. In most cases when the opportunity presented itself, the Yankees burned courthouse records. Peter McColl was clerk of court for Marlboro County, and he somehow persuaded the soldiers not to burn the courthouse. Instead, B. Lundy Griffith, an infantryman from Putnam County, Illinois, wrote in one of the county record books:

"Magnolia" was built in 1853 by Chancellor William Johnson in Bennettsville. It is now the home of Mr. and Mrs. William L. Kinney, Jr. *Suzanne Linder. Courtesy Mr. and Mrs. William L. Kinney.*

General Sherman's army passed through this place. This rebellion must and shall be put down at all hazards. We will fight until every rebel in arms is slain unless they lay down their arms and come back to the union under the old constitution. South Carolina was the root of secession. The South are to blame for this war and none others. Why did not the southern States wait and see whether A. Lincoln would interfere with slavery before they seceded?

We pay respect to all true lovers of the union and the national flag, The Star Spangled Banner.[71]

On Main Street, several blocks from the courthouse was the home of William D. Johnson, a state senator and one of the signers of the Ordinance of Secession. A gracious and imposing structure, the home was a natural target for the Union torch. Just as the soldiers were starting the fire, a Union officer rode up and recognized Johnson as his former roommate at the College of New Jersey (Princeton). The two embraced, and the officer quickly gave the order to put out the fire.[72] The next day the Union troops began moving out towards Fayetteville, North Carolina.[73]

Chesterfield District, one of the first in line to support secession, was the first to commemorate the losses of the Confederacy in 1867. On the face of a memorial column at St. David's Church in Cheraw are carved the words "Fallen but not Dead," and "They have crossed over the river And they rest under the shade of the trees."[74]

The United Daughters of the Confederacy erected a monument in Bennettsville on the courthouse lawn where Union soldiers camped. By some quirk of fate, the soldier on the stone column is wearing a Yankee-style cap.[75]

POST WAR ACTIVITY ON THE RIVERS

In the period just after the Civil War, one of the vessels frequenting the harbor at Georgetown was the steamer *Planter*. It gained fame when a slave named Robert Smalls daringly hijacked her in Charleston harbor and escaped to the Union Navy blockading Charleston. In 1867 her former owner, John Ferguson (who began his career on the Pee Dee), purchased the *Planter*, which fortunately had been improved and repaired while in the service of the Yankees. The *Planter* remained in service on South Carolina rivers until lost in a storm off Cape Romain in July 1876. A new boat built later that year appropriated the name, and this was the *Planter* that frequently stopped at Georgetown through the 1890s.[76] Among other small steamers that operated in the late nineteenth century were the *Merchant* (430 tons), the *Farmer* (430 tons), and the *Eutaw* (430 tons). On the Black River, three small steamers, the *Wildwood*, the *M. W. Gary*, and the *Mingo* brought goods to Georgetown.[77]

In the 1880s and 1890s, Franklin G. Burroughs and B. G. Collins of Conway were merchants who built river steamers to carry merchandise. Some of their steamboats were the *Juniper*, the *Maggie*, the *Ruth*, and the *F. G. Burroughs*, a 283-ton side-wheeler that was 125 feet long, 22 feet wide, with a hold 6 feet deep. It carried passengers and freight between Conway and Georgetown. The *Georgetown Semi-Weekly Times* noted : "The upper deck is fitted up with a commodious saloon, on either side of which are a number of state rooms, and everything about the boat is conveniently arranged. The upper part of the boat is painted white; the hull a dark color."[78]

The most ambitious shipbuilding on the Pee Dee River system was at Bucksville on the Waccamaw River. Henry Buck had moved to Horry County from Maine in the 1830s and had established a flourishing lumber business using steam sawmills. Buck was instrumental in convincing shipbuilders in New England that southern pine was a suitable material. In the early 1870s a Maine shipbuilder, Captain William McGilvery, moved his business to Bucksville where he constructed a three-masted schooner, the *Hattie McGilvery Buck* rated at 240 tons. Then in 1875 with Captain Jonathan C. Nickels, William L. Buck, and a crew of craftsmen recruited in New England, McGilvery directed the building of the *Henrietta*, an ocean-going clipper ship of more than 1,200 tons. Her topmast towered 147 feet; she used twenty-four sails; and she carried a crew of sixteen to twenty. A proud, tall ship, the *Henrietta* had a distinguished career sailing the Pacific to the Orient and Australia. She wrecked in a typhoon near Kobe, Japan, in 1894. The *Henrietta* was the last large wooden ship built in the South.[79]

PLANTERS CLUB ON THE PEE DEE

by Marta Thacker

In November of 1839, most of the great rice planters from the Waccamaw, the Pee Dee, the Black, the Sampit, and Winyah Bay, formed the Planters Club on Pee Dee. The members defined themselves as an agricultural club and sought status from the state legislature for an Act of Incorporation. At the initial meeting, members formed a committee to draft a constitution and by-laws and selected delegates to attend the Agricultural Convention in Columbia later that month.

The Planters Club met in its own clubhouse, constructed by 1844 on land donated by Colonel Peter W. Fraser along the north line of his Enfield plantation. The club assessed members $20 for several expenses relating to this new building. These included the razing of the old clubhouse; costs of supplies such as lime, lathe, and hair for the plaster walls; payment to slave owners for the use of their skilled bricklayers; and the expense of outfitting the clubhouse with suitable "crockery."

While discussing agriculture was the stated objective of the club, members likely gathered for a more social purpose. That club members entertained lavishly among themselves is apparent from a list describing a bountiful "pot-luck." Each member supplied different foods such as ham, turkey, venison, mutton, clams, oysters, shrimp, rice, brandy, madeira, and champagne. Perhaps it was one of these sumptuous entertainments that President Martin Van Buren referred when he spoke of "the cheerful & truly hospitable board" he enjoyed while visiting the club.

Van Buren was one of six men to whom the Planters Club would extend several honorary memberships. It wasn't until 1854 that the club began electing regular members, selecting one or two at almost every meeting. This continued up to their last meeting on April 12, 1861, when the records show the purchase of two dozen plates, two dozen tumblers, and two dozen wine glasses—most likely for a final hurrah.[3]

A monument in Bennettsville stands where the soldiers camped. Although erected by the United Daughters of the Confederacy, the soldier wears a Yankee-style cap. *James Linder.*

MODERNIZATION SILENCES THE STEAMBOAT WHISTLE

The turn of the twentieth century marked a gradual decline of the river as an artery of transportation. Merchants in Cheraw made a last effort in 1907 by creating the Cheraw Georgetown Steamboat Company. Listed on the board of directors were H. P. Duvall, H. E. Clement, W. T. Thrower, William Godfrey, D. S. Matheson, R. T. Caston, and M. W. Duvall, all of Cheraw.[80]

The last period of river traffic was merely a shadow of the steamboats' proud past. The war and the expansion of the railroad lessened the commercial need for the great steamers. The Civil War had brought an end to the plantation era. With the disruptions of labor and capital that followed the war, many large landowners had to break up their property. By the turn of the twentieth century, bright-leaf tobacco would supplant cotton and rice as the most profitable cash crop, while railroads and highways would become the principal transportation routes. Modernization finally silenced the beckoning call of the steamboat whistle, but the sound still echoes on the now quiet corridor of a bygone era.

Heron standing lonely vigil in Winyah Bay. *Robert Clark. Courtesy Department of Natural Resources.*

CHAPTER 10

The Twentieth Century

Gently and without grief the old shall glide into
the New; the eternal flow of things
Like a bright river of the fields of heaven
Shall journey onward in perpetual peace.[1]
J. A. W. Thomas, A History of Marlboro County

Those fortunate enough to see the turn of the twentieth century witnessed significant changes in the role of the Yadkin-Pee Dee. With the competition of the railroad system and better highways, traffic on the river was not the most economical way to transport people and products. This, however, did not diminish its overall importance for the region. In the twentieth century, possibilities for supplying water for drinking and industry became apparent. Some industries required large quantities of water for processing products, but all types could benefit from the hydroelectric power generated by the river. With growing urbanization, appreciation of the river as a scenic and recreational resource increased along with an understanding of its role in conserving the total ecosystem. In many ways, the river became more important to the region as its role in transportation decreased.

THE LAST OF THE STEAMBOAT WHISTLES

The last period of river traffic was merely a shadow of the steamboats' proud past. War and economic recession following the Civil War and later expansion of the railroad lessened the commercial need for great steamers. The final blow came in 1935 when the South Carolina Highway Department built drawbridges over the Pee Dee and Waccamaw rivers and a complex network of roads connected even the most remote areas of the Pee Dee to the rest of the world.

After the turn of the century, river commerce steadily decreased. From 1891 to 1907, 178,798 tons of cotton, rice, timber, and general merchandise valued at 1.8 million dollars traversed the Pee Dee. Between 1908 and 1931, the annual tonnage, mainly stone, sand, and cement for use in highway construction, dropped to 40,314 tons. Finally the average annual commerce on the river amounted to only 10,000 tons worth about $75,000 by 1937.[2]

Tobacco is a major crop in Marion County. *Charles McRae.*

PEE DEE BRIGHT-LEAF TOBACCO FINDS MARKETS ON THE YADKIN

Despite the decline in transportation, the river continued to contribute to a regional identity. The northeast portion of South Carolina is known geographically and politically as "the Pee Dee." True to its past, however, the Pee Dee remains an agricultural community. And, as with changes in the river, changes in the agricultural climate were destined to occur. The production of cotton declined overall in the state after World War II, but remained strong in the Pee Dee. Soybeans became part of the local landscape in the early 1900s although cotton and tobacco were the main money crops. Colonial farmers had grown tobacco on the upper Pee Dee, but it was only after the Civil War that it became the most profitable cash crop in the region below the fall line. Introduced into the Pee Dee in the late 1880s, bright-leaf tobacco was the major crop by 1920.[3]

Cultivation of tobacco along the Pee Dee paralleled the growth of the tobacco manufacturing industry on the Yadkin. The first tobacco factory in Winston produced 20,000 pounds of chewing tobacco in 1871. Hamilton Scales, Pleasant H. Hanes, John W. Hanes, and Major T. J. Brown were among the pioneers in the tobacco industry. Richard J. Reynolds began marketing chewing tobacco in 1874. By 1880 North Carolina factories had tripled the 1870 production. William Cyrus Briggs' machine for making cigarettes increased production significantly after 1892.[4]

The market for cigarette tobacco encouraged Pee Dee farmers to introduce bright-leaf, or flue-cured, tobacco into the region in the late 1880s. Tobacco barns equipped with flue-ventilated furnaces for heating soon dotted the landscape. Processing required hanging the tobacco in the barn and carefully monitoring the heat to cure the leaves. By 1900 flue-cured tobacco was a major cash crop. High profits helped to compensate for the fact that growing tobacco was a labor-intensive endeavor. In 1895 a farmer could reap a net profit of $150 (about $2,700 in 1990s money) to $200 ($3,600) per acre by growing tobacco as compared with $10 ($180) for cotton. Tobacco has remained a staple of the Pee Dee economy in the modern era. In 1995 farmers could average $3,778 profit per acre for tobacco as compared with $416 for cotton.[5]

Yadkin farmers also grew tobacco, but the bright-leaf variety did not flourish in the upland climate. In the piedmont and mountains, farmers air-cured their crop in open barns. Maryland and Burley tobaccos are varieties that suit this method.[6]

DEVELOPMENT OF HYDROELECTRIC POWER—DAMS ON THE YADKIN

The Yadkin River provided hydroelectric power for tobacco factories as well as other manufacturing. In Forsyth County, Idols Dam supplied energy to the first hydroelectric power plant in North Carolina in 1898. Built by Fries Manufacturing and Power Company, the dam provided power to Winston-Salem, thirteen miles away. Thomas Edison was one of the early investors.[7]

About 1900 George Whitney, a Pittsburgh financier, became aware of the possibilities for generating power at the narrows of the Yadkin. He started a development known as "Whitney," but an economic recession in 1907 caused the project to fail. A French syndicate, the Southern Aluminum Company, took over the project in 1912. However, soon World War I made it necessary for the Frenchmen to return to Europe to defend their native land. In 1915, the Aluminum Company of America (ALCOA) through its subsidiary, Tallassee Power Company, purchased the project and continued development, which included the simultaneous construction of a dam, a plant, and homes for the workers. By 1916 the plant was manufacturing aluminum. The Narrows Dam formed a lake extending seven miles up two valleys and covering about seven square miles. Although the French had sold out, the American company kept the town name, Badin, for Adrien Badin, an executive of the French firm. Badin was a company town that included housing, utilities, recreation, an opera house, a school, and a hospital for the workers. In 1919, ALCOA built another dam downstream, which became known as Falls Dam.[8]

The manufacture of aluminum requires large amounts of electricity, and the company found that more power was necessary. ALCOA completed the High Rock Dam in 1927 and the Tuckertown Dam in 1962, both upstream from Badin. The four dams on a thirty-eight-mile stretch of the Yadkin make up the hydroelectric facility that is now owned and operated by Yadkin, Inc., an ALCOA subsidiary. Property owned by Yadkin, Inc., includes the land beneath the waters of the reservoirs as well as many areas of the lakes' shorelines. In addition to hydroelectric power, the lakes provide scenic vistas and recreational opportunities.[9]

Yadkin, Inc., has developed shoreline stewardship and management plans to provide public access and recreation facilities while protecting important natural, environmental, cultural, and scenic

Blewett Falls Lake. *Courtesy Yadkin-Pee Dee Lakes Project.*

resources. The company's stated policy is "to operate in a manner that protects the environment and the health of our employees and of the citizens of the communities where we have an impact."[10]

DAMS ON THE UPPER PEE DEE

Downstream from the dams that power the ALCOA plant are dams at Lake Tillery and Blewett Falls, now owned by Carolina Power and Light Company (CP&L). Hugh MacRae, a businessman from Wilmington, North Carolina, was interested in building a dam at Blewett Falls as early as 1903. The name Blewett comes from William Bluit (or Blewett) who claimed land and built a house at the falls about 1760. He prospered by establishing a fishery and a ferry.[11]

MacRae worked tirelessly to sell the idea of a dam at Blewett Falls. In 1905 the North Carolina legislature chartered the Great Pee Dee Electric & Power Company. It was authorized to build and operate mills, power companies, transmission lines, railways, turnpikes, telephone and telegraph, real estate, and other properties. The incorporators were Hugh MacRae, Charles F. Bolles, Jr., Minor F. H. Gouverneur, and Henry A. Pressy of Wilmington. The incorporators noted that Rockingham, about

The Pee Dee River flooded in 1908, nearly covering the very railroad bridges that hastened the demise of the river's use as a transportation route. *Courtesy Sarah Spruill, Cheraw Visitors Bureau.*

ten miles away, was the site of nine large cotton mills in need of electric power. They changed the name of the company to Rockingham Power Company in 1906.[12]

CONSTRUCTION DIFFICULTIES AT BLEWETT FALLS

Construction of the dam at Blewett Falls began in 1905. Some mischievous boys from Rockingham rode through the countryside "hiring" men to work with the promise of $3 per day. Although their action was intended as a prank, some of the laborers who showed up might have found employment, for as many as 1,200 men worked at the isolated site. A four-mile spur track connected with the Seaboard Air Line at the village of Pee Dee to bring in materials, including thousands of tons of gravel, sand, and cement.

The workers built two 100-foot towers, 1,840 feet apart, on opposite sides of the river. They stretched two immense cableways, weighing twenty tons each, between the towers so men and materials could be shunted from the shores to be suspended above and lowered to work areas in the river.

Badin Lake with the Uwharrie Mountains in the distance. *Suzanne Linder.*

They worked in the blazing sun as well as in freezing or foggy weather at great physical risk. There is no record of exactly how many construction workers lost their lives, but the number was substantial.[13]

An officer hired by the company policed the camp where hastily constructed shanties provided shelter for laborers and sometimes their families. Others who were not employed congregated just outside the camp limits. Liquor was plentiful, and fights were frequent. Henry Garris of Rockingham worked as a water boy. He recalled the stern justice of the camp officer: "He carried his .44s strapped at each side with two belts of ammunition around his waist. He was an expert marksman, quick on the draw and never missed his man."[14]

Besides personnel and safety problems, the builders had to deal with forces of nature. Disaster struck on the night of August 7, 1908, when a flood washed out the cofferdam and took with it a boiler and a derrick. Construction halted, so workers shifted to the Seaboard Air Line trestle, which had also gone with the flood. The order was, "Work until you drop and as soon as you have caught a cat-nap, come back." The men put the bridge back into operation in three days.[15]

Financial difficulties resulting from the flood forced the Rockingham Power Company into receivership on May 8, 1909. Court battles and a fist fight involving some thirty people and two bulldogs ensued. The final outcome was that in 1911 the Yadkin River Power Company gained control of the project. This company had the same officers as CP&L and was managed in conjunction with CP&L until the two merged in 1926. The dam at Blewett Falls was complete by December 15, 1911, when a witness reported it "made a glorious waterfall, the biggest North Carolina has yet seen, 1,650 feet long and 56 feet high. . . . There is backwater forty miles." The power plant went into commercial operation June 1, 1912.[16]

LAKE TILLERY

Just twenty-five miles above Blewett Falls, CP&L began construction of another dam on the Pee Dee to be named for Paul Tillery, chief operating officer and president of the company. Builders noted that a steel and concrete bridge across the river would be covered by the waters of the lake. The company turned the bridge over to the United States military for demolition testing purposes. After surviving artillery shelling and several bombing attempts by 1927, the bridge finally collapsed after being blasted with 2,000 tons of TNT. The experience contributed to bombing techniques utilized in World War II. Thus the "Battle of Swift Island Bridge" initiated the construction of Lake Tillery and the Norwood generating station. Completed in 1928, the dam was 2,800 feet long and 86 feet high, and its four generators could produce 86,000 kilowatts of electricity.[17]

W. KERR SCOTT DAM AND RESERVOIR

A tropical hurricane that swirled out of the Caribbean in September 1945 dumped torrents of rain on the central Carolinas and resulted in major floods. At Blewett, water filled the generator room to a depth of twenty feet, but the dam held. Other smaller dams were not so fortunate.[18] The following year Congress passed the Flood Control Act of 1946. One proposal was the construction of a dam on the Yadkin River approximately 5.5 miles upstream from the twin cities of Wilkesboro and North Wilkesboro. Studies conducted between 1953 and 1959 completed the plan, and actual construction of the W. Kerr Scott Dam began in September 1960 under the direction of the United States Army Corps of Engineers. It completed the project in August 1962.

Besides 1,470 acres of water, the project area includes 2,284 acres of land. About 70 percent of it is devoted to public park and recreational use. The Corps of Engineers maintains five public boat-launching sites, and two others are located at Wilkes County Park and Wilkes Skyline Marina. Recreational fishing attracts many visitors.[19]

Today many fishermen and conservationists are questioning the impact of dams on the environment. Dams change water flows, sediment loads, water temperatures, and oxygen levels. By holding back floodwaters, they harm plant species that have evolved to take advantage of rising and falling waters. They also act as barriers to migrating fish and animals. United States Secretary of the Interior

A view of the Yadkin River from the W. Kerr Scott Dam. *Suzanne Linder.*

Bruce Babbitt participated in the removal of the Quaker Neck Dam near Goldsboro on the Neuse River in eastern North Carolina. He said, "We're removing a dam today in order to restore a river. . . . By restoring a river and a fishery, we will recapture an important part of North Carolina's heritage."[20]

Not all the impacts are negative. Dams can supply electric power and can create a wetland habitat for herons and other wading birds and for fish like largemouth bass and crappie, thus providing fishing and other recreational opportunities. And by creating reservoirs, dams can help supply reliable drinking water.

Nevertheless, some dams have outlived their usefulness, and current thinking is that if these dams can be removed, it would be a good thing for the environment. Fishermen are again catching spring stripers on the Neuse. "I'm glad they removed the dam," says retired Wake County well driller, N. W. Poole. "It sure has helped the fishing here."[21]

FISHING—RECREATIONAL AND COMMERCIAL

Throughout history recreational fishing has been popular on the Yadkin-Pee Dee. What is less well known is that commercial fisheries operated on the Pee Dee in the first half of the twentieth century. When Douglas Rights, a Moravian minister and historian, made a voyage down the Yadkin-Pee Dee

Recreational fishing has always been popular on the Yadkin-Pee Dee. *Charles McRae.*

in the mid-1920s, he encountered four fisheries in splendid condition and several others needing some repair in an eight-mile section of the river near Cheraw. He said, "A row of rocks runs across the river, supporting a fence-work of logs and planks. Several boxes are placed at intervals, through which the water runs freely, and at several places large frames are placed, which have flooring of laths with openings for water passage."[22]

Bernard Stubbs of Cheraw recalled visiting the Coward and Pegues fisheries on the Pee Dee for a fish dinner in his youth. He said, "If the weather was good, we'd eat on the riverbank out of tin plates and tin cups; if bad in the cook sheds." The menu was fried shad, red horse bread (named for the red horse sucker fish), shad roe, and black coffee. Stubbs confessed that although Cheraw High School had a National Honor Society for gifted students, he and some friends formed their own NHS (National HOOKEY Society), and about once a week, the president would call a meeting at the fishery.[23]

FISH DIPPERS AND FALL TRAPS

Stubbs believed the foundations of the fisheries were ancient fish dams built by Native Americans. The dams contained seven dippers to catch fish on the way upstream and four fall traps for fish headed

THE RIVER FISHERIES OF THE ATLANTIC STATES.
Fish-nets in the Peedee River. (Sect. v, vol. i, p. 624.)
From a photograph.

Fish dippers on the Pee Dee. *NOAA National Marine Fisheries Service Photo Collection.*

downstream. A dipper was a three-pronged contraption mounted on a mulberry or white cedar axle. The arms and baskets were of split white oak. Workers placed the dippers in small openings in the dam, and as the pent-up water rushed through, it turned the dippers. Fish trying to swim upstream would enter the small openings in the dam. The dippers would pick them up, and at the top of the arc of their circle, their slanted bottom would allow the fish to slide into a box placed in the water, where they would be picked up later.

Constructed of large rocks, the fall traps formed a v-shaped break in the dam, with the smaller end downstream. Planks driven into the river bottom were underwater at the upper end and rose to some four feet above the water at the downstream end. Fish moving downstream entered the v of swift water and were washed up on the incline and held there by the current.[24]

Shad was the principal catch. The shad is an anadromous fish, meaning that it lives mainly in the ocean, but swims up a freshwater river to spawn. The eggs of the shad, called roe, are considered a rare delicacy. The shad, the largest member of the herring family, runs in the Pee Dee in March or April. In addition to shad, the fisheries caught red horse, carp, catfish, herring, rockfish, and occasionally sturgeon. Carnell Hatcher, whose father operated one of the fisheries, recalled a twenty-six-pound rockfish that almost tore up the box before it was removed. Once in a while an Atlantic sturgeon of up to nine feet and several hundred pounds would become entrapped. The fishermen butchered the huge fish on the bank, carefully preserving the eggs, or caviar, for shipment to Baltimore.[25]

Caviar sold for a high price, but shad brought only two dollars for a fish with roe and seventy-five cents for one without the eggs. The fishermen had to pay a tax of five cents on each shad and two dollars on each dipper. They could use the dippers only four days a week; then they had to remove them so that fish could proceed upstream. If the water was too high, the dippers would float away; if it was too low, not enough would flow to make the dippers "dip." On a good day the fishery might get 30 to 40 fish, but with a short season and limited operating days, the margin of profit was not great. The Pee Dee fisheries ceased to operate about 1946.[26]

"RIVER PEOPLE" SOLD FISH AND GAME

After the commercial fisheries closed there were still "River People" who supported themselves and their families by selling fish and game, a practice now illegal. Bernard Stubbs recalled his father buying squirrel, rabbit, quail, bream, and redbreast. Douglas Rights observed a fisherman on the Yadkin, named S. D. Frey, who said he had caught as many as 270 fish in one haul of his bounce net, another practice now illegal. Rights photographed a bounce net that appeared to be a pole attached to a tripod made of branches on the land side and supported by a forked stick, possibly four feet tall, in the ground.[27]

Another unusual type of fishing Rights described was "grabbling." The fisherman waded into the river in the heat of the day when the fish had taken refuge under the rocks at the bottom. He explored the rocky cavities with deft and gentle movements of the hands, and when he located a fish, he quickly closed his fingers around his prey and brought it to the surface. Rights reported, "Some of these grabblers even go so far as to say that they rub the fish with their fingers while in the water and apparently mesmerize him. We have this information from reliable sources, but we have never grabbled, nor have we ever seen any grabbling. We would like to know, too, if mud turtles and water moccasins are grabbled in this way."[28]

POLLUTION BECOMES A PROBLEM

When Douglas Rights completed his voyage down the river in 1928, pollution was not a problem. A little more than half a century later another reporter made a trip down the Yadkin-Pee Dee in an effort to stimulate public awareness and concern about protecting the river from pollution.

In the 1960s and 1970s, environmental awareness intensified nationwide, and interested citizens in the Carolinas feared that urban growth would accelerate in the North Carolina piedmont and along

"Sunday morning on the Yadkin River can be a religious experience . . . " Caldwell County, North Carolina, near Scenic Byway 268. *Suzanne Linder.*

the South Carolina Grand Strand. Both these areas depend on the Yadkin-Pee Dee for water resources. In the 1970s effects of pollution were surfacing in complaints about the city of Winston-Salem's sewage treatment plant and problems with drinking water in the city of Salisbury.

STATES CONSIDER CONSERVATION MEASURES

In response to these issues, North and South Carolina jointly asked for and received money from the United States Water Resources Council to plan for the rapid economic development that, unchecked, could further threaten water quality. This resulted in a three-year study in which local, state, and federal governments cooperated with private citizens to hear public opinion on the river and plan for the future. The group held twenty-one public meetings and published a report in 1981 that outlined a plan for the entire river basin to be implemented by the North Carolina Department of Natural Resources and the South Carolina Water Resources Commission (now part of the Department of Natural Resources). The report noted that the basin's water quality had improved greatly from the past

The swampy Little Pee Dee River is a popular destination for canoeists. *Charles McRae.*

when raw sewage and industrial chemicals flowed untreated into the river. Nevertheless, there would be a limit as to how much the river could dilute and carry away, and vigilance was necessary to protect water resources for the future.[29]

CITIZENS' GROUPS GET INVOLVED

A citizens' group called the Yadkin-Pee Dee River Basin Committee with the leadership of Robie Nash, a North Carolina legislator from Salisbury, worked to sustain public interest in the basin. Joe Matthews, director of the Northwest Piedmont Council of Governments, represented the committee and approached Joe Goodman, managing editor of the *Winston-Salem Journal*, about sending a reporter on a trip down the river—one similar to that made by Rights some fifty-four years earlier. Goodman chose Floyd Rogers, whose book *Yadkin Passage* tells about life *of* the river and *on* the river in 1982.[30]

Rogers' book has become a classic of river lore, and its purpose of stimulating interest in conservation apparently bore fruit. Today agencies like the Land Trust for Central North Carolina, the Bi-State

Yadkin-Pee Dee River Task Force, the Yadkin River Commission, the Yadkin River Basin Association, and the Yadkin-Pee Dee Lakes Project work diligently to protect the waterway. In May 1998 the North Carolina Department of Environment and Natural Resources published the *Yadkin-Pee Dee River Basinwide Water Quality Management Plan*, a comprehensive outline that demonstrates the state's commitment to environmental integrity. Also in 1998 another book based on newspaper articles about the Yadkin River was published by the *Salisbury Post*. Mark Wineka and Wayne Hinshaw combined substantial facts with beautiful descriptions and photographs in their book, *A River Runs Through Us*. Wineka began his account by saying, "Sunday morning on the Yadkin River can be a religious experience. On the water, you feel close to a higher being and, maybe, it's the river itself. Fog lies just above the water like the whitest of table cloths draped over a communion table." Wineka went on to say that the river has 525 permitted dischargers now. He asked, "How many more can it stand? Will the biggest dischargers—municipal waste treatment plants—commit the public resources necessary to protect the river as their systems expand?"[31]

CONSERVATION EFFORTS IN SOUTH CAROLINA

In South Carolina, officials of the Department of Natural Resources are asking similar questions. The Land, Water, and Conservation Division published a statewide water plan in 1998 that included the Pee Dee watershed, describing policies for the efficient, equitable, and environmentally-responsible science-based management of water resources. In addition to watershed planning projects, the Department's River Conservation Program includes outreach and education efforts and scenic river projects. The "Adopt-a-Landing" program encourages private groups to make a commitment to keeping a river landing free of litter. The third Saturday of September is "Beach Sweep/River Sweep" day, co-sponsored by the South Carolina Sea Grant Consortium. The month of June is designated Rivers Month, and four times a year a newsletter, *South Carolina River News*, is available.[32]

The Department of Health and Environmental Control (DHEC) administers water quality control in South Carolina. DHEC's *Watershed Water Quality Management Strategy: Pee Dee Basin* describes, at the watershed level, all activities related to water quality that may potentially have a negative impact. Each watershed in the Pee Dee Basin is evaluated and a strategy described to address impaired streams. The department operates a permanent statewide network of monitoring stations to determine long-term water quality trends and identify locations in need of additional attention. Permits for wastewater discharges are also the responsibility of DHEC.[33]

THE SCENIC RIVERS PROGRAM

Governor John West signed the original South Carolina Scenic Rivers Act into law in July 1974. Governor Carroll Campbell signed an updated law in 1989, which established the Scenic Rivers Trust

Late fall afternoon on Hurricane Branch, Great Pee Dee Heritage Preserve, near Darlington. *Charles McRae.*

Fund to provide financial backing. Although the legislature has yet to make an appropriation, the framework is available to receive private contributions. Designation of the rivers is by voluntary conservation easements by landowners and through purchase, but rivers must meet certain standards to be eligible, and their designation as scenic must be ratified by the General Assembly. The management of the protected river is through a cooperative, voluntary process, which involves landowners, community interests, a local scenic river advisory council, and the South Carolina Department of Natural Resources working together. Under the act, two sections of the Pee Dee watershed have gained scenic river designation. The segment of the Little Pee Dee was designated in 1990 from the point where US 378 crosses from Marion to Horry County to the point of confluence with the Great Pee Dee. This segment of the Little Pee Dee runs through extensive swamp. It forms the boundary between Horry and Marion counties and on the Marion County side borders the Britton's Neck community.[34]

In 1994 a fifty-four-mile segment of the Lynches River from US 15 near Bishopville to the Lynches River State Park in Florence County officially became a scenic river. An active advisory council developed a plan for long-term management of the river, addressing such issues as water quality, recreational use, public access, scenic quality, fish and wildlife, and management of river-bordering land. The council sponsors an annual festival held at Lee State Park near Bishopville.[35]

HERITAGE TRUST PRESERVES

In addition to scenic river designation, South Carolina uses its Heritage Trust Program to protect those natural features and cultural remains that are quickly disappearing as the state's population increases. Land donated or purchased by the trust includes some 75,000 acres. The aim is to protect permanently the best examples of rare plants, animals, birds, archaeological sites, and other significant features. Within the Lynches River watershed are Heritage Preserves at Forty Acre Rock on Flat Creek, Lynchburg Savanna, and Savage Bay. The Great Pee Dee River Preserve is in Darlington County. The Little Pee Dee watershed includes Ervin Dargan, Horace Tilghman, Cartwheel Bay, and the Little Pee Dee River Heritage Preserves. Lewis Ocean Bay and Waccamaw Preserves are in the Waccamaw region.

PALMETTO CONSERVATION FOUNDATION PROTECTS SNOW'S ISLAND

Snow's Island at the intersection of Lynches River and the Great Pee Dee is the site most closely associated with the Revolutionary War General Francis Marion. In the spring of 2000, Sonoco, one of the largest manufacturers of packaging materials for industrial and consumer markets, donated a conservation easement on 70 acres of Snow's Island to the Palmetto Conservation Foundation. The company will still harvest timber from the site, but the easement prohibits deep plowing. The site is protected from development, and will be available for professional archaeological investigations.[36]

WINYAH BAY FOCUS AREA

Another type of preservation effort focuses on wetlands. The Atlantic Coast Joint Venture of the North American Waterfowl Management Plan, a cooperative effort among the United States, Canada, and Mexico, sponsors special focus areas. The Winyah Bay Focus Area includes the lower drainages of the Black, Pee Dee, Sampit, and Waccamaw rivers as well as Winyah Bay, the mouth of the Yadkin-Pee Dee System.

Objectives of the Winyah Bay Focus Area include permanent protection of 85,000 acres of wetlands and associated upland habitats as well as the enhancement of 1,500 acres managed for wildlife. The primary method of protection is through conservation easements on private lands. Such easements allow land to remain in private ownership while providing protection in perpetuity for important natural resources. Landowners can retain the right to pursue wildlife management, recreation, forestry, and agriculture while achieving certain tax advantages. Advocacy groups for land protection work with owners to secure easements. These groups include the Winyah Bay Focus Area task force, The Nature Conservancy, Ducks Unlimited, South Carolina Coastal Conservation League, Lowcountry Open Land Trust, and Historic Ricefields Association.[37]

This bridge once afforded passage over a small creek in the Uhwarrie National Forest. *Richard Watkins.*

UWHARRIE NATIONAL FOREST

Federal conservation efforts are prominent in the Yadkin-Pee Dee Basin in one national forest and two national wildlife refuges. Created in 1961, the Uwharrie National Forest includes nearly 50,000 acres in the North Carolina counties of Montgomery, Randolph, and Davidson.

Badin Lake and the Pee Dee River border the forest on the west, while the Uwharrie River winds its way through the mountain range by the same name.

The Uwharrie Mountains are remnants of an ancient chain of island volcanoes that were active some 600 million years ago at the edge of an ancient ocean. Some experts believe they are the oldest mountains in the world, and over the millennia they have worn down to an elevation of under 1,000 feet.

Forest management for pine and hardwoods and conservation of fish and wildlife still leave room for numerous recreational opportunities. Hiking trails through the scenic mountains or along the many streams give the visitor an opportunity to search for Indian artifacts and to see nature at its best. A covered bridge lends nostalgia to the landscape. Trails for horses, all-terrain vehicles, dirt bikes, and four-wheel drive vehicles are available. One can choose primitive camping or visit an established campground. The Cove boat landing provides access to The Narrows Reservoir and Badin Lake.

Some of the first gold mined in North America came from this region, and the convenience store at the little community of Eldorado sells gold mining equipment to tourists.[38]

NATIONAL WILDLIFE REFUGES

The Pee Dee National Wildlife Refuge, located in Anson and Richmond counties, North Carolina, encompasses 8,443 acres of various habitats including crop fields, wetlands, pine forests, and native hardwoods. A large concentration of wintering waterfowl finds its wetlands an attraction. Some of the best deer hunting in the state is available by permit, and the various ponds and streams offer fishing opportunities from April to October. In the spring and fall, migrating songbirds are frequent visitors. The refuge includes fifty miles of trails and roads. A covered bridge trail is a feature.

GADDY'S GOOSE POND

In the 1930s, a local hunter, Lockhart Gaddy, used live Canada geese as decoys in fields near the Pee Dee River. Gaddy decided in 1934 that he would rather provide food, shelter, and sanctuary for these majestic birds than hunt them. The first year, nine wild geese visited his private pond, but by the 1950s the flock had grown to an estimated 10,000. The project grew to such proportions that visitors came from all over the world to observe, and Gaddy's geese were on the cover of *Life* magazine on March 18, 1953.

Lockhart Gaddy had a special personal rapport with the geese. They seemed to appreciate that they were safe on his land. Usually the pond was alive with their movement, and the sound of their honking was quite loud. When Gaddy died, the geese seemed to know. The pond was quiet during the time of his funeral, and later, geese made a practice of visiting his grave. After the deaths of Gaddy and his wife, their refuge was closed to the public, but in 1963, the Pee Dee National Wildlife Refuge was established only a few hundred yards from Gaddy's pond.[39]

CAROLINA SANDHILLS NATIONAL WILDLIFE REFUGE

A part of President Franklin Roosevelt's New Deal program, the Resettlement Administration purchased unproductive land to retire the soil from sub-marginal agriculture. The federal government began purchasing land in the South Carolina sandhills in 1939. The badly eroded sandhills land could not provide a suitable environment for wildlife. Under federal management, sound soil, wildlife, and forestry conservation techniques have restored the natural habitat. The Carolina Sandhills National Wildlife Refuge includes some 46,000 acres in northeastern South Carolina near the town of Patrick.

A large cypress tree from lower Marion County. *Charles McRae.*

Among its goals, the refuge wants to provide wildlife with its natural habitat and particularly to provide protection for endangered and threatened species, including the red-cockaded woodpecker, the southern bald eagle, and the eastern cougar. The refuge also offers opportunities for environmental education, interpretation, and wildlife-oriented recreation.[40]

WACCAMAW NATIONAL WILDLIFE REFUGE

The United States Fish and Wildlife Service proposed a new refuge in 1995 in the vicinity of the Great Pee Dee and Waccamaw Rivers in Georgetown, Horry, and Marion counties. Included within the project area will be historic Sandy Island, noted as the location of several ante-bellum rice plantations and large-scale lumber operations after the Civil War. The Waccamaw Refuge could eventually protect some 50,000 acres, including the largest contiguous block of freshwater tidal wetlands in South Carolina. The project gained official approval in 1997, and since that time USFWS has been in the process of acquiring land through purchase and conservation easement.[41]

Above: The Black River—a tributary of the Pee Dee—was an early trading route. Note Cherokee roses in the foreground. Photo from Black River House Plantation. *Suzanne Linder.* Below: Winter on the Pee Dee River. Photo from Cashaway Ferry Bridge. *Jim Linder.*

STATE PARKS AND WILDLIFE MANAGEMENT

Among the many state parks in the North Carolina river basin are Stone Mountain, Pilot Mountain, Boone's Cave, and Morrow Mountain. In the South Carolina river basin they are Cheraw and Lee state parks. In addition, the North Carolina Wildlife Resources Commission oversees "Gamelands" for wildlife protection and controlled hunting. In South Carolina, the Department of Natural Resources administers "Wildlife Management Areas." Both state agencies sponsor and maintain river access points with boat landings. Thousands of acres are open to the public for hiking, bird watching, canoeing, or just enjoying nature.

TWENTIETH-CENTURY CHANGES

As the importance of the Yadkin-Pee Dee as a means of transportation dwindled, its role as a water source, a vehicle for hydroelectric power, and a recreational resource increased dramatically. The growth of population brought more water usage and more potential for pollution. Clearing land for timber and agriculture as well as real estate developments poured silt into the river. For a time, untreated sewage and chemicals polluted the precious waters. In the 1970s efforts to clean up the river intensified, so that by the century's end, despite greater demands for water usage, the river was cleaner than it had been around mid-century. New laws regulate "point-source" pollution such as discharges from a sewage plant or industrial facility. The river still has some problems because of "non-point source" pollution from run-off associated with agricultural or lawn chemicals, construction sites, landfills, or timber harvesting.[42]

Increased access to the river and the land along its banks provided by state and federal agencies means that more people have a stake in preserving its natural beauty and wildlife. A greater appreciation of this great natural resource has prompted private citizens to donate conservation easements through land trusts and conservation organizations in the private sector. Governmental and private interests have combined to make a significant impact. Nevertheless, a challenge remains for each individual who loves the river to endeavor to protect it. Perhaps the lesson of the twentieth century is that the river belongs to all of us, and it is up to us to preserve it.

Catfish Creek Swamp awash in color near the Great Pee Dee River. *Charles McRae.*

EPILOGUE

*"They'll build great engines yet, and grander towers, but
always the rivers run, in the day, in the night, in the dark,
draining immensely their imperial tides out of the wilderness. . . .
the river, always the river, the dark eternal river, full of strange
secret time, washing the city's stains away, thickened and
darkened by its dumpings, is flowing by us, by us to the sea."*
— Thomas Wolfe[1]

In the preface, we asked the question, "How does one capture the essence of a river?" Essence is its true identity or ultimate nature. It includes physical and geographical aspects, but it also encompasses what the river means to people in an intangible way. There can be many answers to our question. Scientists tell us that the river is water in a never-ending hydrologic cycle. Lawrence Earley, editor of *Wildlife in North Carolina*, said, "Rivers run with water as old as the planet itself. The same 326 million cubic miles of water . . . on Earth today was present 3 billion years ago, not a jot more or less." The same water circulates continually, falling as rain, seeping into the ground or running into streams, rising through plants or evaporating from the ocean to enter the atmosphere as vapor, and falling again as rain or snow. "Our landscape is alive with the urgency of moving water, whether it's boiling and tumbling in mountain headwater streams or meandering in lazy loops through a coastal floodplain."[2] Being aware of this cycle makes us realize what a responsibility human beings have to preserve this precious resource.

Cartographers know the river as a geographical entity. They plot its course on maps that show its length and the varied terrain through which it flows. As a feature of the landscape, the Yadkin-Pee Dee influenced settlement patterns. Native Americans gravitated to the river, moving up and down its course to hunt and fish in season. European settlers came up the river by boat to build homes in the Pee Dee Basin, while others, mostly of Scots-Irish or German descent, came down the great wagon road from Pennsylvania and Virginia to settle the Yadkin portion of the river. The fertile valleys and many creeks of the Yadkin attracted colonists and provided resources for agriculture as well as water-power for early gristmills and later development of hydroelectric plants. The river still attracts people who want to build homes along its banks, and experts today are questioning how much development the river can stand.

Ecologists see the river in terms of the interactions of all living things with the environment. Technological development and population growth cause serious problems in preserving the quality of water and the habitat of wildlife. As civilization becomes increasingly complex, the interconnectedness of all things becomes more apparent.

Historians seek stories of the human beings who have populated the river basin. We have shared the stories of many people who have lived all or part of their lives on its banks—John Lederer as he

Uwharrie River from Low Water Bridge. *Suzanne Linder.*

explored unknown territory, William Waties as he pursued trade with Native Americans, the Witherspoon family as they faced the dangers of the wilderness, Elizabeth Steele as she faced the rigors of Revolution. We have heard the voices of people throughout history, and we have heard many voices in the present day that express a love for the river and a sincere concern for protecting it. In the words of Norman McLean, "Eventually, all things merge into one, and a river runs through it. The river was cut by the world's great flood and runs over rocks from the basement of time. On some of the rocks are timeless raindrops. Under the rocks are the words, and some of the words are theirs."[3] Through the centuries the people who have followed the river, fought it in flood stage, or found a final resting place along its banks have left their mark. If their words are not literally under the river's rocks, they are recorded in its history.

The river is biology, geography, ecology, and history. Yet it is much more than any of those. The secret of the river's essence is that each person must find it for himself. The spirit of the river that prompted Native Americans to worship on its banks and early congregations to baptize converts in its waters offers to some a place of solitude to escape from the stress of modern life. Drifting along in a canoe or just sitting quietly on the bank can be an inspirational experience. To others the river means a place to gather for recreation with friends, to picnic, fish, or water ski. Some people see it as a place to build a home, others as a habitat for fish and wildlife. The river has its own voice that speaks to each of us in its own way. The words are there. Listen.

Endnotes

PREFACE

1. Trevor Fairbrother and Chiyo Ishikawa, *Leonardo Lives: The Codex Leicester and Leonardo da Vinci's Legacy of Art and Science* (Seattle: Seattle Art Museum, 1997), 17.

2. Barry Beasley and Tom Blagden, Jr., *The Rivers of South Carolina* (Englewood, Colorado: Westcliffe, 1999), 110.

CHAPTER 1

1. William Cumming, *The Discoveries of John Lederer* (Charlottesville: University of Virginia Press, 1958), passim.

2. Ibid., viii, 71.

3. Ibid., 15–16.

4. Ibid., 17.

5. Ibid., 18.

6. Ibid., 77.

7. Indian scholar Douglas L. Rights identified the Sara with the Cheraws. By 1701 they had moved to the Dan River near the Virginia line. Then due to Iroquois attacks, they moved to the lower Yadkin or Pee Dee. Barnwell's map about 1722 and Moseley's 1733 map show them on the east bank of the Pee Dee near the confluence of Rocky River. Douglas L. Rights and William P. Cumming in *The Discoveries of John Lederer*, 123.

8. Cumming, *The Discoveries of John Lederer*, 29. See also: Peter P. Cooper, "An Archaeological Survey of a Portion of Stanly County, North Carolina," (Salisbury: Catawba College, 1974), 15. Cooper found salt licks in the nearby area of Stanly County.

9. Cumming, *The Discoveries of John Lederer*, 29.

10. Ibid, 81, 85, 91.

11. Ibid, x.

12. John R. Swanton, *The Indians of the Southeastern United States* (Washington: United States Government Printing Office, 1946), 218.

13. James A. Rogers, *Theodosia* (Columbia: R. L. Bryan, 1978), xxi–xxii. See also Susan L. Allston, "The Peedee," *Names in South Carolina*, (1959), VI: 6–8; and W. L. McDowell, ed., *Journals of the Commissioners of the Indian Trade, September 20, 1710–August 29, 1718* (Columbia: South Carolina Archives Department, 1955), 93. Historian Alexander Gregg theorized that the name might have originated when a white man like Patrick Daly carved the initials "P.D." on a tree; even Gregg, however, discounts this explanation. See Gregg, *History of the Old Cheraws* (Columbia: The State Company, 1925. Reprint Spartanburg, S. C.: The Reprint Company, 1982), 20.

14. Douglas L. Rights, *The American Indian in North Carolina* (Durham: Duke University Press, 1947), 67–69. On 103, Rights cites William Byrd, *Dividing Line Histories* (Raleigh, North Carolina: William K. Boyd, 1929), n.p.: "The soil is exceedingly rich on both sides of the Yadkin, abounding in rank grass and prodigiously large Trees. . . . " According to Rights, "This seems to verify the name 'Yadkin' as derived from a Siouan term referring to large trees."

15. Floyd Rogers, *Yadkin Passage* (Winston-Salem, North Carolina: Hunter Publishing Company, 1983), 3.

16. United States Water Resources Council, *Comprehensive Water Resources Study, Level B, Yadkin-Pee Dee River Basin Plan of Study* (Columbia: South Carolina Water Resources Commission, 1979), 1, 4; See also James L. Michie, *Expectations of Archeological Site Location Within Floodplains and Peripheral Upland Areas* (Columbia: Institute of Archeology and Anthropology, 1980), 1, "This area covers approximately 100 miles northeast to southwest, and about 200 miles in a northwest to southeast direction, an expanse which drains about 20,000 square miles." Slightly different figures (9,280 square miles in North Carolina and 6,880 square miles in South Carolina) are given in Christopher Brooks, et al., eds., P*ee Dee River Basin Framework Study* (Columbia: South Carolina Water Resources Commission, 1977), 16.

17. John Lawson, surveyor general of North Carolina in 1711, called the Yadkin River "Sapona" and "Reatkin" and supposed that it was the West Branch of the Cape Fair [*sic*]. John Lawson, *Lawson's History of North Carolina* (London: W. Taylor and F. Baker, 1714. Reprint Richmond, Virginia: Garrett and Massie, 1937), xi, xii, 44.

18. Bailey Willis, "The Northern Appalachians," in National Geographic Society, *The Physiography of the United States* (New York: American Book Company, 1896), 185–187; William D. Thornbury, *Principles of Geomorphology* (New York: John Wiley & Sons, Inc., 1969), 120.

19. Daniel A. Fairey, *South Carolina's Land Resources: A Regional Overview* (Columbia: South Carolina Land Resources Commission, 1988), 5; Floyd Rogers, *Yadkin Passage*, 51.

20. Michie, *Expectations of Archeological Site Location*, 2; Donald Colquhoun, *Geomorphology of the Lower Coastal Plain of South Carolina* (Columbia: Division of Geology, State Development Board, 1969), 4.

21. Mary L. Medley, *History of Anson County North Carolina 1750–1976* (Wadesboro: Anson County Historical Society, 1976), 226–227; *Cheraw Intelligencer and Southern Register*, July 1, 1825. In the *Georgetown Gazette* of May 30, 1804, Farquhard Campbell, proprietor of a

public house at Sneydsborough known as the "Spread Eagle," advertised that he would open another public house at the Rocky River Springs for the "ensuing season."

22. The author swam at Riverton as a child.

23. U. S. Army Corps of Engineers, *Review of Reports Yadkin-Pee Dee River North Carolina and South Carolina*, Serial No. 82 (Charleston: Corps of Engineers, 1973), 4–7; Michie, 3; Brooks, 16.

24. Tom Cameron, interview with the author, July 4, 1990; Floyd Rogers, 42. Rogers quotes an informant who reported that Pee Dee cottonmouths could grow to five and a half feet long and as thick as a telephone pole.

25. Charles F. Kovacik and John J. Winberry, *South Carolina: The Making of a Landscape* (Columbia: University of South Carolina Press, 1989), 21.

26. Fairey, *South Carolina's Land Resources*, 9. See also Henry Savage, *The Mysterious Carolina Bays* (Columbia: University of South Carolina Press, 1982), passim. Savage supports the meteorite explanation.

27. E. Thomas Hemmings, "Early Man in the South Atlantic States," *South Carolina Antiquities,* vol. IV, bk. 2 (1972), 98–99; James Michie has demonstrated that sea level 3,500 years ago may have been eight to ten feet lower than at present. See James Michie, "Archeological Indications for Sea Level, 3,500 Years Ago," *South Carolina Antiquities*, V, I (1973), 116.

28. Michie, *Expectations of Archeological Site Location*, 5.

29. Kovacik and Winberry, *South Carolina: The Making of a Landscape*, 56.

30. For a list of sites see Michie, *Expectations of Archeological Site Location*, 20–22.

31. Joffre Lanning Coe, "The Formative Cultures of the Carolina Piedmont," Transactions of the American Philosophical Society (1964). Reprint Philadelphia: The American Philosophical Society, 1987), 54: 81. Coe qualified his work by stating: "It should be emphasized, however, that this evidence represents only a few events isolated from the continuum of life and preserved at this one spot on the earth's surface. It should not be assumed that these data are in any sense a complete inventory of cultural changes within this area or even at this site." Coe, 54.

32. Coe, "The Formative Cultures of the Carolina Piedmont," 9.

33. Stanley South, *Indians in North Carolina* (Raleigh: State Department of Archives and History, 1964), 18.

34. Charles Hudson, *The Southeastern Indians* (Knoxville: The University of Tennessee Press, 1976), 282.

35. South, *Indians in North Carolina* , 25, 26, 33.

36. Theda Perdue, *Native Carolinians: The Indians of North Carolina* (Raleigh: Division of Archives and History, 1988), 10–12;

SIDE BAR CHAPTER I

1. Cumming, *The Discoveries of John Lederer*, 41–42.

2. Ibid., 40–41.

CHAPTER 2

1. Peter Martyr D'Anghera, *De Orbe Novo*, trans. Francis A. MacNutt (New York and London: The Knickerbocker Press, 1912), II: 255. D'Anghera, hereinafter cited as Peter Martyr, was the first historian of the New World. He was a member of the Spanish Court and was attached to the Imperial Council of the Indies. He knew many explorers personally and sometimes entertained Ayllon and his Indian friend at his table (258). Paul Quattlebaum identified the promontory as Pawley's Island, South Carolina, Paul Quattlebaum, *The Land Called Chicora* (Gainesville, Florida: University of Florida Press, 1956), 10.

2. See John R. Swanton, *The Indians of the Southeastern United States*, Smithsonian Institution, Bureau of American Ethnology, Bulletin 137 (Washington: Smithsonian Institution Press, 1946), 183.

3. Quattlebaum, *The Land Called Chicora*, 11.

4. Martyr, *De Orbe Novo*, 256; Quattlebaum, 12–13.

5. Martyr, *De Orbe Novo*, 267–268.

6. Martyr, *De Orbe Novo*, 259; Steven G. Baker, "Cofitachique: Fair Province of Carolina" (Ph.D. diss., University of South Carolina, 1974), 64–65.

7. Martyr, *De Orbe Novo*, 261, 268.

8. Quattlebaum, *The Land Called Chicora*, 4–6. A translation of Ayllon's patent is reproduced on 135–144. Quattlebaum was trained as an engineer. A native of Horry County, South Carolina, he was familiar with the terrain.

9. Paul E. Hoffman, *A New Andalucia and a Way to the Orient: The American Southeast During the Sixteenth Century* (Baton Rouge and London: Louisiana State University Press, 1990), x, 321, 328.

10. Quattlebaum, *The Land Called Chicora*, 18–24. Archaeologist James Michie of Coastal Carolina College of the University of South Carolina explored the area in January, 1991, but did not find evidence of Spanish settlement. See the *State*, Jan. 28, 1991. Smithsonian ethnologist, John R. Swanton, linguistically analyzed the list of "provinces" described by Francisco Chicora in 1521 and identified Chicora's "Yenyohol" with Winyah and "Guacaya" with Waccamaw. See John R. Swanton, *The Indians of the Southeastern United States*, Smithsonian Institution, Bureau of American Ethnology, Bulletin 137 (Washington: United States Government Printing Office, 1946), 203, 206.

11. Quattlebaum, *The Land Called Chicora,* 16, 26.

12. Ibid., 21.

13. Ibid., 23–24.

14. Ibid., 26.

15. Ibid., 26–27.

16. Their mounted lancers, arquebuses, crossbows, and war dog gave the Spaniards overwhelming military superiority. Chester de Pratter, "The De Soto Trail in South Carolina," address at the South Carolina State Museum, October 12, 1989. Because usage for centuries has made it customary, Hernando de Soto will be referred to as De Soto rather than Soto.

17. Since 1939 when the United States De Soto Commission outlined the route, new evidence has become available. Archaeological research has established new understandings of sixteenth-century aboriginal settlement patterns. Advances in the dating of historic artifact types have made it possible to identify objects carried by the Spanish explorers, and the sites where these items occur suggest visitation by Europeans. Previously unavailable documents also contribute to revision. Captain Juan Pardo explored the interior of the Carolinas between 1566 and 1568, visiting some of the same sites as De Soto. A document by Juan de la Vandera [also written Bandera], scribe for Juan Pardo's second expedition, has greatly amplified understanding of Pardo's route as well as that of DeSoto. Charles Hudson, Marvin T. Smith, and Chester B. DePratter collaborated on revising the route. An additional consideration was that sixteenth-century Spaniards used two leagues in measuring distances, the *legua comun* which was 5.57 kilometers and the *legua legal*, which was 4.19 kilometers. The De Soto Commission used the *legua legal*, but Hudson, Smith, and DePratter found evidence that support the use of the *legua comun*. Research is continuing at the Institute for Southern Studies at the University of South Carolina under the direction of Stanley South and Chester DePratter. See: U. S. De Soto expedition Commission, *Final Report of the United States De Soto Expedition Commission*, House Document 71, 76th Congress, 1st Session (Washington: Smithsonian Institution, 1939, report, 1985); Swanton, *Indians of the Southeastern United States*, plate facing 40; Charles Hudson, Marvin T. Smith, and Chester B. DePratter, "The Hernando De Soto Expedition: From Apalachee to Chiaha," *Southeastern Archaeology*, 3 (1984), 1: 65–77. Reprint South Carolina Institute of Archaeology and Anthropology, *Notebook*, (1987), 19: 18, 22, 24; Chapman J. Milling, *Red Carolinians* (Chapel Hill: University of North Carolina Press, 1940), 65.

18. Hudson, Smith, and DePratter, "De Soto Expedition," 24.

19. Fidalgo of Elvas, *True Relation of the Vicissitudes that Attended the Governor Don Hernando De Soto and Some Nobles of Portugal in the Discovery of the Province of Florida*, trans. by Buckingham Smith, excerpt in South Carolina Institute of Archaeology and Anthropology, *Notebook* (1987), 19: 16. Another chronicler referred to the young lady as the niece of the Lady of the town. See Luys Hernandez de Biedma, *Relation of the Conquest of Florida*, trans. by Buckingham Smith, excerpt in *Notebook*, 19: 12.

20. The above description is a composite taken from the eyewitness accounts of the Gentleman of Elvas, Luys Biedma, and Rodrigo Ranjel. The accounts differ slightly as to the parts played by the kinswoman and the Senora or Lady of Cofitachequi. See Elvas, *True Relation of the Vicissitudes*, 16; Biedma, *Relation of the Conquest of Florida*, 12; and Rodrigo Ranjel, *A Narrative of De Soto's Expedition Based on the Diary of Rodrigo Ranjel, His Private Secretary by Gonzalo Fernandez de Oviedo y Valdes*, excerpt reproduced in Charles Hudson, et al, *Notebook*, 19: 6.

21. Elvas, *True Relation of the Vicissitudes*, 16; Ranjel, *A Narrative of De Soto's Expedition*, 9.

22. Ranjel, *A Narrative of De Soto's Expedition*, 9. *Liquidambar Styraciflua*, also called copalm balsam, is commonly known as sweet gum.

23. Henry Dobyns, *Their Number Become Thinned* (Knoxville: University of Tennessee Press, 1983), 262–264. Dobyns found evidence that an overland spread of infectious disease occurred along Native American inland trade routes in the narrative of Alvar Nunez Cabeza de Vaca. "In 1535, Nunez and his companions crossed from Texas to Sinaloa. Sickness broke out among the hundreds of Native Americans accompanying them. They halted their march; more than 300 Native Americans fell ill. Many of them died. Whatever killed Nunez's companions may have been the disease that reached the Creeks on the Atlantic Coast, perhaps in 1536, 1537, 1538, or 1539, depopulating entire settlements."

24. Elvas, *Relation of the Vicissitudes,* 17.

25. Steven G. Baker, *Cofitachique: Fair Province of Carolina* (Thesis University of South Carolina, 1974), 37–38; Elvas, *Relation of the Vicissitudes,* 17. Elvas states that the outer limit of the territory of the Lady of Cofitachequi was at Guaxule which was beyond Xuala. Hudson, Smith, and DePratter, "De Soto Expedition," 25. Hudson, Smith, and DePratter located Xuala slightly north of Marion, North Carolina. See also Charles Hudson, *The Southeastern Indians* (Knoxville: University of Tennessee Press, 1976), 78.

26. Elman Service defined chiefdom as a redistributional society having a permanent central coordinating agency for economic, social, and religious activities. The society was dominated by the office of chieftain, the ultimate authority in coordination of these affairs. Centers for such coordination provide a major distinction between chiefdoms and tribal societies. Chiefdoms also had some degree of territoriality. See: Elman R. Service, *Primitive Social Organization: An Evolutionary Perspective* (New York: Random House, 1965), 143–177, as cited in Baker, *Cofitachique: Fair Province of Carolina*, 2–3.

27. Stanley South of the South Carolina Institute of Archaeology and Anthropology has led excavations on Paris Island over the past twenty years, proving the location of Charlesfort and demonstrating that Santa Elena was a thriving village. Research using Spanish documents and artifacts from Santa Elena is continuing in cooperation with the Institute for Southern Studies at the University of South Carolina. For a synopsis of the data see Walter Edgar, *South Carolina: A History* (Columbia: University of South Carolina Press, 1998), 26–34; see also Charles Hudson, et al, *Notebook* (1987), 19: 2.

28. Chester B. DePratter and Marvin T. Smith, "Sixteenth Century European Trade in the Southeastern United States: Evidence from the Juan Pardo Expeditions (1566–1568)," *Notebook* (1987), 19: 53–54.

29. Juan Pardo, "Report of the Entry and Conquest made by Order of Pedro Menendez de Aviles 1565 into the Interior of Florida," *Notebook* (1987), 19: 29–30.

30. Pardo, "Report of the Entry and Conquest," *Notebook* (1987), 19: 30–31.

31. Chester B. DePratter , Charles M. Hudson, and Marvin T. Smith, "The Route of Juan Pardo's Explorations in the Interior Southeast, 1566–1568," *Notebook* (1987), 19: 47.

32. Pardo, "Report of the Entry and Conquest," *Notebook* (1987), 19: 31.

33. Abstract of the Vandera Document in Herbert E. Ketcham, "Three Sixteenth Century Spanish Chronicles Relating to Georgia," *Georgia Historical Quarterly* (1954), 38 : 66–82. Reprint *Notebook* (1987), 19: 33; DePratter, Hudson, and Smith, "The Route of Juan Pardo's Explorations," *Notebook* (1987), 19: 38, 47.

34. DePratter, Hudson, and Smith, "The Route of Juan Pardo's Explorations," *Notebook* (1987), 19:47. The Pee Dee region was noted for good corn crops. In 1889, Captain Zachariah J. Drake, a Pee Dee planter, established a world record by growing 255 bushels of corn on an acre. See David D. Wallace, *South Carolina: A Short History, 1520–1948* (Columbia: University of South Carolina Press, 1969), 645.

35. DePratter, Hudson, and Smith, "The Route of JuanPardo's Exlorations," *Notebook* (1987), 19:48.

36. William Hardy McNeill found that once European contact was established, the populations of Mexico and Peru became victims on a mass scale of common childhood diseases of Europe and Africa producing a ninety per cent drop in population within 120 years. The Indians saw epidemics as indications of God's wrath towards them and approval of the Spaniards who had immunity. This contributed to their docility. See William Hardy McNeill, *Plagues and Peoples* (Garden City, New York: Anchor Press/Doubleday, 1976), 202, 205, 208. Ann Ramenofsky noted, "Repetition of the breakdown of burial practices in different regions suggests that death from disease may have been causal." See: Ann Ramenofsky, *Vectors of Death: The Archaeology of European Contact* (Albuquerque: University of New Mexico Press, 1987), 23; also Marvin T. Smith, *Archaeology of Aboriginal Culture Change in the Interior Southeast* (Gainesville: University of Florida Press/Florida State Museum, 1987), 7, 143.

37. Dobyns, *Their Number Become Thinned*, 338; Charles F. Kovacik and John J. Winberry, *South Carolina, A Geography* (Boulder and London: Westview Press, 1987), 60. Ethnohistorian Henry Dobyns said, "Early historic depopulation and especially the apparent 95 percent decline in population between 1519 and 1617, created a major biological and cultural discontinuity." Kovacik and Winberry estimated that the Indian population of 15,000 in 1600 had declined to half that by 1715 [in South Carolina].

38. For a thorough discussion of archaeological excavations of Santa Elena see Stanley South, Russell Skowronek, and Richard E. Johnson, *Santa Elena* (Columbia: South Carolina Institute of Archaeology and Anthropology, 1988), passim.

SIDE BAR CHAPTER 2

1. N. Brent Kennedy, *The Melungeons, The Resurrection of a Proud People* (Macon, GA: Mercer University Press, 1994), 122.

CHAPTER 3

1. Hugh Talmage Lefler, ed., *A New Voyage to Carolina by John Lawson* (Chapel Hill: University of North Carolina Press, 1967), x, xi.

2. Ibid., 50.

3. Ibid.

4. Ibid., 52.

5. Ibid.

6. Ibid., 53–55.

7. Ibid., 56. At the confluence of the Yadkin and the Uwharrie stands Morrow Mountain, used for centuries as a quarry site by Native Americans. The author has observed a proliferation of stones that appeared to have been worked and discarded.

8. Ibid., passim.

9. George C. Rogers, Jr., *The History of Georgetown County, South Carolina* (Columbia: University of South Carolina Press, 1970), 12.

10. W. L. McDowell, ed., *Journals of the Commissioners of the Indian Trade* (Columbia: South Carolina Archives Department, 1955), ix. Hereinafter cited as *JCIT*. A complete text of the act is printed in the appendix, 325–329.

11. *JCIT*, July 10, 1716, 74.

12. Ibid., July 31, 1716, 96. Later the instructions specified that the slaves were not to be branded with the iron, but instead marked by powder or other means. Commissioners to Waties, *JCIT*, Dec. 10, 1716, 138.

13. Ibid., November 26, 1716, 132.

14. Ronald E. Bridwell, *'That We Should Have a Port . . .'* (Georgetown: *Georgetown Times*, 1982), 3; Rogers, 13.

15. *JCIT*, August 11, 1716, 104. For other rate schedules see 210, 269, 281. "Strouds" referred to a coarse woolen cloth named after Stroud in Gloucestershire, England, where woolens were made. Likewise, the town of Duffel near Antwerp gave its name to a coarse woolen cloth having a thick nap, *Random House Dictionary*, 440, 1409.

16. *South Carolina Gazette*, (Charleston), August 17, 1738.

17. *JCIT*, June 18, 1717, 192.

18. Verner W. Crane. *The Southern Frontier, 1670–1732* (Ann Arbor, Michigan: University of Michigan Press, 1956), 170. Crane said: "That South Carolina escaped complete ruin was due to the energy of a gallant governor, to the skill of the seasoned Indian fighters who commanded her militia, to assistance in arms and men from neighboring provinces, and the conversion of the Cherokee at a critical moment to peace and friendly assistance." See also: Walter Edgar, *South Carolina: A History* (Columbia: University of South Carolina Press, 1980), 101.

19. *JCIT*, August 10, 1717, 202. The location on Black River was near the old Prince Frederick Parish Cemetery off Highway 51 north of Georgetown.

20. Ibid., September 11, 1717, 206.

21. Ibid., Jan. 31., 1718, 254.

22. Ibid., May 22, 1718, 275; June 27, 1718, 297.

23. John R. Swanton, *The Indians of the Southeastern United States* (Washington: Smithsonian Institution Bureau of American Ethnology, Bulletin 137, Government Printing Office, 1946), 203; "A letter to Mr. Boone, June 24, 1720," *Calendar of State Papers, Colonial Series, 1720–1721*, ed Cecil Headlam (London, 1933), 58, as cited in Rogers, *The History of Georgetown County*, 11.

24. Rogers, *The History of Georgetown County*, 14–15. Profitable trade with the Cherokee continued, however. See Crane, *The Southern Frontier, 1670–1732*, 298–299.

25. Crane, *The Southern Frontier, 1670–1732*, 165–166.

Side bar Chapter 3

1. See Janet Schaw, *Journal of a Lady of Quality* (New Haven, Yale University Press, 1939. Reprint Spartanburg: Reprint Company, 1971), 13. Schaw reported that a planter near Wilmington had "a very fine boat with an awning to prevent the heat and six stout Negroes in neat uniforms to row her down. . . . " See also John Brickell, *The Natural History of North Carolina* (Dublin: James Carson, 1737) as cited in Frank Roy Johnson, *Riverboating in Lower Carolina* (Murfreesboro, North Carolina: Johnson Publishing Company, 1977), 11. Johnson reported that some of the larger craft could carry forty or fifty barrels of pitch and tar. The derivation of the word, periauger, is from Carib, via Spanish, *piragua*, a dugout. The word is variously spelled perriauger, pettiauger, periago, etc. See Jess Stein, ed., *The Random House Dictionary of the English Language* (New York: Random House, 1966), 1071. See also C. Cristopher Crittenden, *The Commerce of North Carolina* (New Haven: Yale University Press, 1936), 16. Crittenden reported that a large craft could carry 100 barrels.

2. *JCIT*, 93, 162. On January 7, 1917, the commissioners paid John Barnwell three pounds, six shillings, eight pence for the hire of his Indian man for 25 days to and from the Northward Factory. *JCIT*, 146.

Chapter 4

1. A. S. Salley, Jr., *Georgetown Times*, July 19, 1935, as cited in Rowena Nylund, "The Historical Background of the Brown's Ferry Vessel," (Master's thesis, University of South Carolina, 1989), 50.

2. South Carolina Colonial Plats XII, 12, 15, 16; Charleston Deeds, Book 3T, 254, South Carolina Department of Archives and History [hereinafter cited as SCDAH], as cited in Nylund, "The Historical Background of the Brown's Ferry Vessel," 17.

3. Elizabeth W. Allston Pringle, *The Register Book for the Parish Prince Frederick Winyaw* (Baltimore: Williams and Wilkins Company, 1916), 1.

4. "George Hunter's Map of the Cherokee Country and the Path thereto in 1730," *Bulletin No. 4 of the Historical Commission of South Carolina* (Columbia, S. C., 1917), as cited in George Rogers, *The History of Georgetown County, South Carolina* (Columbia: University of South Carolina Press, 1970), 18.

5. Thomas Cooper and David J. McCord (eds.), *The Statutes at Large of South Carolina* (Columbia: 1836–1841), II, 615–617. Hereinafter cited as *S. C. Statutes*.

6. Ronald E. Bridwell, '. . . *That We Should Have a Port. . .': A History of the Port of Georgetown, South Carolina, 1732–1865* (Georgetown: *Georgetown Times*, 1982), 3.

7. *S. C. Statutes*, III: 171–172.

8. Commons House Journal, No. 6 (1722–1724), 307–308; as cited in Rogers, *The History of Georgetown County*, 19; Elizabeth W. Allston Pringle, ed. *The Register Book for the Parish Prince Frederick Winyaw* (Baltimore: Published for the National Society of the Colonial Dames of America, Williams and Wilkins Company, 1916), iii–iv.

9. Harvey Toliver Cook, *Rambles in the Pee Dee Basin* (Columbia: The State Company, 1926), 16, 17, 148.

10. Loulie Latimer Owens, *Saints of Clay: The Shaping of South Carolina Baptists* (Columbia: The South Carolina Baptist Convention, 1971), 26; Cook, *Rambles in the Pee Dee Basin*, 151.

11. J. P. McPherson, "History of the Presbyterian Church in Williamsburg, S. C.," *Southern Presbyterian*, February 8, 1850.

12. George Howe, *History of the Presbyterian Church in South Carolina* (Columbia: Duffie and Chapman, 1870), I: 282.

13. Nylund, "The Historical Background of the Brown's Ferry Vessel," 50; J. Harold Easterby, *The South Carolina Rice Plantation as Revealed in the Papers of Robert F. W. Allston* (Chicago: University of Chicago Press, 1937), 10.

14. *S. C. Statutes,* VII: 486–488.

15. Rogers, *The History of Georgetown County, South Carolina,* 46.

16. In the *Georgetown Gazette and Commercial Advertiser* of July 6, 1808, was printed a notice from the Customs House: "Vessels in loading up the river must previous to clearing out produce a certificate to the collector . . . of the particular kind and quality of produce on board and specify the day shipped."

17. Bridwell, '. . . *That We Should Have a Port. . .*'3, 6.

18. Converse D. Clowse, *Economic Beginnings in Colonial South Carolina, 1670–1730* (Columbia: University of South Carolina Press, 1971), 166–167.

19. George C. Rogers, Jr., *The History of Georgetown County, South Carolina* (Columbia: University of South Carolina Press, 1970), 39.

20. Clowse, *Economic Beginnings in Colonial South Carolina,* 172.

21. Francis Yonge, *A View of the Trade of South-Carolina, With Proposals humbly Offer'd for Improving the Same* as cited in H. Roy Merrens, *The Colonial South Carolina Scene* (Columbia: University of South Carolina Press, 1977), 70. For instructions as to how to make tar by the Scandinavian method as required by the British, see Joseph J. Malone, *Pine Trees and Politics* (Seattle: University of Washington Press, 1964), Appendix D, 152. See also Percival Perry, "The Naval-Stores Industry in the Old South, 1790–1860," *Journal of Southern History* (Nov. 1968) XXXIV: 511.

22. Clowse, *Economic Beginnings in Colonial South Carolina, 1670–1730,* 177–178.

23. Commons House Journal, No. 6 (1722–1724), 171, South Carolina Department of Archives and History (SCDAH).

24. British Public Records Office (1725–1727) XII: 196–197, SCDAH, as cited in Rogers, *The History of Georgetown County, South Carolina,* 31.

25. Rogers, *The History of Georgetown County, South Carolina,* 31.

26. British Public Records Office (1730) XIV: 20, SCDAH; "George Hunter's Map of the Cherokee Country and the Path thereto in 1730," *Bulletin No. 4 of the Historical Commission of South Carolina* (Columbia, 1917), as cited in Rogers, 31–32.

27. British Public Records Office, Naval Office Shipping Returns, MS, MF Reel 89, SCDAH, passim. On June 9, 1736, the snow *Martha* owned by Jacob Kollock and sailing under Master Cornelius Kollock cleared inwards. Cornelius Kollock (1824–1897) would become well known in the Pee Dee area in the next century in the field of medicine. Perhaps this ship's master was his ancestor. See Suzanne Linder, *Medicine in Marlboro County, 1736–1980* (Baltimore: Gateway Press, 1980), 132.

28. Robert Meriwether, *The Expansion of South Carolina, 1729–1765* (Kingsport, Tennessee: Southern Publishers, Inc., 1940), 19–20.

29. Public Records of South Carolina, MS, XIV: 174–177, British Public Records Office, SCDAH; Meriwether, *The Expansion of South Carolina,* 19–22; Julian J. Petty, *The Growth and Distribution of Population in South Carolina* (Columbia: State Planning Board, 1943. Reprint Spartanburg: The Reprint Company, 1975), 222.

30. Public Records of South Carolina, MS, XIV: 176–177, SCDAH; Meriwether, *The Expansion of South Carolina,* 19.

31. Charles F. Kovacik and John J. Winberry, *South Carolina: The Making of a Landscape* (Columbia: University of South Carolina Press, 1989), 79; Meriwether, *The Expansion of South Carolina, 1729–1765,* 86.

32. "A Gentleman's Account of His Travels, 1733–34," as quoted in Merrens, ed., *The Colonial South Carolina Scene,* 114, 118.

33. Ibid., 119. Charleston Deeds, Y: 281. Gordon's land became part of Springfield Plantation.

34. Ibid., 114.

35. The author recalls as a child hearing the pileated woodpecker referred to as the "chicken woodpecker" because it was about the size of a chicken. In 1734, ivory-billed woodpeckers were also available, although they are now thought to be extinct.

36. "A Gentleman's Account," 115.

37. Ibid., 116. "Champaign land" refers to level, open country.

38. There is a location on the Waccamaw still known as Bear Bluff. It is located about eighteen miles due west of Calabash, North Carolina, or eleven miles northeast of Conway, South Carolina, across the river from state road 905. It may be nearer thirty miles by boat because of the bends in the river; certainly it might seem like thirty miles to those paddling a canoe upstream.

39. "A Gentleman's Account," 116.

40. Ibid., 117.

41. Journal of the Council, Jan. 24, 1744, as cited in Meriwether, *The Expansion of South Carolina, 1729–1765,* 87. See also 86.

42. Meriwether, *The Expansion of South Carolina,* 87.

43. Journal of the Council, February 7, 1737; May 4, 1745; as cited in Meriwether, *The Expansion of South Carolina, 1729–1765, 87.*

44. Cainhoy was located on the Wando River about twelve miles from Charleston. George Howe, *History of the Presbyterian Church in South Carolina* (Columbia: Duffie and Chapman, 1870), I: 185, 282.

45. *South Carolina Gazette,* December 8, 1759, as cited in Meriwether, *The Expansion of South Carolina, 1729–1765,* 88.

46. Elmer T. Clark, ed., *The Journal and Letters of Francis Asbury* (Nashville, Tennessee: Abingdon Press, 1958), I: 485, 667; II: 69.

47. *South Carolina Gazette* (Charleston, S. C.), May 2, 1768, as cited in Meriwether, *The Expansion of South Carolina*, 87–88.

48. Easterby, *The South Carolina Rice Plantation*, 7.

49. David D. Wallace, *South Carolina A Short History, 1520–1948* (Columbia: University of South Carolina Press, 1951, repr. 1969), 49.

50. Clowse, *Economic Beginnings in Colonial South Carolina, 1670–1730*, 122, 123, 168, and Appendix, Table III, n.p.

51. See Charles Joyner, *Down by the Riverside* (Chicago: University of Illinois Press, 1984), 41; Duncan Clinch Heyward, *Seed from Madagascar* (Chapel Hill: University of North Carolina Press, 1937), 41; Rogers, *The History of Georgetown County*, 324, 343.

52. Charles Joyner, *Down by the Riverside*, 13–14. See also Daniel C. Littlefield, *Rice and Slaves: Ethnicity and the Slave Trade in Colonial South Carolina* (Baton Rouge: Louisiana State University Press, 1981), 74–114, passim.

53. Laurence Oliphant, *Patriots and Filibusters; or Incidents of Political and Exploratory Travel* (Edinburgh, 1860), 141; Welcome Bees [*sic*], in WPA MSS. South Caroliniana Library, University of South Carolina, as cited in Joyner, *Down by the Riverside*, 15–16.

54. Council Journal, Jan. 18, 24, 25, 1743/4; SCDAH.

55. Clowse, *Economic Beginnings in Colonial South Carolina, 1670–1730*, 252. Clowse estimates the population in 1730 at 10,000 whites to 20,000 blacks. See also: David Duncan Wallace, *South Carolina: A Short History* (Columbia: University of South Carolina Press, 1969), Appendix III, 709. Wallace cites Public Records, XIV: 143, giving the opulation in 1730 as 3000 families or 15,0000 whites. Drayton's *View of South Carolina*, 193, estimates 7,333 whites, 22,000 Negroes. Wallace indicates that the estimate of whites is probably low. Governor Glen in *Carroll's Collections*, II, 218, gives estimates for 1749 at 25,000 whites and 39,000 Negroes. See also Petty, *The Growth and Distribution of Population in South Carolina*, 222.

SIDE BARS CHAPTER 4

1. Clowse, *Economic Beginnings in Colonial South Carolina, 1670–1730*, 171–172, 176–177. See also W. W. Ashe, "The Forests, Forest Lands and Forest Products of Eastern North Carolina," *North Carolina Geological Survey Bulletin*, No. 5 (1894), 83, 94.

2. Rassie Wicker, *Miscellaneous Ancient Records in Moore County* (Southern Pines, North Carolina: Moore County Historical Association, 1971), 45–50, as cited in Suzanne Linder, *They Came By Train and Chose to Remain* (Hamlet, North Carolina: Richmond Technical College, 1982), 8–10; Charles Christopher Crittenden, *The Commerce of North Carolina* (New Haven: Yale University Press, 1936), 56.

3. Institute of Archeology and Anthropology, University of South Carolina, Permanent Site Survey Record No. 38GE57.

4. J. Richard Steffy, "Preliminary Report Hull Construction Features of the Brown's Ferry Vessel," *Notebook*, X (February 1979), Institute of Archeology and Anthropology, University of South Carolina, 1, 18, 20–21.

5. Nylund, "The Historical Background of the Brown's Ferry Vessel," 5. Nylund states that the location was a few miles from Prince Frederick's Church, established in 1726, which places Brown's Ferry about twenty miles up river.

6. The teredo or shipworm is a salt-water bivalve mollusk that feeds on wood and minute organisms. Shipworms do enormous damage to wooden hulls. See William Bridgwater and Seymour Kurtz, eds., *The Columbia Encyclopedia* (New York, 1963), 1950.

7. Steffy, 24. The *Georgetown Chronicle* of January 19, 1797, advertised for sale "A four oar'd Boat, fit for carrying rice, wood or corn about 30 feet keel, 10 feet beam in the clear, 4 feet in depth, for terms. Apply to Abel Goodwin." Although smaller, this boat sounds similar to the Brown's Ferry Vessel.

CHAPTER 5

1. William Willis Boddie, *History of Williamsburg* (Columbia: The State Company, 1923. Reprint Spartanburg, S. C.: The Reprint Company, 1980), 8. The white pine is not native to South Carolina. It was probably a Walter's pine, which resembles the white pine. See W. C. Coker and H. R. Totten, *Trees of the Southeastern States* (Chapel Hill, University of North Carolina Press, 1934), 27–29. For a discussion of the mast trade and the marking of trees suitable for masts with an arrow, see Joseph J. Malone, *Pine Trees and Politics* (Seattle, Washington: University of Washington Press, 1965), 6, 10. The town of Kingstree, which developed at this site, is only about forty miles from Georgetown by highway. The journey by water was longer because of the many bends and curves in the Black River.

2. *South Carolina Gazette* (Charleston, S. C.), October 28, 1732.

3. Boddie, *History of Williamsburg*, 10.

4. Robert Meriwether, *The Expansion of South Carolina, 1729–1765* (Kingsport, Tennessee: Southern Publishers, Inc., 1940), 79.

5. J. G. Wardlaw, *Genealogy of the Witherspoon Family* (Yorkville, South Carolina: no publisher, 1910), 6–8. Wardlaw quotes a document written by Robert Witherspoon dated at Williamsburg, S. C., in 1780, which recalls his experiences as an immigrant in 1734. The original manuscript has disappeared. A photo-offset reproduction of an 1835 copy of the original provides a slightly different version from that in the Wardlaw book. See *An Early Manuscript Copy of the Witherspoon Family Chronicle and Later Notes on Related Families* (Columbia: reproduced for the Williamsburg County Historical Society by the State Printing Company, June 1967), 1–15; as cited in H. Roy Merrens, *The Colonial South Carolina Scene* (Columbia: University of South Carolina Press, 1977), 122–129.

6. Wardlaw, *Genealogy of the Witherspoon Family,* 8.

7. The location is about fifteen miles in a direct line from Georgetown, but the many curves in the river made the distance by boat considerably farther.

8. Samuel Davis McGill, *Narrative of Reminiscences in Williamsburg County* (Columbia: The R. L. Bryan Company, 1897), 277.

9. Wardlaw, *Genealogy of the Witherspoon Family,* 9. For an estimate of distances see Robert Mills, Map of Williamsburg County, *Atlas of the State of South Carolina,* Facsimile of 1825 edition. (Easley, S. C.: Southern Historical Press, 1980.) n.p. Maps are arranged alphabetically.

10. Wardlaw, *Genealogy of the Witherspoon Family,* 9–10. Robert Witherspoon says his mother died January 22, 1777 (15), in the 72nd year of her age, and on 13 he mentions that she married at age twenty, which would have placed the marriage of James Witherspoon and Elizabeth McQuoid in 1725. Since Robert was born in 1728, it seems reasonable that his older brother, David, was born in 1726 and his younger brother, John, in 1730, followed by Sarah in 1732. On 12, Robert states, "About the same time, 1737, my father had a daughter, Elizabeth, that died, aged 3 years, born at the place called the Bluff, where we lived." It is not clear whether the child, Elizabeth, was born or died in 1737. The 1835 version of the chronicle, however, reads: About the same time [1737] my father had a daughter died, named Elizabeth, born at the Bluff, about 3 years old." [Merrens, 127] If she died in 1737, it would have meant that Mrs. Witherspoon was pregnant on the journey and delivered soon after having arrived and having lost daughter Sarah in Charleston. The difficulties of being a mother under such circumstances are incomprehensible in the modern day. It is interesting that Robert says "my *father* had a daughter."

11. Wardlaw, *Genealogy of the Witherspoon Family* , 10.

12. Ibid., 10–11.

13. Ibid.

14. Ibid., 11.

15. Ibid., 10.

16. Thomas Cooper and David J. McCord, eds., *The Statutes at Large of South Carolina* (Columbia: 1836–1841), III, 436–437; hereinafter cited as *S. C. Statutes.*

17. *Colonial Records of Georgia,* XXV: 15–19; as cited in Meriwether, 83.

18. Meriwether, *The Expansion of South Carolina, 1729–1765,* 82–83. King George's War was the American phase of the War of the Austrian Succession (1740–1748). The British joined Austria against France, Spain, Saxony, Bavaria and Prussia. The British aspect of the war against Spain was known as the "War of Jenkin's Ear." The British-French conflict in America was King George's War. Paul Bernstein and Robert W. Green, *History of Civilization* (Totowa, New Jersey: Rowman and Allanheld, 1962), II: 57–58.

19. *Indigofera Tinctoria* had showed promise in the early years of the settlement of Carolina, but attempts to make it profitable were abandoned both because it was difficult to cultivate and because of the success of rice. See Robbie L. Alford, "Historic Georgetown County Leaflet" No. 6 (Georgetown, South Carolina: The Rice Museum, 1975, repr. Georgetown County Historical Commission, 1989), 1. See also Julian J. Petty, The Growth and Distribution of Population in South Carolina (Columbia: State Planning Board, 1943), 56.

20. Charles F. Kovacik and John J. Winberry, *South Carolina: The Making of a Landscape* (Columbia: University of South Carolina Press, 1989), 74–75; Eliza Lucas Pinckney to Charles Cotesworth Pinckney, September 10, 1785, as cited in H. Roy Merrens, ed., *The Colonial South Carolina Scene, Contemporary Views, 1697–1774* (Columbia: University of South Carolina Press, 1977), 145–146. For a contemporary account of growing indigo, see 146–160.

21. *Further Observations Intended for Improving the Culture and Curing of Indigo, etc. in South-Carolina* (London, 1747), as cited in Merrens, *The Colonial South Carolina Scene,* 157.

22. The inventory of James Armstrong, Dec. 7, 1751, lists indigo and provisions valued at 162 pounds 10 pence. The inventory of John Fleming, April 6, 1751, mentions "Indigo boxes." Charleston Inventories, Book R(1), 152; Book B, 47; SCDAH.

23. Boddie, *History of Williamsburg,* 42.

24. Boddie, *History of Williamsburg,* 89–90. In 1786, an English visitor to Sierra Leone wrote, "The best indigo in the world, if we may judge from the deep indelible blues the natives give their cloths, grows wild in every part of the country: and the Portuguese, when settled here, had large indigo works in several places, the ruins of which are still remaining." See John Matthews, *A Voyage to the River Sierra-Leone* (London: B. White and Son, 1788. Reprint. London: Frank Cass and Company Limited, 1966), 52; See also: Daniel Littlefield, *Rice and Slaves* (Baton Rouge: Louisiana State University Press, 1981), 76. Littlefield cites a report of indigo in the Senegal-Gambia region in 1749.

25. Merrens, *The Colonial South Carolina Scene,* 155–157.

26. John J. Winberry, "Indigo in South Carolina: A Historical Geography," *Southeastern Geographer,* XIX, No. 2 (Nov. 1979), 96.

27. Boddie, *History of Williamsburg,* 43.

28. Merrens, *The Colonial South Carolina Scene,,* 128; Charleston Inventories, Book X, 428, South Carolina Department of Archives and History. Colonial currency was worth approximately one-seventh of the British pound sterling. Walter Edgar estimated that the salary of the colonial governor in 1760, £1500 sterling, would be worth $126,000 in modern money. The personal estate of £5028 colonial would convert to £718 sterling or less than half of $126,000 or roughly $60,000. The value of the land is difficult to estimate without knowing the extent of cultivation or improvements. Information on the land comes from Colonial Plats, 3: 182; Royal Grants, 34: 412. See Walter Edgar, *South*

Carolina: A History (Columbia: University of South Carolina Press, 1998), 11–114, notes 15 and 18. The Thorntree House has been moved from its original location near Salters to Kingstree. It was restored by the local historical society and is open to the public.

29. Laurens, Letter Books, June 30, July 2, 31, 1755; as cited in Meriwether, *The Expansion of South Carolina, 1729–1765,* 83. Meriwether notes that the militia census of 1757 lists 155 male slaves from 16 to 60 years of age, indicating a total for the township of over six hundred.

30. Journal of the Council, May 4, 1737; as cited in Meriwether, *The Expansion of South Carolina, 1729–1765,* 84.

31. Robert Meriwether noted that the establishing of a Presbyterian church in Kingston was an indication that a number of the Scotch-Irish settled there. Meriwether, *The Expansion of South Carolina, 1729–1765,* 87.

32. Meriwether, *The Expansion of South Carolina, 1729–1765,* 80–81.

33. George Howe, *The History of the Presbyterian Church in South Carolina* (Columbia: Duffie and Chapman, 1870), I: 282–283. See also: Harvey Toliver Cook, *Rambles in the Pee Dee Basin South Carolina* (Columbia: The State Company, 1926), 118. A letter from Thomas Morritt to Rev. Mr. Humphreys, Secretary of the Society for the Propagation of the Gospel, Feb. 3, 1727, mentions a meeting house erected by Anabaptists and dissenters.

34. Boddie, *History of Williamsburg,* 45–47.

35. Wardlaw, *Genealogy of the Witherspoon Family,* 12.

36. Boddie, *History of Williamsburg,* 47–48.

37. Richard J. Hooker, ed., *The Carolina Backcountry on the Eve of the Revolution: The Journal and Other Writings of Charles Woodmason, Anglican Itinerant* (Chapel Hill: Published for the Institute of Early American History and Culture at Williamsburg, Virginia by the University of North Carolina Press, 1953), 134–135, 198. On July 8, 1761, Rachel Rae put up for sale "Some black cattle, horses, household furniture and a choice library of books." See Cook, 152. Woodmason stated further (135) that the widow married the pastor who succeeded her husband.

38. "Ancient Records," *Southern Presbyterian,* February 22, 1850, 136.

39. William H. Chandler, "Religion and Churches in Williamsburg County, South Carolina 1726–1850," unpublished MS. Chandler is an attorney in Hemingway, South Carolina.

40. Historian William Boddie stated, "Not more than one man out of the first one hundred wills and transfers of property made and recorded between 1765 and 1775 had to make his mark, nor did a greater per centum of women releasing rights fail to write legibly their names. Out of more than three hundred of Marion's Men from Williamsburg who filed their statements for pay, only six made their marks where they should have signed their names." See Boddie, *History of Williamsburg,* 91. For regulation regarding schoolmasters, see Public Records of South Carolina, British Public Records Office MS, SCDAH, XIV: 196.

41. Hooker, *The Carolina Backcountry on the Eve of the Revolution,* 98–101, 118.

42. Ibid., 123.

43. Meriwether, *The Expansion of South Carolina, 1729–1765,* 83–84.

CHAPTER 6

1. South Carolina Colonial Plats, I, 512; II, 160, 172, 427; as cited in Robert L. Meriwether, *The Expansion of South Carolina, 1729–1765* (Kingsport, Tennessee: Southern Publishers, Inc., 1940), 89.

2. Robert K. Ackerman, *South Carolina Colonial Land Policies* (Columbia: University of South Carolina Press, 1977), 94, 95, 97, 99.

3. Commons House Journal, November 17, December 6, 1733; Council Journal, March 7, 29, 1735; as cited in Meriwether, *The Expansion of South Carolina, 1729–1765,* 89.

4. Combined Alphabetical Index, 25579–25580, South Carolina Department of Archives and History.

5. Combined Alphabetical Index, 25582.

6. Meriwether, *The Expansion of South Carolina, 1729–1765,* 89, 91; Meriwether lists Gordon's acreage at 3100 acres, but the author could locate only 3000 in the Combined Alphabetical Index. George Rogers, Jr., *The History of Georgetown County, South Carolina* (Columbia: University of South Carolina Press, 1970), 35; Harvey Toliver Cook, *Rambles in the Pee Dee Basin, South Carolina* (Columbia: The State Company, 1926), 32. For biographical information on Lewis, see: Walter B. Edgar and N. Louise Bailey, eds., *Biographical Directory of the South Carolina House of Representatives, The Commons House of Assembly,* Vol. II, 1692–1795 (Columbia: University of South Carolina Press, 1977), 228.

7. Combined Alphabetical Index, 25579, 25581, SCDAH; Council Journal, March 16, 1731, as cited in Alexander Gregg, *History of the Old Cheraws* (New York: Richardson and Company, 1867. Reprint Spartanburg, S. C.: The Reprint Company, 1982), 43.

8. Council Journal, September 16, 1738; Combined Alphabetical Index, 25579, 25581. Gregg, 76, gives nationality of Buckholt. A creek near Society Hill is named for the family that included Abraham and Peter in addition to Jacob. Gregg said, "They were men of enterprise, but of a roving disposition, and left the Pedee at an early period."

9. During the Revolution, "Swamp Fox" Francis Marion would make use of this area to hide from the British. His famous hideout was at Snows Island at the intersection of Lynches River with the Pee Dee. See Robert D. Bass, *Swamp Fox* (London: Alvin Redman Limited, 1960), 104.

10. Meriwether, *The Expansion of South Carolina, 1729–1765*, 89–90.

11. Edgar and Bailey, *Biographical Directory* , 228; Meriwether, *The Expansion of South Carolina, 1729–1765*, 91.

12. Council Journal, August 13, 1736, in Brent Holcomb, ed., *Petitions for Land from the South Carolina Council Journals*, I: 1734/5–1748 (Columbia: SCMAR, 1996), 53. "The nearest tributary of the Peedee that could be called its main branch was Little River, seventy miles north of Queensboro and twenty miles beyond the North Carolina line as later surveyed." Meriwether, *The Expansion of South Carolina, 1729–1765*, 91. Gregg, *History of the Old Cheraws* (50), thought the reference was to the Rocky River or the Uwharrie, both of which intersect the Pee Dee in North Carolina.

13. Council Journal November 16, 1736, as cited in Gregg, *History of the Old Cheraws*, 47.

14. Gregg, *History of the Old Cheraws*, 50.

15. *Records of the Welsh Tract Baptist Meeting, Pencader Hundred, Newcastle County, Delaware, 1701–1728* (Wilmington, Delaware: 1904), 17; See also Leah Townsend, South Carolina Baptists (Florence, South Carolina: The Florence Printing Company, 1935), 61–63. Townsend gives other names who immigrated at later dates. See South Carolina Colonial Plats, III: 375, 412; as cited in Meriwether, *The Expansion of South Carolina, 1729–1765*, 91.

16. Meriwether, *The Expansion of South Carolina, 1729–1765*, 92. Meriwether lists Griffith John, but the Alphabetical Index lists Griffith Jones, which agrees with the church list in Townsend, 62. The Alphabetical Index does not confirm Thomas Evans's plat.

17. Gregg states that the Welsh settled first at Catfish and then moved up the river to the Welsh Neck. See Gregg, *History of the Old Cheraws*, 51. Meriwether, however, shows that there was no general removal. See Meriwether, *The Expansion of South Carolina, 1729–1765*, 92, and n. 13: South Carolina Colonial Plats, IV: 145–146, 188–189, 297.

18. Bureau of Soils, Marlboro, 59, and South Carolina Colonial Plats, IV: 187, 190–194, 394; XVII, 228, as cited in Meriwether, *The Expansion of South Carolina, 1729–1765*, 92.

19. Combined Alphabetical Index, 33046.

20. Meriwether, *The Expansion of South Carolina, 1729–1765*, 92–93. Thomas Elerby [later Ellerbe] was an Englishman who came from Virginia. Roderick McIver and John Macintosh were Scots. James Gillespie was Scots-Irish; Francis Young was supposed Irish; and Claudius Pegues was French Huguenot. See Gregg, *History of the Old Cheraws*, 63, 88, 89, 61–62, 94–95.

21. Journal of the Commons House of Assembly, January 26, 1737/8, 430.

22. Some of the Cheraws had joined the Catawba. See James Adair, *History of the American Indians* (London: 1775), 224; Council Journal, June 8, 1739, SCDAH. David J. McCord, *The Statutes at Large of South Carolina* (Columbia: A. S. Johnston, 1840), III: 525; hereinafter cited as *Statutes*.

23. Council Journal, July 5, December 15, 1742; November 9, 1743, as cited in Brent H. Holcomb, *Petitions for Land from the South Carolina Council Journals*, I: 1734/5–1748 (Columbia: SCMAR, 1996), 152, 159. Other non-Welsh were Daniel Manahan, James Jones, William Smith, and William Hemsworth. Council Journal, February 14, 1745/6; December 15, 1742; March 12, 1745/6, in Holcomb, 246, 159, 252.

24. Council Journal of September 16, 1736, authorized Gillespie to trade with the Cherokee. Appointment as deputy surveyor, Secretary of State, Recorded Instruments, Miscellaneous Records, 2-D, 187, March 24, 1735. Gillespie was a Justice of the Peace in 1750 when he petitioned for help, stating that he and militia captain William James were the only magistrates within a hundred miles, and some of the settlers were "Living very Riotous." Council Journal, May 29, 1750. Deed, Provost Marshall to Christopher Gadsden, Charleston Deeds, TT: 85. The deed was for 1280 acres, but in the new survey, the plat showed 1300 acres. Colonial Plats, 6: 213; caption reads: "I have admeasured unto Christopher Gadsden a tract of thirteen hundred acres of land in Craven county on the S. W. side of Pee Dee River Bounded N'wardly by James Gillespies land, and SE'ly by Nicholas Roger's land, Nerd on said Pee Dee River, SW by vacant land: And hath such shape, form and marks as the above plat represents which tract is supposed to contain about four hundred plantable acres. Certified the 15th day of April 1757. John Wade D.S. [Deputy Surveyor]" The boundary between North and South Carolina was unclear. James Gillespie received a patent for 1280 acres and another for 200 acres in Anson County, North Carolina on October 2, 1751. The question arises if this land was actually in South Carolina. *Colonial Records of North Carolina*, William Saunders, ed., IV: 1047; 1251. See also: Gregg, *History of the Old Cheraws*, 62; Meriwether, *The Expansion of South Carolina*, 95; Richard Walsh, ed., *The Writings of Christopher Gadsden* (Columbia: University of South Carolina Press, 1966), xvii, 311; Christopher Gadsden *vs.* William Terrill [regarding debt], Court of Common Pleas, #195A (1762). Advertisement, *South Carolina Gazette*, March 14, 1761.

25. Council Journal, July 7, 1739, SCDAH.

26. Council Journal, Jan. 26, 1743; as cited in Gregg, 58–59.

27. Gregg, *History of the Old Cheraws*, 109–110; See deed of Joseph Holland to Gideon Gibson, Miscellaneous Records, WPA Transcripts, Vol. 86 (1758–1763), 1052–1053, SCDAH; Holland "Doth bargain and Sell and in open market deliver unto him the said Gideon Gibson All that parcel or Stock of Cattle I am now possessed with Containing Fifty Head Rainging near Peedee River and Jeffreses Creek marked with same thereof with an under Square in one Ear and two under half penny's in the other . . . some branded thus H with fifty head of Swine marked with a Crop and under bit in one Ear other whole with Eight head of horse kind sume thereof branded thus H others thus 3. . . ."

28. "Records of Welsh Neck Baptist Church, 1737–1935," Typed transcript, South Caroliniana Library, University of South Carolina, 1.

29. Charleston Inventories, Book T, 486–487; SCDAH.

30. The author visited the Calvert Marine Museum, Solomons, Maryland, which provides an exhibit illustrating the process of caulking with oakum. For a definition of oakum, see Clarence L. Barnhart, ed., *The World Book Dictionary* (Chicago: Field Interprises Educational Corporation, 1972), 1416.

31. Charleston Inventories, Book X, 408.

32. Charleston Wills, Will Book TT, 11–12; Charleston Inventories, Vol. AA, 6–10; SCDAH.

33. "Diary of Evan Pugh," Transcript in Darlington County Historical Commission. Hereinafter cited as Pugh Diary. Pugh mentions the following crops: corn—May 30, 1791; indigo—May 20, 1788, rice—May 3, 1777, flax—October 2, 1781, wheat—July 22, 1791. The author worked from the typescript, but the diaries have since been published. Horace F. Rudisill, ed., *The Diaries of Evan Pugh, 1762–1801* (Florence, SC: St. David's Society, 1993). For biographical information on Pugh, see Eliza Cowan Ervin and Horace Fraser Rudisill, *Darlingtoniana* (Columbia: R. L. Bryan Company, 1964), 257–259.

34. Rachel N. Klein, *Unification of a Slave State: The Rise of the Planter Class in the South Carolina Backcountry, 1760–1808* (Chapel Hill: University of North Carolina Press, 1990), 5.

35. Klein, *Unification of a Slave State,* 50–51, 67n.

36. For extensive treatment of the Regulator Movement, see Gregg, Chapter VII; Richard Maxwell Brown, *The South Carolina Regulators* (Cambridge, Massachusetts: The Belknap Press of Harvard University Press, 1963); Klein, *Unification of a Slave State,* 64–77. The Regulator documents are published in Richard J. Hooker, ed. *The Carolina Backcountry on the Eve of the Revolution* (Chapel Hill: University of North Carolina Press, 1953).

37. Townsend, *South Carolina Baptists,* 68. Pugh's journal records attending meetings of the Regulators. See Gregg, 151n. Townsend suggests that association with the Regulators may have been the reason for dislike of Pugh, but Rachel Klein (*Unification of a Slave State* 67, n. 44) notes that a number of leading regulators had close ties to the Welsh Neck and Cashaway Baptist Churches.

38. Pugh Diary, June 9 and 10, 1762. Pugh "lay in the woods" on a trip to the Yadkin from the Welsh Neck. Ervin and Rudisill, 257.

39. Pugh Diary, May 16, August 11, 28, 1766; October 19, 25, 1768. See also: Suzanne C. Linder, *Medicine in Marlboro County, 1736 to 1980* (Baltimore, Maryland: Gateway Press, Inc., 1980), 2.

40. "Diary of Evan Pugh," Notes at end of 1762, 1770, and 1773.

41. "Records of Welsh Neck Baptist Church," July 1, April 5, 1759; May 1, 1819; October 6, 1820; December 23, 1817; and passim. The Cashaway Baptist Church Book, 6, June, 1770, recorded, "William Owens lodged a complaint against Big Benjamin James for having sold a mare to him but would not deliver the mare, the matter was settled between them by the church. . . ." See "Cashaway Baptist Church Book," Transcript, South Caroliniana Library, University of South Carolina.

42. "Records of the Welsh Neck Baptist Church," October 6, 1759, and "Cashaway Baptist Church Book," September 12, 1759. Transcripts, South Caroliniana Library.

43. Richard K. Showman, ed., *The Papers of General Nathanael Greene* (Chapel Hill: University of North Carolina Press, 1991.), VI: xvii–xviii; Nathanael Greene to Thomas Jefferson, Dec. 6, 1780, VI: 513.

44. George Washington to Nathanael Greene, Nov. 8, 1780, as cited in Showman, *The Papers of General Nathanael Greene,* VI: 470. Washington also wrote to Thomas Jefferson about having similar boats built in Virginia. He said, "Major General Greene is perfectly acquainted with the kind of Boats I have mentioned, and with the mode of fixing them." Washington wrote to Major General William Heath on Dec. 19, 1780, requesting a written description of such "flat-bottomed boats as are most convenient to be transported on carriages . . . two things are to govern; convenience of the Men, and the transportation of the Boats on Wheels. Then, on December 27, Washington sent the dimensions of "the most convenient Flat Boats, either for transportation upon carriages, or for transporting Men." Unfortunately, the dimensions are not included in either the Washington Papers or the Jefferson Papers. See John C. Fitzpatrick, ed., *The Writings of George Washington, from the Original Manuscript Sources, 1745–1799* (Washington: U. S. Government Printing Office, 1931–1944), Washington to Jefferson, Nov. 8, 1780, 20: 326–327; Washington to Heath, Dec. 19, 1780, 20: 447; Washington to Jefferson, Dec. 27, 1780, 21: 21.

45. Nathanael Greene to Edward Stevens, Dec. 1, 1780; Showman, *The Papers of General Nathanael Greene,* VI: 512–513. Batteaus, also known as "mountain boats," were used to haul heavy loads over rapids in rivers. They were approximately 56 feet long by 6.5 to 7.5 feet wide with pointed ends, shallow draft, and a rudder attached to a long pole. See Mark M. Newell, *The Santee Canal Sanctuary* (Columbia: University of South Carolina, Underwater Antiquities Management Program of the Institute of Archaeology and Anthropology, September, 1989) Part II, 60–61. The term "batteau" was also applied to much smaller vessels. It is impossible to determine exactly what Greene had in mind. Greene also had Colonel Thaddeus Kosciuszko survey the Catawba River. Green to Kosciuszko, Dec. 3, 1780; Showman, VI, 515.

46. Greene to Stevens, Dec. 1, 1780; Showman, *The Papers of General Nathanael Greene,* VI: 513.

47. Nathanael Greene to Thomas Jefferson, Dec. 6, 1780; Showman, *The Papers of General Nathanael Greene,* VI: 530–531.

48. Showman, *The Papers of General Nathanael Greene,* VI: 578.

49. Gregg, *History of the Old Cheraws,* 352–353.

50. Nathanael Green to General [Alexander] Lillington, January 16, 1781, Greene Letterbook, MS, Library of Congress, MFM, South Caroliniana Library.

51. Nathanael Greene to Daniel Morgan, Dec. 16, 1780; Showman, *The Papers of General Nathanael Greene,* VI: 589–590.

52. Elswyth Thane, *The Fighting Quaker: Nathanael Greene* (New York: Hawthorn Books, Inc., 1964), 193.

53. Nathanael Greene to Morgan Brown, Jan. 2, 1781; Greene Letterbook, Brown later represented the St. David's Parish in the state legislature both as a representative and a senator. In 1791 he was a county court judge for Marlboro County. See Gregg, *History of the Old Cheraws*, 445–446, 448, 452.

54. Nathanael Greene to Henry Lee, Jan 26, 1781; Henry Lee, *The Campaign of 1781 in the Carolinas* (Philadelphia: E. Littell, 1824. Reprint Spartanburg, S. C.: The Reprint Company, 1975), Appendix, viii.

55. Major Ichabod Burnet to John Ingram, Irvin's Ferry, Virginia, February 15, 1781, Clements Library, University of Michigan. John Ingram was assistant commissary of issues at Cross Creek [now Fayetteville, North Carolina], and Ichabod Burnet was aide to Nathanael Greene. See Showman, *The Papers of Nathanael Greene*, VI: 603n, 431n.

56. Nathanael Greene to Daniel Morgan, January 19, 1781, Greene Letterbook.

57. Thane, *The Fighting Quaker: Nathanael Greene,* 202. Thane gives the date of Cowpens as Jan. 19 [200].

58. Thane, *The Fighting Quaker: Nathanael Greene,* 204.

59. Colonel Thomas Wade of Anson County, North Carolina, had previously [1761–1774] owned land on Lynches River, a tributary of the Pee Dee. His name appears in Anson County deeds on July 15, 1770. He was colonel of the Salisbury District minutemen and later colonel of militia. He served as commissary general of purchase in South Carolina. After the Revolution, the county seat of Anson County was named Wadesboro in his honor. Streets were named for other Revolutionary heroes, including Nathanael Greene. Wade reportedly sought to build three hundred flat-bottomed boats. See Mary L. Medley, *History of Anson County, North Carolina, 1750–1976* (Wadesboro, North Carolina: Anson County Historical Society, 1976), 40–41, 44, 66.

60. Colonel Lewis Morris, Jr., to Colonel Thaddeus Kosciuszko, Feb. 1, 1781, George W. Greene Transcript, Huntington Library. "Artificers" are skilled craftsmen, possibly boat builders.

61. Thane, *The Fighting Quaker: Nathanael Greene,* 207–208.

62. Thane, *The Fighting Quaker: Nathanael Greene,* 212. Thane calls Greene the victor [218], while Henry Lumpkin calls Cornwallis the victor. Henry Lumpkin, *From Savannah to Yorktown* (New York: Paragon, 1981), 175.

63. N. Louise Bailey and Elizabeth Cooper, *Biographical Directory of the South Carolina House of Representatives* (Columbia: University of South Carolina Press, 1981), BDHR, III: 477–479.

64. See Robert D. Bass, *Swamp Fox* (London: Alvin Redman Limited, 1960), 104 and passim.

65. Chris Horn, "20th Century Fox Hunt," *Carolina: The University of South Carolina Magazine* (October 1994), IV: 5.

66. Horn, "20th Century Fox Hunt," 6.

67. Deed from William Pegues to Achilles Knight, Marlboro County Deed Book F, 227; Marlboro Estate Papers, Office of Judge of Probate, Box E, No. 1; also copied in Book A, No. 3, 237. Marlboro County Courthouse, Bennettsville, South Carolina.

68. Stephen Parker had both a father and a son named Elisha. Gregg, 98; and Will of Stephen Parker, Marlboro County Estate Papers, Box 17, No. 9, Office of Judge of Probate, Bennettsville, South Carolina. Because of the date, it is more likely that this Elisha was the son. The names of Elisha Parker and wife Elizabeth appear in the records of the Pine Grove Monthly Meeting of the Society of Friends, which met in Marlboro County from about 1755 to 1815. The meeting was discontinued because so many members had moved west in opposition to slavery. Achilles Knight is not specifically mentioned, but there are several Knights listed. See William Wade Hinshaw, *Encyclopedia of American Quaker Genealogy* (Ann Arbor, Michigan: Edwards Brothers, Inc., 1936), I: 832, 1065, 1070.

69. Will of Stephen Parker, Marlboro County Estate Papers, Box 17, No. 9. Cannon and Massey Weaver moved in 1828 through Tennessee into Monroe County, Mississippi, where Cannon earned a living as a wagon maker. Ray L. Weaver (a descendant) to the author, June 23, 1992.

70. Colonial Plats, I: 77.

71. Gregg, 98; Brent H. Holcomb, ed., *Marlboro County, South Carolina, Minutes of the County Court, 1785–1799, and Minutes of the Court of Ordinary, 1791–1821* (Easley, South Carolina: Southern Historical Press, 1981), 33, 54.

72. Thomas Cooper and David J. McCord, eds., *The Statutes at Large of South Carolina* (Columbia: 1836–1841), IX: 144; hereinafter cited as *Statutes.*

73. Ibid., 145–146.

74. Ibid., 211–212.

75. Ibid., 223–224.

76. Daniel B. Thorpe, "Taverns and Tavern Culture on the Southern Colonial Frontier: Rowan County, North Carolina, 1753–1776," *The Journal of Southern History,* LXII: 663.

77. Ibid., 674.

78. Ibid., 681.

79. *Statutes*, IX: 258, 372. The first mention of the Cheraw Ferry was in 1784 when Thomas Lyde was licensed. (286). Kershaw's Ferry, however, operated at that location during the Revolution. See Showman, *The Papers of Nathanael Greene*, map 8, back endpaper. Other ferries that may have operated earlier were officially sanctioned by the legislature: Gallivant's Ferry on the Little Pee Dee at Ellerslie's Landing in 1792 (350); Cashua Ferry, near Brownsville in Marlboro County in 1792 (354); a ferry over the Little Pee Dee at the plantation of Stephen Gibson in 1792 (353); a ferry over Lynch's Creek at the mouth of Sparrow's swamp on land belonging to Robert Nettles, Jr. in 1789 (322); a ferry over the Pee Dee near Jeffries Creek operated by Joseph Burch in 1792 (247). For location of Ports Ferry and Burch's Ferry, see Robert Mills, *Atlas*

of the State of South Carolina, Facsimile of 1825 edition (Easley, South Carolina: Southern Historical Press, 1990), Marion District, n.p. (Districts are listed alphabetically).

80. Statutes, VII: 489, 532, 538–539, 584–586.

81. Loulie L. Owens, *Saints of Clay: The Shaping of South Carolina Baptists* (Columbia: South Carolina Baptist Convention, 1971), 30.

82. Horace Fraser Rudisill, ed., *Minutes of Saint David's Society (1771–1835)* (Florence, South Carolina: The Saint David's Society, 1986), i–iv, 1–2.

83. Rudisill, ed., *Minutes*, iii–iv.

84. For a discussion of partisan fighting in the Pee Dee, see Gregg, *History of the Old Cheraws*, 300–414, passim.

85. The author has visited the Pegues Place and the Robertson home. For the story of Poelnitz, see James A. Rogers, *Theodosia and other Pee Dee Sketches* (Columbia: R. L. Bryan Company, 1978), 134–139.

SIDE BAR CHAPTER 6

1. Thomas Cooper, ed., *Statutes at Large of South Carolina* (Columbia: A.S. Johnston, 1838), IV: 300.

2. Rudisill, ed., *Minutes*, April 12, 1773, 13.

3. Alexander Gregg, *History of the Old Cheraws* (New York: Richardson and Company, 1867. Reprint Spartanburg, South Carolina: The Reprint Company, 1982), 52, 77.

4. Walter B. Edgar and N. Louise Bailey, *Biographical Directory of the South Carolina House of Representatives* (Columbia: *The Expansion of South Carolina, 1729–1765*, University of South Carolina Press, 1977), II: 514–515.

5. See Suzanne Linder, *Anglican Churches in Colonial South Carolina* (Charleston: Wyrick and Company, 2000), passim.

CHAPTER 7

1. These generalizations will be documented below.

2. William H. Foote, *Sketches of North Carolina* (New York: Robert Carter, 1846), 187–188.

3. Kenneth P. Bailey, *Christopher Gist* (Hamden, Connecticut: Archon Books, 1976), 23–24.

4. James S. Brawley, *Rowan County: A Brief History* (Raleigh: North Carolina Department of Cultural Resources, 1974), 3.

5. *The Colonial Records of North Carolina* (Raleigh, Department of Cultural Resources, 1988), IV: xxi; V: 24–25 as cited in Samuel J. Ervin, Jr., *A Colonial History of Rowan County, North Carolina*, The James Sprunt Historical Publications, 16 (Chapel Hill: University of North Carolina Press, 1917), 12.

6. *The Colonial Records of North Carolina*, IV: 1073–74.

7. "Germans" refers to people who spoke the German language. In the eighteenth century, there were numerous German states. Germany was not consolidated until the nineteenth century.

8. Robert W. Ramsey, *Carolina Cradle* (Chapel Hill: University of North Carolina Press, 1964), 10, 17. Ramsey [18] found that in 1750, a 50-acre farm in Pennsylvania would sell for £7 10s whereas in the Granville district of North Carolina land was selling in 1753 at the rate of 5s. per hundred acres regardless of acreage. See also Carl Hammer, Jr., *Rhinelanders on the Yadkin: The Story of the Pennsylvania Germans in Rowan and Cabarrus* (Salisbury, N. C.: Rowan Printing Company, 1943), 25. Indian attacks caused severe losses in Augusta County, Virginia, in 1745. See Lyman Chalkley, ed., *Chronicles of the Scotch-Irish Settlements in Virginia Extracted from the Original Court Records of Augusta County, 1745–1800*, 3 vols. (Rosslyn, Virginia: Commonwealth Printing Company, 1912), I: 15.

9. Ramsey, *Carolina Cradle*, 21–22. Ramsey studied county records, particularly will books, and found numerous examples of movement of families immediately after the death of the patriarch. He stated, "There can be no doubt that the patriarchal position of the father in colonial America was a powerful controlling factor in the westward—and southward—movement of population."

10. James G. Leyburn, *The Scotch-Irish* (Chapel Hill: University of North Carolina Press, 1962), 215.

11. The elder McCulloh did not come to North Carolina. Until his death he resided at Turnham Green, Essex. Ramsey, 93; James G. Leyburn, *The Scotch-Irish* (Chapel Hill: University of North Carolina Press, 1962), 213.

12. Robert J. Cain, ed., *Records of the Executive Council, 1735–1754, The Colonial Records of North Carolina*, VII: xxiii; Hugh Talmage Lefler and Albert Ray Newsome, *North Carolina* (Chapel Hill: University of North Carolina Press, 1973), 156–157. "Proclamation money" was local Carolina currency worth about $1/7$ of the British pound sterling.

13. *The Colonial Records of North Carolina*, IV: 1086. For a thorough treatment of McCulloh's land dealings in America, see Charles G. Sellers, Jr., "Private Profits and British Colonial Policy: The Speculations of Henry McCulloh," *William and Mary Quarterly*, Third Series (October, 1951), VIII: 535–551.

14. The map was originally drawn in 1751. Additions to the western part of the 1755 edition indicate how rapid settlement increased geographical knowledge. William P. Cumming, *The Southeast in Early Maps* (Chapel Hill: University of North Carolina Press, 1962), 52–53; Plates 57, 58; Carl Bridenbaugh, *Myths and Realities* (New York: Atheneum, 1952), 129.

15. To review the story see page 52 of this book.

16. Harriette Simpson Arnow, *Seedtime on the Cumberland* (New York: Macmillan, 1960), 104–105, 171.

17. Land Grant Records of North Carolina, Office of the Secretary of State, Raleigh, Land Grant Book VI: 114, as cited in Robert W. Ramsey, "James Carter: Founder of Salisbury," *North Carolina Historical Review* (Spring, 1962), XXXIX: 132.

18. "An Account of Claims Laid on the County of Rowan for the Year 1764," Rowan County Court Minutes, 1755–1767, 551–552. One of the recipients of a bounty of 10s. for a wolf was Daniel Boone.

19. R. B. Hardison and R. C. Jurney, *Soil Survey of Rowan County, North Carolina* (Washington, D. C.: Government Printing Office, 1915), 23–25, 27–33, 47, as cited in Ramsey, 151.

20. In present-day Czechoslovakia.

21. Daniel B. Thorp, *The Moravian Community in Colonial North Carolina* (Knoxville: The University of Tennessee Press, 1989), 11, 23, 29. There was a colony of Moravians already established at Bethlehem, Pennsylvania, but this was a proprietary colony where William Penn had established freedom of religion.

22. Spangenberg to White, Jan. 17, 1754; and Spangenberg to van Laer, Jan. 22, 1754, Library of Congress, Moravian Church Records, R. 14.Ba.Nr.2b: 117, and R.14.Ba.Nr.2b: 124–127, as cited in Thorp, *The Moravian Community*, 24.

23. Ibid., 26–28.

24. Ibid., 29.

25. Adelaide L. Fries, ed., "The Spangenberg Diary," *Records of the Moravians in North Carolina* (Raleigh: North Carolina Historical Commission, 1922), 40, 55.

26. Ibid., 59.

27. Joffre Lanning Coe, "The Formative Cultures of the Carolina Piedmont," *Transactions of the American Philosophical Society*, 54, Part 5 (1964), 14.

28. Fries, ed., *Records of the Moravians*, 59–60.

29. Ramsey, *Carolina Cradle*, 192.

30. Thorp, *The Moravian Community*, 81, 41, 71–72.

31. Fries, *Records of the Moravians*, I: 73–75.

32. Ibid., 74, 79.

33. Hugh T. Lefler and Albert Ray Newsome, *North Carolina, the History of a Southern State* (Chapel Hill: University of North Carolina Press, 1973), 87.

34. Fries, *Records of the Moravians*, I: 104–105, 234; Philip M. Hamer and George C. Rogers, Jr., eds., *The Papers of Henry Laurens* (Columbia: University of South Carolina Press, 1972), 56.

35. Rowan Court Minutes, I: 37, 59; Rowan County Deed Books, III: 395, as cited in Ramsey, 173.

36. "Journal of an Officer, who travelled over a part of the West Indies and of North America in the Course of 1764 & 1765," King's Mss. 213, British Library, London, in British Records (MFM Reel Z.5.162p.), North Carolina State Archives, Raleigh, North Carolina.

37. H. Roy Merrens, *Colonial North Carolina in the Eighteenth Century: A Study in Historical Geography* (Chapel Hill: University of North Carolina Press, 1964), 72.

38. Rowan Court Minutes, I: 34.

39. Land Grant Records of North Carolina, Office of the Secretary of State, Raleigh, Land Grant Book VI: 114, as cited in Robert W. Ramsey, "James Carter: Founder of Salisbury," *North Carolina Historical Review* (Spring, 1962), XXXIX: 132.

40. *Colonial Records of North Carolina*, V: 355–356.

41. Ibid., 355.

42. Rowan Court Minutes, I: 5.

43. *Colonial Records of North Carolina*, V: 357.

44. Taxables were described by an act of the Assembly of 1749 as all white males over sixteen, all Negroes and mulattoes over twelve, and all white persons over twelve who intermarried with Negroes. Walter Clark, ed., *The State Records of North Carolina* (Winston, Goldsboro, and Raleigh: State of North Carolina, 1895–1914), XXIII: 345. In the absence of census records, tax records offer some indication of demographic changes.

45. Ramsey, *Carolina Cradle*, 193.

46. The Dunkards were also German pietists. They practiced baptism by immersing communicants three times, and also practiced footwashing and the lovefeast. Today the denomination is "Church of the Brethren." See William Bridgwater and Seymour Kurtz, eds., *The Columbia Encyclopedia* (New York and London: Columbia University Press, 1963), 269.

47. Fries, *Records of the Moravians*, I: 133–134.

48. Ibid., 134.

49. Possibly a relative of Christopher Gist. The Gist home was near present-day Wilkesboro, North Carolina, at the point where the Yadkin River is closest to Virginia, therefore on the extreme frontier at that time. Christopher Gist had left North Carolina for the Ohio country by

1752. See Bailey, *Christopher Gist*, 24, 62. A man they called Guest had befriended the Moravians on several occasions. See Fries, *Records of the Moravians*, I: 110, 85, 102.

50. Fries, *Records of the Moravians*, I: 169–171. For further information on Bethabara see: Stanley South, *Historical Archaeology in Wachovia: Excavating Eighteenth-Century Bethabara and Moravian Pottery* (New York: Kluwer Academic/Plenum, 1999).

51. Fries, *Records of the Moravians*, I: 171; Brawley, *Rowan County*, 9.

52. Ervin, *A Colonial History*, 28–29; Fries, *Records of the Moravians*, I: 210.

53. Fries, *Records of the Moravians*, I: 227, 230, 232, 211, 274. On December 24, 1756, "The watch Meeting began at 10 o'clock, eight musicians leading the congregation [with their instruments.]" For an account of Attakullakulla's career as a diplomat, see Harriet Simpson Arnow, *Seedtime on the Cumberland* (New York: The Macmillan Company, 1960), 172–202.

54. Fries, *Records of the Moravians*, I, 233; South, *Historical Archaeology*, 46.

55. David Duncan Wallace, *South Carolina: A Short History* (Columbia: University of South Carolina Press, 1951), 179–181.

56. Merrens, *Colonial North Carolina*, 54.

57. Brawley, *Rowan County*, 2, 12–13.

58. Rowan Deeds, IV: 241, 763; V: 307, 308, as cited in Ramsey, *Carolina Cradle*, 168–169. In 1763, Elizabeth Gillespie married William Steele of Lancaster County, Pennsylvania. Their son, John Steele, became a prominent North Carolinian, served in Congress, and was appointed the first Comptroller of the Treasury of the United States. Margaret Gillespie, daughter of Elizabeth by her first husband, married Samuel E. McCorkle, a co-founder of the University of North Carolina.

59. Johanna Miller Lewis, "Women Artisans in Backcountry North Carolina, 1753–1790," *North Carolina Historical Review* (July, 1991), LXVIII: 231.

60. See Julia Cherry Spruill, *Women's Life and Work in the Southern Colonies* (Chapel Hill: University of North Carolina Press, 1938), 81; Carl Bridenbaugh, *The Colonial Craftsman* (Chicago: University of Chicago Press, 1950), 1–32, passim; Hugh Talmage Lefler and Albert Ray Newsome, *North Carolina: The History of a Southern State* (Chapel Hill: University of North Carolina Press, third edition, 1973), 122, as cited in Lewis, "Women Artisans," 215–216.

61. Lewis, "Women Artisans," 232–235.

62. Rowan County Apprentice Bonds, April 15, 1781, March 1, 1785, as cited in Lewis, "Women Artisans," 227.

63. Lefler and Newsome, *North Carolina*, 128.

64. In his study of the Carolina frontier from 1747–1762, Robert Ramsey identified 36 persons who owned between one and four slaves. Ramsey, *Carolina Cradle*, 176–178. Sam, a slave, was admitted into the Moravian congregation in 1771. Between March and October of that year the Moravians bought four additional slaves. They also leased slaves from time to time. See Thorp, *The Moravian Community*, 54–56.

65. Lefler and Newsome, *North Carolina*, 129.

66. Merrens, *Colonial North Carolina*, 176.

67. Brawley, *Rowan County*, 16.

68. Hugh T. Lefler and William S. Powell, *Colonial North Carolina* (New York: Charles Scribner's Sons, 1973), 220–222.

69. Ibid., 222–223. The earliest printed version of the ballad dates from 1826.

70. Brawley, *Rowan County*, 16–18.

71. Brawley, *Rowan County*, 22. James Mooney, *Myths of the Cherokee* (New York: Johnson Reprint Company, 1970), 48–50.

72. Elizabeth Gillespie Steele to Ephraim Steele, July 13, 1780, MS, John Steele Papers, Southern Historical Collection, University of North Carolina at Chapel Hill.

73. Henry Lumpkin, *From Savannah to Yorktown* (Columbia: University of South Carolina Press, 1981), 85.

74. Brawley, *Rowan County*, 25; C. L. Hunter, *Sketches of Western North Carolina* (Raleigh: The Raleigh News Steam Job Print, 1877), 184.

75. Elizabeth Steele to Ephriam Steele, [month omitted], 19th, 1781, Transcript, John Steele Papers, Southern Historical Collection, University of North Carolina at Chapel Hill.

76. William K. Boyd, ed., and Charles A. Krummel, trans., "German Tracts Concerning the Lutheran Church in North Carolina During the Eighteenth Century," *North Carolina Historical Review*, VII (April, 1930), 234–235.

77. Boyd and Krummel, "German Tracts," 261. Roschen's statement does not necessarily contradict Johanna Miller Lewis's findings about artisans in Rowan County because women artisans worked in their own homes, and barter was common. It is possible, however, that some plantations were relatively self-sufficient.

CHAPTER 8

1. Mary L. Medley, *History of Anson County, North Carolina 1750–1976* (Wadesboro, North Carolina: Anson County Historical Society, 1976), 72. For the romantic story of Richard Edgeworth, founder of Sneedsboro or Sneydesboro as he originally spelled it, see Medley, 78–83.

Richard Edgeworth of Edgeworth Town, Ireland, left his home after a duel over a lady. When his ship was wrecked, Moses Knight of Cheraw District saved his life and brought him to Cheraw. Edgeworth supposedly named Sneydesboro for his stepmother, Honora Sneyd, who had been courted by Major John Andre, hung as a British spy in the American Revolution. The *Georgetown Gazette*, May 30, 1804, published a notice from Farquhard Campbell saying that he planned to open a public house at Rocky River Springs, but that his other public house at Sneydsborough at the sign of the *Spread Eagle* would be continued under the direction of his brother. The *Winyah Intelligencer*, April 3, 1819, noted that Knox and McKinzie's boat from Sneedsborough arrived with cotton, flour, and bacon.

2. G. Terry Sharrar, "The Indigo Bonanza in South Carolina, 1740–1790," *Technology and Culture*, 12 (July, 1971), 447–455; Marjorie S. Mendenhall, "A History of Agriculture in South Carolina, 1790–1860," (Ph.D. dissertation, University of North Carolina at Chapel Hill, 1940), 93–132, as cited in Lacy K. Ford, Jr., *Origins of Southern Radicalism* (New York: Oxford University Press, 1988), 6–7.

3. *City Gazette and Daily Advertiser,* Dec. 6, 1787; May 29, June 24, 1788; as cited in Rachel N. Klein, *Unification of a Slave State* (Chapel Hill: Published for The Institute of Early American History and Culture, Williamsburg, Virginia, by the University of North Carolina Press, 1990), 246–247. John E. McIver, brother of Evander McIver, represented the Cheraws District in the South Carolina Senate in 1798. He entered into partnership in the firm of Childs, McIver & Co. in Charleston in 1785. In 1794 the *City Gazette and Daily Advertiser* was issued by Markland and McIver. They sold out to Frenau and Payne, who continued to the end of the century. In 1801 David R. Williams became, with his brother-in-law John McIver, joint editor and proprietor of the *City Gazette* and the *Weekly Carolina Gazette*. See Harvey Toliver Cook, *The Life and Legacy of David Rogerson Williams* (New York: [no publisher given] 1916), 52–53. Williams later founded one of the first cotton manufacturing plants in the South.

4. William Bridgwater and Seymour Kurtz, *The Columbia Encyclopedia* (New York: Columbia University Press, 1963), 2322.

5. Klein, *Unification of a Slave State,* 247.

6. Ford, *Origins of Southern Radicalism,* 7.

7. David Ramsay, *The History of South Carolina*, 2 vols. (Charleston, S. C., 1809), II: 120–121, 139–191, 230–246, as cited in Ford, *Origins of Southern Radicalism,* 11.

8. Rusty Fleetwood, *Tidecraft* (Savannah, Georgia: Coastal Heritage Society, 1982), 87–88. Ulrich B. Phillips stated that the standard weight of a bale of cotton in 1826 was 320 pounds. See U. B. Phillips, *A History of Transportation in the Eastern Cotton Belt to 1860* (New York: Columbia University Press, 1908), 134.

9. U. B. Phillips, *History of Transportation,* 69–70.

10. Thomas A. Bailey and David M. Kennedy, *The American Pageant* (Lexington, Massachusetts: D. C. Heath and Company), 202–203.

11. Daniel W. Hollis, "Costly Delusion: Inland Navigation in the South Carolina Piedmont," *Proceedings of the South Carolina Historical Association* (1968), 29.

12. Williams built a cotton mill for spinning yarn on Cedar Creek, Darlington District, about 1812. Later he also produced cotton bagging, twine, cotton oznaburgs, and "Negro winter clothing." Labor was supplied by slaves. The first superintendent was a white man from the North, but later a Negro was employed as superintendent. As cited by Harvey Cook, the Columbia *Telescope* stated, "General Williams will make a thorough experiment on the capacity of slave labor for manufacturing. If it shall be successful and large capital be invested in this way, we may expect an immediate repeal of the tariff." The store operated under the name of Bruce and Williams. See Cook, *David Rogerson Williams,* 140, 141, 143.

13. *Camden* [S. C.] *Gazette*, November 26, 29, 1816, as cited in Hollis, "Costly Delusion," 30.

14. *Acts and Resolutions of the General Assembly of South Carolina,* 1817, 21; 1818, 12, 33, as cited in Hollis, 30–31.

15. "Report of the Civil and Military Engineer of the State of South Carolina for the Year 1818," as reproduced in David Kohn, ed., *Internal Improvements in South Carolina, 1817–1828* (Washington, D. C.: Privately Printed: 1938), A8. How the boats from the boatyard at Marks Creek and from Sneedsboro navigated this portion of the river is a mystery unless they waited for a freshet to bring high water.

16. Dana Crosland, Bennettsville, SC., interview with the author, October 23, 1992. After hearing the story from old-timers, Mr. Crosland took a canoe to the spot, found the large marked rock, and touched bottom with his paddle to prove the veracity of the story.

17. Kohn, *Internal Improvements,* A9.

18. Ibid., A9.

19. Ibid., A14.

20. In another part of his report, Wilson said, "The logs must be sawed and raised by a Crane or Windlass, and ought to be removed out of the reach of freshets." See Kohn, *Internal Improvements,* A16.

21. *Winyah Intelligencer* (Georgetown, S. C.), May 8, 1819.

22. Williams to Wilson, in Kohn, *Internal Improvements,* 9.

23. David Rogerson Williams to John Wilson, Centre Hall, October 20, 1819, as reproduced in Kohn, *Internal Improvements,* 7–10. Williams must have been meticulous to figure the costs to a half-cent.

24. Hollis, "Costly Delusion," 31. Kohn, *Internal Improvements,* viii. Blanding was a native of Massachusetts. He was D. R. Williams's roommate at Rhode Island College, later Brown University, where he studied with Dr. Jonathan Maxcy, who later became the first president

of South Carolina College. It is said that Maxcy suggested that Blanding come to South Carolina. His friendship with Williams may also have been influential. He became an attorney, engineer and banker. See Kohn, *Internal Improvements,* 599; Cook, *David Rogerson Williams,* 51.

25. The workers were slaves hired from their owners. Williams said, "Unfortunately, one person fell overboard, while at work, and was drowned. This owner is in very moderate circumstances, and his loss is respectfully submitted for your consideration." David R. Williams to J. R. Poinsett, Nov. 3, 1820, as reproduced in Kohn, *Internal Improvements,* 57–58.

26. Williams to Poinsett in Kohn, *Internal Improvements,* 58.

27. David R. Williams to Messrs Follet and Smith of Petersburg, Virginia, May 13, 1830, as quoted in Joseph S. Ames, *The Williams Family of Society Hill* (Columbia, S. C.: The State Printers for the Pee Dee Historical Association, 1910), 16. Ames states [11] that Williams began building levees at the suggestion of his father-in-law, Nicholas Power of Providence, Rhode Island. Dana Crosland of Bennettsville explored the levees or "slave dams" as they were colloquially called. He said there was a metal pipe about two feet in diameter inserted in one of the dams to drain the water that might be caught behind it. Local folk recalled that Williams had sent all the way to Rhode Island for it, and the story has persisted to the present day. In another place Mr. Crosland observed a large brick culvert that provided a way for a creek to reach the river. The total drainage system was intricate and very impressive. Crosland also said that Ansel Brigman, a resident of the Brownsville section of Marlboro County, told him that his grandfather, Malachi Brigman, recalled that "Cap'n Williams" [Nicholas Power Williams, son of D. R. Williams] had a ditch dug across the peninsula at the downriver side of Robbins Neck. The ditch was designed to serve as a property line, but the river gradually cut a new channel, forming Byrd Island. About the time of the Civil War, it became impossible to jump across the ditch, and today the main bed of the river flows through that route. Dana Crosland, interview with the author, October 23, 1992.

28. "Report of the Superintendent of Public Works for the Year 1828," as reproduced in Kohn, *Internal Improvements,* 565–566.

29. Fleetwood, *Tidecraft,* 87. In the report of the commissioner for roads, rivers and canals for 1820, the section of Black Creek Navigation stated, "This creek can be rendered navigable by boat 60 feet long, 12 wide and drawing 2 feet water in the driest seasons, for 35 miles by land from its confluence with the Pee Dee." Kohn, *Internal Improvements,* 61. The boat described was probably a flat used to transport goods from Darlington District to the Pee Dee where they could be loaded on a boat of deeper draft for the trip to Georgetown. Williams's quotation: Kohn, *Internal Improvements,* 9. The (Georgetown) *Winyah Intelligencer* of Dec. 15, 1819, reported the arrival of David R. Williams's two flats from Society Hill with 258 bales of cotton. The Dec. 18, 1819, issue of the paper reported Mr. J. Ford's flat from Marion with cotton. Flats continued to be used on the Pee Dee and its tributaries in the 1840s and 1850s. The (Georgetown) *Winyah Observer,* November 26, 1842, noted A. Sparks and Son's boat and flat from Society Hill with 621 bales of cotton, and on November 30, 1842, Purvis's flat from Cheraw with 199 bales cotton, and Punche's flat with 193 bales. On December 3, 1842, Kirton's flat arrived from Little Pee Dee. On December 18, 1846, the newspaper mentioned the arrival of Snow's flat from Black Mingo, a tributary of Black River. The (Georgetown) *Pee Dee Times,* November 25, 1853, reported the arrival of nine rafts and a flat with 650 barrels of rosin from Lumberton,[Lumber River] North Carolina.

30. Ulrich B. Phillips, *History of Transportation in the Eastern Cotton Belt to 1860* (New York: Columbia University Press, 1908), 71–72.

31. Ashpole Swamp in Dillon County is located in the drainage area of the Lumber River. Durward T. Stokes, *The History of Dillon County* (Columbia: University of South Carolina Press, 1978), Map 1, 2.

32. Fleetwood, *Tidecraft,* 88–89.

33. "Hands" referred to laborers who might be either slave or free. Negro hands in this case were slaves. A hand was one person.

34. David Gregg McIntosh, *Reminiscences of Early Life in South Carolina* (Florence, S. C.: Saint David's Society, 1985), ed. Horace Rudisill, 5–6.

35. McIntosh, *Reminiscences,* 5–6. The (Georgetown) *Winyah Observer,* November 23, 1842, noted that J. H. McIntosh's boat from Society Hill arrived with 389 bales of cotton for E. Waterman and B. King.

36. William W. Boddie, *History of Williamsburg* (Columbia: The State Company 1923, repr. Spartanburg, S. C.: The Reprint Company, 1980), 319, 333, 334; *Winyah Observer* (Georgetown, S. C.) mentions Belin's boat from Black Mingo on December 2, 1846. On February 4, 1852, the boat *Wiltown* from Black Mingo arrived. *Pee Dee Times* (Georgetown) of November 23, 1853, noted that Belin's Boat for Black Mingo had cleared. The church has burned since the author visited.

37. Account Books of Bright Williamson, 1804–1805, facsimile in South Caroliniana Library, University of South Carolina. Biographical sketch in Harvey Toliver Cook, Rambles in the Pee Dee Basin (Columbia: The State Company, 1926), 443–444.

38. W. W. Sellers, *A History of Marion County, South Carolina* (Columbia: R. L. Bryan Company, 1902), 342; See also William Curry Harllee, *Kinfolks* (New Orleans: Search & Pfaff, Ltd., 3 vols., 1934), I: 343–345, 393, 410, 493–499. In 1819, Thomas Harllee agreed with his son David S. Harllee to run his store in Marion County on a partnership basis. David later moved to Cheraw and then to Marlboro County. Thomas Harllee died in 1827.

39. Williams to John Wilson, October 20, 1819, as reproduced in Kohn, *Internal Improvements,* 9. A teamboat was used as a ferry on the Ashley River near Charleston. In 1820 the *Genius of Georgia,* a teamboat, was launched on the Savannah River. See Fleetwood, *Tidecraft,* 92. See also Donald G. Shomette, "Heyday of the Horse Ferry," *National Geographic* 176, no. 4, 548; Kevin Crisman and Arthur Cohn, *When Horses Walked on Water* (Washington: Smithsonian Institution, 1998). In a letter dated 13 May 1930, Williams stated that he was the first person who attempted the use of mules, "certainly in the Southern States, if not in the United States, for the purpose of agriculture." Ames, *The Williams Family,* 16.

40. "Plans and Progress of Internal Improvement in South Carolina, 1820," as reproduced in Kohn, *Internal Improvements,* 85–86.

41. *Winyah Intelligencer* (Georgetown, S. C.), October 8, 1819; December 18, 1819.

42. "Report of the Board of Public Works, 1821," as reproduced in Kohn, *Internal Improvements,* 121.

43. William S. Powell, *North Carolina through Four Centuries* (Chapel Hill: University of North Carolina Press, 1989), 253–255.

44. A. D. Murphey to Hamilton Fulton, August 10, 1919, "A view of the Internal Improvements contemplated by the Legislature of North Carolina," as reproduced in William Henry Hoyt, ed., *The Papers of Archibald D. Murphey* (Raleigh: E. M. Uzzell & Co., State Printers, 1914), II: 120–121, 140.

45. *Western Carolinian*, January 2, 1821. For further references to stockholders' activities, see issues for October 16, 1821, and March 15, 1825.

46. Thomas Carter Ruffin (1787–1870) completed his preparation for the bar in Murphey's office. He served in the legislature of North Carolina and on the state supreme court. He was also noted as a financier and agriculturist. See Hoyt, *Murphey Papers,* I: 18. Murphey to Ruffin, March 29, 1819; Hoyt, *The Papers of Archibald D. Murphey,* I: 130–132. Richmond Pearson died in 1819. See John H. Wheeler, *Historical Sketches of North Carolina* (New York: Frederick H. Hitchcock, 1925), 385.

47. Jacob Hanes, a local citizen, sold lots in 1819 for another town on the Yadkin to be named Fulton, but the town never developed. James Wall, *Davie County: A Brief History* (Raleigh: North Carolina Department of Cultural Resources, Division of Archives and History, 1976), 41.

48. Wall, *Davie County,* 56–57. Judge Peter Hairston, Cooleemee Plantation, interview with the author, October 30, 1992.

49. Hiram Jennings to Archibald Murphey, August 8, 1820; Hoyt, *The Papers of Archibald D. Murphey,* I: 170–171. In 1978, part of the retaining wall was visible along one bank of the river in the Pilot Mountain State Park. See Wall, *Davie County,* 38.

50. Thomas E. Jeffrey, "Internal Improvements and Political Parties in Antebellum North Carolina, 1836–1860," *North Carolina Historical Review,* LV: 2 (April, 1978), 114–116. Spaight was governor of North Carolina from 1835 to 1836. Wall, 38.

SIDE BARS CHAPTER 8

1. Dumas Malone, ed., *Dictionary of American Biography* (New York: Charles Scribner's Sons, 1935), 8: 106.

2. "The Log-book of the 'Savannah,'" *Harper's New Monthly Magazine,* vol. 54, # 321 (Feb. 1877).

3. James A. Rogers, "First Atlantic Steamboat Captain," *Theodosia and Other Pee Dee Sketches* (Columbia: R. L. Bryan, 1978), 53.

4. Dumas Malone, ed., *Dictionary of American Biography* (New York: Charles Scribner's Sons, 1935), 8: 106–107.

5. Frank O. Braynard, *S.S. Savannah: The Elegant Steamship* (New York: Dover, 1963), 206.

6. Ibid., 207.

7. Ibid.

8. James A. Rogers, *Theodosia* (Columbia: R.L. Bryan, 1978), 135–136.

9. Ibid.

10. Ibid., 137; Marlboro County Deeds, AA: 341–342, SCDAH.

11. Rogers, *Theodosia,* 134.

12. Ibid., 138.

13. Inglis Fletcher, *Wicked Lady* (New York: Bobbs Merrill, 1962).

CHAPTER 9

1. *Cheraw Gazette*, December 29, 1835.

2. Ibid; 1840 Census, *Fayetteville* [N. C.] *Observer,* June 4, 1850, as cited in Joyce M. Gibson, *Scotland County Emerging, 1750–1900* (Laurel Hill, N. C.: Joyce M. Gibson, 1995), 77.

3. Memoirs of Mrs. S. G. Godfrey, as cited in James A. Fitch, "Down the Mighty River—Steamboats on Our Waters," *Pee Dee Magazine,* VII, #1 (Jan./Feb. 1994), 11.

4. *Winyah Observer* (Georgetown, SC), December 11, 1850.

5. *Pee Dee Gazette,* October 4, 1839.

6. Cashaway was near where Highway 301 crosses the Pee Dee from Florence County to Marlboro.

7. E. W. Charles to Mrs. Jane Charles, Darlington, SC, 19 January 1846, Darlington County Historical Commission. The author is indebted to Horace Rudisill for identification of the passengers.

8. Fitch, *Pee Dee Magazine,* 10.

9. James A. Fitch, "Down Our Mighty Rivers," *Mortar & Pestle,* Georgetown, The Rice Museum, Spring/Summer, 1995, 3.

10. Fitch, *Pee Dee Magazine,* 11. This quotation was from Franklin Burroughs regarding the steamer, *Burroughs,* which operated much later than the antebellum period, but the situation on board was probably much the same.

11. James A. Fitch, "Down Our Mighty Rivers," *Mortar and Pestle,* (Spring/Summer 1995).

12. J. Eli Gregg and Son, Mars Bluff, Day book, 1842–1843, and "Goods Bought" 1844–1849, MS (#860) South Caroliniana Library. The author is indebted to Alexander Gregg of Georgetown for bringing this material to her attention. Act of Incorporation, South Carolina *Statutes*, David J. McCord, ed., (Columbia: 1837), VIII: 458. Gregg became president of the company June 1, 1838. Merchants and Planters Account Book, 1838–1840, MS, Darlington County Historical Commission.

13. "Terrible Casualty," *Winyah Observer*, January 17, 1849; "The Late Disaster," (Charleston) *Courier*, November 23, 1853. Faulkner and Carns et al *vs.* Wright, Coker and Tuttle, December 1838, Reports, Court of Appeals and the Court of Errors of South Carolina, Dec. 1838–May 1839, Wm. Rice, Vol. 1, 1839, 107–126.

14. Hugh Talmadge Lefler and Albert Ray Newsome, *North Carolina: The History of a Southern State* (Chapel Hill: University of North Carolina Press, 1973), 384.

15. *Carolina Watchman* (Salisbury, NC) Oct. 23, 1855. This and the following citations from the *Carolina Watchman* came from transcriptions in the Rowan County Public Library, Salisbury, NC. Subscription list, MS, from the W. A. Whitaker Papers, Southern Historical Collection, University of North Carolina, Chapel Hill, #3433, 1852–1859. See also: "Reports of Charles B. Fisk, Esquire, Chief Engineer to the Stockholders of the Yadkin Navigation Company on Recognizance and a Survey of the Yadkin River," (Salisbury: J. J. Bruner, 1856), passim., Rowan Public Library.

16. *Carolina Watchman* (Salisbury, NC) April 10, 1884.

17. *Carolina Watchman* (Salisbury, NC), March 13, 1879.

18. The *Osceola* was launched January 31, 1837. In 1841, she ran aground at Wright's Bluff and stove in her hull. She was repaired by J. Hanahan and Company in Georgetown and resumed service. On May 17, 1839, the *Cheraw Gazette* reported that D. Malloy had received a shipment of Irish potatoes via the *Osceola*. The *Winyah Observer* of January 20, 1844 reported her arrival from Cheraw with the lighter *Ann Eliza*. After the boiler burst at Cheraw in 1846, no further mention of the *Osceola* has been found on the Pee Dee. See Ronald E. Bridwell, '. . . *That We Should have a Port. . .*" (Georgetown: Chamber of Commerce, 1982), 48.

19. *Charleston Courier*, January 19, 1849; *Winyah Observer*, January 17, 1849; Edward A. Mueller, "Jacob Builds a Fleet: the Brock Line—the Old Reliable," *Steamboat Bill, Journal of the Steamship Historical Society of America*, #132 (Winter 1974), 51–52. Edward D. Sloan to Jack Brock, June 8, 1998, copy in possession of the author. Sloan is related to Ferguson.

20. *Marion Star*, November 22, 1853. C. Carroll White, captain, wrote an account of the accident that was published in the (Charleston) *Courier* stating that of the twenty-seven people, seventeen survived. The explosion took place about 6:30 AM when some passengers had not yet boarded. "Ben Williams, the cook, Peter, one of the firemen, Joe, 2nd engineer, are all missing. Simon [the pilot], Stephen, and four other deck hands, were killed; one of the above died this morning; they have been buried. Dandy, Bob and Burns are wounded , but I think not seriously. The boat is literally torn to pieces."

21. *Winyah Observer*, November 25, 1846. The article stated that William B. Graham of Horry came to town to procure some family supplies. The wind was high and his boat heavily loaded with cargo and five persons. Two drowned including Mr. Graham, a father of seventeen. The same newspaper of January 6, 1847, reported, "During the severe and excessively high wind of Monday evening one of the Little Pee Dee boats from Harleesville with 60 bales of cotton . . . was filled with water from the violence of the sea in the bay near the entrance of our harbor and sank in shoal water." The cotton was salvaged. J. B. McDaniel of Marion was the owner.

22. The Steamer *Pee Dee*, Captain Christian, from Cheraw bound for Charleston with 1,069 bales of cotton cleared the port of Georgetown December 1, 1846. *Winyah Observer*, issues of November 16, 26 and December 10, 1842 and December 2,and 16, 1846. The newspaper does not always give first names. Harlee was possibly Thomas Harllee of the Little Pee Dee. Bright Williamson of Oaklyn Plantation near Darlington operated boats out of Black Creek to the Pee Dee. A. P. LaCoste was a merchant in Cheraw. For a sketch of Williamson's career, see Harvey T. Cook, *Rambles in the Pee Dee Basin* (Columbia: The State, 1926, rpt. Greenville: Southern Historical Press, n.d.), 441–446. Other boats were operated by Alexander Sparks, Caleb Coker, [Nicholas?] Williams, and John F. Wilson of Society Hill; Foxworth and McCorkle of Mars Bluff, and owners named Fuller, Richardson, and Kirton from the Little Pee Dee. Ibid., January 13, 14, 20, 1844.

23. Merchants and Planters Steam Boat Co., Account Book, 1838–1840, MS, Darlington County Historical Commission. The log book of the *Bennettsville* at the same location gives details on supplies for the crew, etc.

24. *Winyah Observer*, December 29, 1847.

25. *Winyah Observer*, December 29, 1847; December 11, 1850; November 25, 1853; Bridwell, ". . .*That We Should have a Port . . . ,*" 45–46.

26. Henry A. McKinnon, Jr., "Navigation on the Lumber River—Part II," *NEWS* (Lumberton, NC), March 29, 1989; Bridwell, 46.

27. Bridwell, ". . .*That We Should have a Port . . . ,*" 46; *Pee Dee Times* (Georgetown), September 21, 1853, reported Freeman's Lighter from Black Mingo with 212 barrels of naval stores and Abraham's Lighter from Black River with 117 barrels, the steamer, *Fairy*, with 379 barrels from Black River, and October 5, 1853, the paper reported the steamer, *Fairy*, with 254 barrels from Conwayboro, and Freeman's Lighter from Black Mingo with 210 barrels.

28. South Carolina *Statutes*, 7: 7.

29. Gibson lived in Darlington County. He attended the College of South Carolina. He was the only one of the Marion County planters listed who owned more than 100 slaves in that district. Chalmers Davidson, *The Last Foray* (Columbia: University of South Carolina Press, 1971), 201.

30. United States Census, 1860, Agricultural Schedule, Marion District.

31. Davidson, *The Last Foray,* 241.

32. United States Census, 1860, Agricultural Schedule, Marlboro District. The initials for Mr. Evans were difficult to decipher, but Samuel Wilds Evans seems the most likely.

33. Ibid., Darlington District.

34. Davidson, *The Last Foray,* 224.

35. United States Census, 1860, Agricultural Schedule, Chesterfield District.

36. Rogers, *History of Georgetown County,* 324–325; Davidson, *The Last Foray,* 170–267, passim, John R. Hetrick, "Treatise on the Economics of Rice production in Georgetown County South Carolina: The Middle Period, 1786–1860," M. A. Thesis, University of South Carolina, 1971, A84–A88.

37. George C. Rogers, Jr., *The History of Georgetown County,* (Spartanburg, SC: The Reprint Co., 1995), 253. Marion County was 48 percent black; Marlboro, 57 percent; Darlington, 59 percent; and Chesterfield, 38 percent.

38. See Chapter 4 this volume.

39. Amelia Wallace Vernon, *African Americans at Mars Bluff, South Carolina* (Columbia: University of South Carolina Press, 1993), 157–158. It is beyond the scope of this work to discuss in detail the preservation of African culture in the Pee Dee, but for further information, the reader is referred to Mrs. Vernon's study as well as to the classic work by Charles Joyner, *Down by the Riverside* (Urbana and Chicago: University of Illinois Press, 1984).

40. Charles Joyner, *Down by the Riverside* (Chicago: University of Illinois Press), 242.

41. Alberta Morel Lachicotte, *Georgetown Rice Plantations* (Georgetown: Georgetown County Historical Society, 1993), 122.

42. N. Louise Bailey, Mary Morgan, and Carolyn Taylor, eds., *Biographical Directory of the South Carolina Senate* (Columbia: University of South Carolina Press, 1986), I: 51–55.

43. Elizabeth Allston Pringle, *Chronicles of Chicora Wood* (New York: Charles Scribner's Sons, 1922), and *A Woman Rice Planter* (New York: Macmillan, 1913. Reprint Columbia: University of South Carolina Press, 1992), 13–14; 27–30.

44. Lachicotte, 124. See also: Elizabeth Allston Pringle, *Chronicles of Chicora Wood* (New York: Charles Scribner's Sons, 1922), and *A Woman Rice Planter* (New York: Macmillan, 1913. Reprint Columbia: University of South Carolina Press, 1992).

45. Susan Lowndes Allston, *Sketches Along the Pee Dee River,* Pamphlet, South Caroliniana Library, 1.

46. Lachicotte, *Georgetown Rice Plantations,* 124–125, Jamie Constance, interview with the author, May 12, 1999.

47. Lon D. Outen, *Horton's on Lynches River and Red Oak Plantation* (Greenville, S. C.: A Press, 1989), 13.

48. Ibid., 17.

49. Ibid., 18.

50. Ibid.

51. Peter W. Hairston, *The Cooleemee Plantation and Its People* (Winston-Salem, NC: Hunter , 1986. Reprint Lexington, NC: Davidson County Community College, 1998), 38–39. See also: Henry Wiencek, *The Hairstons: An American Family in Black and White* (New York: St. Martin's Press, 1999), 4. This book explores the history of the Hairston family and the families of their former slaves over many generations. It is a fascinating account of how black and white families interacted through the years. For clarification, it should be noted that the name "Peter" has been passed down through the generations, so that at any given date for the last 200 years, the owner of the plantation was likely Peter Hairston. The name is pronounced Harston.

52. Peter W. Hairston to George Hairston, September 1850, reproduced in Hairston, *The Cooleemee Plantation and Its People,* 35. See also: James W. Wall, *Davie County: A Brief History* (Raleigh: North Carolina Department of Cultural Resources, Division of Archives and History, 1976), 38–39.

53. Wiencek, *The Hairstons,* 8–9.

54. Ibid.

55. S. David Carriker, *Railroading in the Carolina Sandhills: Volume 1: The 19th Century (1825–1900)* (Ellerbe, NC: S. David Carriker, 1985), 30–34, 136.

56. August Kohn, *The Cotton Mills of South Carolina* (Columbia: S. C. Department of Agriculture, Commerce, and Immigration, 1907), 18–19; J. A. W. Thomas, *A History of Marlboro County* (Atlanta: 1897. Reprint Baltimore: Regional Publishing Company, 1971), 267.

57. Joe M. McLaurin, "Richmond County and the Civil War," *Richmond County Record, Journal of the Society of Richmond County Descendants* (Rockingham, NC), Issue 22, 418.

58. Diffee W. Standard and Richard W. Griffin, "The Cotton Textile Industry in Ante-bellum North Carolina: Part II," *North Carolina Historical Review* (April 1957), 34: 161–163; Bridwell, 45. *Carolina Watchman* (Salisbury, NC) of February 3, 1848, noted that Maxwell Chambers bought the Salisbury Cotton Factory for $30,000. The newspaper noted in the June 24, 1852, issue that the Rowan Factory was undergoing a variety of changes in order to resume operations. A new steam engine of 90 horsepower replaced the old machine. On February 3, 1853, the same paper noted that Chambers sold his interest in the Rowan Factory to J. S. and P. B. Chambers. J. G. Cairns would endeavor to run the mill.

59. Kohn, *The Cotton Mills of South Carolina,* 16.

60. David Duncan Wallace, *South Carolina—A Short History, 1520–1948* (Columbia: University of South Carolina Press, 1951), 457.

61. James McBride Dabbs, *Pee Dee Panorama* (Columbia: University of South Carolina Press, 1951), 24.

62. Bridwell, *". . . That We Should have a Port. . . ,"* 49. See also: *Official Records of the Union and Confederate Navies in the War of the Rebellion,* Series I, (Washington: Government Printing Office, 1895), 2: 60; 13: 193, 256–257, 259.

63. Dabbs, *Pee Dee Panorama,* 6.

64. Leah Townsend, "The Confederate Gunboat 'Pedee'," *South Carolina Historical Magazine,* 60: 67.

65. Ibid., 68.

66. Ibid., 70.

67. Townsend, "The Confederate Gunboat 'Pedee'," 67; James A. Rogers, *Theodosia and Other Pee Dee Sketches* (Florence, SC: James A. Rogers, 1978), 25.

68. Larry E. Nelson, "Sherman at Cheraw," *South Carolina Historical Magazine,* 100, 349.

69. Joe McLaurin, "Richmond County and the Civil War," Issue 19, 354; Issue 20, 375; Issue 22, 418–419.

70. William Light Kinney, Jr., ed., *Sherman's March—A Review* (Bennettsville, SC: W. L. Kinney, Jr., 1962), 264–266.

71. Ibid., 224–225. Drawing in *Frank Leslie's Illustrated Newspaper,* April 3, 1864, shows tents.

72. William Light Kinney, Jr., personal communication with the author. The house, now known as "Magnolia," is the home of Mr. and Mrs. William Light Kinney, Jr. Johnson was later elected judge of the Court of Equity and is usually given the title "chancellor."

73. "Special Orders No. 59," quoted in Kinney, *Sherman's March,* 256–266.

74. Dabbs, 27.

75. Kinney, *Sherman's March,* 278–279; Suzanne Linder, personal observation of the statue. The author recalls seeing this anomaly reported in *Ripley's Believe It or Not.*

76. Ronald Bridwell, *"Gem of the Atlantic Seaboard"* (Georgetown: Chamber of Commerce, n.d.), 11.

77. Ibid., 21.

78. Ibid., 36–37.

79. Ibid., 14–15. See also Bridwell, ". . . That We Should have a Port. . . ," 45. The town of Bucksville no longer exists. The landing has been relocated. The community of Bucksport preserves the Buck family name in the area. See Catherine Lewis, *Horry County, South Carolina, 1730–1993* (Columbia: University of South Carolina Press, 1998), 111–112.

80. Claudia B. Kizer, "River Traffic on the Pee Dee Between Cheraw and Georgetown," Typescript, Historic Cheraw Foundation, 9.

SIDE BARS CHAPTER 9

1. Kenneth Emerson, *Doo-Dah: Stephen Foster and the Rise of American Popular Culture* (New York: Simon & Schuster, 1997), passim.

2. Adolph L. Dial, "Lumbees" in Charles Reagan Wilson and William Ferris, eds., *Encyclopedia of Southern Culture* (New York: Doubleday, 1989), 2: 64–65; Henry A. McKinnon, Jr., " The Great State of Robeson," *The News* (Lumberton, N. C.) March 15, 1989.

3. Records of the Planters Club on Pee Dee, Sparkman Papers, 2732 #1, South Caroliniana Library; Rogers, *The History of Georgetown County,* 288–290, 340.

CHAPTER 10

1. J. A. W. Thomas, *A History of Marlboro County, S.C.* (Baltimore: Regional Publishing Company, 1978), 290.

2. Ronald E. Bridwell, "The Gem of the Atlantic Seaboard" (Georgetown: *Georgetown Times,* 1991) 58; James A. Fitch, "Down Our Mighty Rivers," *Mortar & Pestle,* Georgetown, The Rice Museum, Spring/Summer, 1995, 3.

3. Charles F. Kovacik and John J. Winberry, *South Carolina: The Making of a Landscape* (Columbia: University of South Carolina Press, 1989), 162.

4. Hugh T. Lefler and Albert R. Newsome, *North Carolina: The History of a Southern State* (Chapel Hill: University of North Carolina Press, 1963), 476–477; Adelaide Fries, Stuart T. Wright, and J. Edwin Hendricks, *Forsyth: The History of a County on the March* (Chapel Hill: University of North Carolina Press, 1976), 180–183, 187. Biggs's machine was not the first of its kind, but it was the first in Winston.

5. Walter Edgar, *South Carolina: A History* (Columbia: University of South Carolina Press, 1998), 479.

6. *Encyclopedia Britannica* (Chicago: Encyclopedia Britannica, Inc., 1958), XXII: 263.

7. Ibid., 548; Mark Wineka, *A River Runs Through Us* (Salisbury, NC: Salisbury Post, 1998), 4. Southern Public Utilities Company, which became Duke Power, bought the plant in 1913. In 1983 an engineers' association designated Idols Dam a historical engineering landmark.

8. *Greensboro Daily News,* March 9, 1924; *The Stanly News & Press Spectrum,* April 30, 1991.

9. Mark Wineka, *A River Runs Through Us* (Salisbury, NC: The Salisbury Post, 1998), 34; North Carolina Division of Water Quality, Water Quality Section, *Yadkin-Pee Dee River Basinwide Water Quality Management Plan* (Raleigh: North Carolina Environmental Management Commission, 1998), Chapter 2: 20; hereinafter cited as *NC River Management Plan.*

10. Yadkin, Inc., "Shoreline Management Plan Summary," July 1, 1999, 2.

11. Jack Riley, *Carolina Power & Light Company, 1908–1958* (Raleigh: Carolina Power & Light Company, 1958), 131.

12. Ibid., 131–132.

13. Ibid., 133–134.

14. Ibid., 135.

15. Ibid., 137.

16. Ibid., 141–146.

17. *Spotlight*, CP&L Employee Communication, April, 1987.

18. Riley, *Carolina Power & Light Company*, 149–151.

19. U. S. Army Corps of Engineers, *W. Kerr Scott Reservoir, Shoreline Management Plan* (Wilmington, NC: U. S. Army Engineer District, 1997), 3.

20. Rodney Foushee, "Harnessing Rivers: Dams," *Wildlife in North Carolina* (Special Rivers Issue, November 1999), 109–111.

21. Ibid., 113.

22. Douglas Rights, *A Voyage Down the Yadkin-Great Pee Dee River* (Winston-Salem: 1928; rpt. Winston-Salem Journal, 1983), 58. This is published in the same volume with Floyd Rogers' *Yadkin Passage.*

23. Bernard Stubbs, interview with the author, November, 1995, and clipping of article, in possession of author, written by Stubbs for the *Cheraw Chronicle*, n.d.

24. Ibid.

25. Ibid. For a photo of a 334-pound sturgeon caught by Charles Tolson, see *Cheraw Chronicle*, April 3, 1943.

26. Ibid.

27. Ibid.; Rights, *A Voyage Down the Yadkin-Great Pee Dee River,* 29, 39, 61. Rights made his journey down the river in three stages at different times. On the first leg of the trip in 1925 he observed bounce nets. By the time he completed the last stage in 1928, bounce nets had been declared illegal.

28. Rights, *A Voyage Down the Yadkin-Great Pee Dee River,* 8.

29. Joe Goodman, "Editor's Preface," in Floyd Rogers, *Yadkin Passage* (Winston-Salem Journal, 1983), viii–ix, 53–54; Comprehensive Water Resources Study, *Yadkin-Pee Dee River Basin*, Level B, Draft Recommended Plan (Winston-Salem, NC: April 1981), frontispiece.

30. Rogers, *Yadkin Passage,* viii–ix, 3.

31. Wineka, *A River Runs Through Us*, 1, 56.

32. "South Carolina River Conservation Program," information sheet published by South Carolina Department of Natural Resources (SCDNR). The author thanks Bill Marshall for supplying this information.

33. South Carolina Department of Health and Environmental Control, Bureau of Water, *Watershed Water Quality Management Strategy: Pee Dee Basin*, Technical Report No.001-97 (Columbia: SCDHEC, 1997), 2, 10.

34. Ibid., South Carolina Water Resources Commission, *South Carolina Scenic Rivers Program Administrative Handbook*, Report No. 172 (Columbia: Water Resources Commission, 1991), 7–10, 43.

35. Ibid.

36. *Post and Courier* (Charleston), April 11, 2000.

37. "South Carolina Focus Areas," typescript, August 1994, provided by SCDNR.

38. "Uwharrie National Forest," brochure provided by Jake Cebula, Uwharrie Supervisory Research Specialist, Troy, NC.

39. U. S. Fish & Wildlife Service, "Pee Dee National Wildlife Refuge," (Wadesboro, NC: Information Pamphlet, December 1997), n.p.; Janet Watson, staff person with PDNWR, interview with the author, June 20, 2000.

40. U. S. Fish & Wildlife Service, "Carolina Sandhills National Wildlife Refuge," (McBee, SC: Information Pamphlet, January 1985), n.p.

41. *Georgetown* (SC) *Times*, July 9, 1998; U. S. Fish and Wildlife Service, "Coastal South Carolina," Fact Sheet (Atlanta: Spring 1995), n.p.

42. North Carolina River Management Plan, Chapter 3, 1–36.

EPILOGUE

1. Thomas Wolfe, *Of Time and the River* (New York: Charles Scribner's Sons, 1935), 860.

2. Lawrence Earley, "From the Mountains to the Sea," *Wildlife in North Carolina,* Special Issue on Rivers, November, 1999.

3. Norman McLean, *A River Runs Through It* (Chicago: University of Chicago Press, 1976. Reprint New York: Pocket Books, 1992), 113.

Index

Cape Romain 133

Carloss, Mary Ann 107

Carolina bays 8, 9

Carolina Power and Light Company 140, 143

Carolina Sandhills National Wildlife Refuge 154–155

Carp 147

Carter, James 85

Carteret, John 79

Carteret, John (Earl Granville) 79, 86
    and sale of lands 82

Cartwheel Bay 152

Cashaway 112

Cashaway Baptist Church 66, 69

Caston, R. T. 135

Catawba County, North Carolina 111

Catawba Indians
    words of 4

Catawba River 70, 92, 106

Catawba Valley 80

Catfish 147

Catfish Creek 61

Catfish Creek Swamp 158

Cathey, John 85

Caviar 147

Cedar Creek 128
    ferry for 73

Centenary viii

Charles, Edgar Welles 112, 119

Charles, Jane 112

Charles V of Spain 16, 18

Charlesfort 23

Charleston 27, 29, 31, 38, 40, 43, 50, 52, 60, 61, 67, 80, 89,
        90, 96, 97, 112, 122, 128
    and land transctions 60
    and railroads 127
    and trade from North Carolina 85
    collector of customs in 40
    courts in 56, 66
    merchants in 54, 63, 85
    port of 37–38, 49, 105, 109, 112, 115

Charleston harbor
    Union blockade of 133

Charleston newspapers 96

Charlotte Journal 111

Charlotte, North Carolina 69, 111

Charlottesville, Virginia 1

Chatham. *See* Cheraw

Cheraw 24, 63, 70, 75, 97, 100, 115, 123, 128, 135, 145
    and commerce 111
    and navigation of Pee Dee 98, 99, 105, 106
    and the Civil War 127, 130, 131, 133
    exports from 106, 109, 115
    plantations in 119
    population of 106
    steamboat company in 115

Cheraw and Darlington Railroad 127

Cheraw ferry 74

Cheraw Georgetown Steamboat Company 135

Cheraw High School 145

Cheraw Indians 31, 32, 63

Cheraw newspapers 111

Cheraw State Park 157

Cheraws District 74

Cherokee Indians 31, 89, 92, 120

Cherokee War 89

Chesapeake River 97

Chesterfield County
    cotton planters in 119

Chesterfield District
    and the Civil War 128, 133

Chicora 16

Chicora, Francisco 16–18

Chicora Wood Plantation 119, 122–124

Christian Reid (steamer) 115

Christy's Minstrels 116

Churton, William 86

City Gazette and Daily Advertiser (Charleston) 96

Civil War 135
    and the Pee Dee area 128–133

Clark family 79

Clay, Henry 96

Clement, H. E. 135

Clermont Plantation 119

Clinton, North Carolina 108

Clipper ships 133

Cloth
    prehistoric 13

Coe, Joffre Lanning 10–11

Cofitachequi 20–24

Coit, Hercules 60

College of New Jersey 132

Collins, Andrew 32

Martyr, Peter 16–17
Maryland tobacco 139
Mask, William 71
Matheson, D. S. 135
Matthews, Joe 149
McCall, George Jay Washington 119
McCall, J. N. 118
McClelland, James 56
McColl, Peter 131
McCollum, John 115
McCotery, William 74
McCulloh, Henry 80, 86
McCulloh, Henry Eustace 80
McDonald, Adam 49
McDonald, John 60
McDougal, John 45
McFarlands Turnpike 120
McGilvery, William 133
McIntosh, David Gregg 102
McIntyre, S. E. 118
McIver, Allen Evander 119
McKeithen, Dugal 35
McLean, Norman 160
McLeod, Alexander 119
McPherson, James 60
McQueen, Alexander 119
McQueen, John 60, 128
Mecklenburg County, North Carolina 111
Melungeons 19
Menendez de, Pedro 23
Merchant (steamer) 133
Merchants and Planters Steamboat Company 114, 115
Mercury 2
Methodists 45
Mica 2
Michie, James 9
Michigan (schooner) 118
Middleton, Arthur 38
Middleton, Henry A. 119
Middleton, John I. 119
Militia
    return of 43
Milldam Plantation 119
Miller, Samuel 35

Mills 128, 131
Millwood Plantation 112
Milton Plantation 119
Mingo (steamboat) 133
Mining, gold 154
Minto 107
Mississippians 24
    culture of 11–13, 23
Mocksville Cotton Factory 128
Mocksville, North Carolina 126
Money, Thomas 61
Montero, Sebastian 23
Montgomerie, Archibald 89
Montgomery County, North Carolina 13, 111, 153
Moore County, North Carolina 7
Moravians 79
    and military service 87
    settlements of 81–85, 93. *See also* Bethabara; Salem, North Carolina
Morgan, Abel 61
Morgan, Daniel 70, 71, 92
Morning News Review 130
Morris, Lewis, Jr. 71
Morrow Mountain 26
Morrow Mountain State Park 157
Morven 122
Mound-builders 11
Muddy Creek, North Carolina 82
Mules 105
Murphey, Archibald DeBow 106–109
Murray, John 73

N

Narrows Dam 139
Narrows Reservoir 153
Nash, Robie 149
Native Americans 3, 27, 93, 159.
    and Chicora 16
    and destruction of culture 33
    and fish dams 145–146
    and spread of epidemics 24

Rutherford, Griffith 92
Ryle, John 89